POLICING THE RAINBOW

POLICING THE RAINBOW

by David Webb

To Bettan Sunit & family wishing you good health, happiness & prosperity. It was nice to meet you & your husband on my birthday.

[signature]

13.4.12.

Published by
King Lion Publishing Ltd

Printed by
Fluid Edge Ltd

Written by David Webb with Peter Bidulph
Original Cover Design By Rob Macauley
©King Lion Publishing
Sunrise House
103 Adelaide Street
Blackpool
Lancashire
FY1 4LU
01253 295577
ISBN 0-9545215-9-5
Printed by Fluid Edge Ltd
01253 401404

To my wife Betty, my daughter Caroline and husband Nigel, my son Andrew and wife Tracey, my daughter Debbie and husband Andrew, and my grandchildren Rosie, Sam, Max, Liberty, Amy and Alex, in whose love I found courage through the darkest days.

CONTENTS

ACKNOWLEDGEMENTS

I made many good friends throughout my career. All have contributed directly or in other ways to my understanding of inner city problems, and without such understanding, I could never have attempted this project.

To John Brown, a close and good colleague, who sadly died at the height of his career and so soon after the publication of his second study of Handsworth. He loved inner city people of all racial origins, moving easily among them, rich and poor. He loved the clubs, the churches and our old Thornhill Road Police station. His Cranfield conferences for Police officers from all over the world are legendary. What contribution to society's self-knowledge might he have made with a full three score and ten?

To Lord Scarman, the distinguished judge who walked with me along the streets of Handsworth, at home and at ease among the poor, a man both interested and caring.

To my friends in the Walsall Police force. Bob Snee still serves as an executive on NARPO. Ken Perry, who was my superintendent when I left Walsall, is a staunch friend. Keith Ashton achieved senior rank in other divisions of the force. Jim Collins, in retirement, still walks his beloved Walsall Town Centre.

To those inspectors, sergeants and constables at Thornhill Road who, day by day, gave all in their efforts to keep the suburb living and working together in peace and harmony. Especially to Joe Matthews, Jerry Finch and Keith Dickens who looked after me in my early years of command, and kept me - not always successfully! - on the straight and narrow. And to Chief Inspector Martin Burton, an important cog in the wheel as my deputy - an experienced man. I recommended him to succeed me on my retirement in 1981. To former Chief Superintendent David Baker and Chief Superintendent Geoff Rees, both good men who did their best to implement their version of community policing in difficult circumstances and through turbulent years. Both David and Geoff have received well-deserved recognition with the award of the Queen's Police Medal. Joe Matthews also received the Queen's Police Medal prior to his well-earned retirement, and his successor Don Wilson received the MBE for his continuing good work.

To Bernard Francis and the members of the Faith and Confidence Fellowship Social Club. The old place is still there and I pop in occasionally to share a pint and fight the good fight. To Mr. and Mrs Knights of the Monte Carlo Club, and Lee Baker of the Alcazar Club. To Norman Townsend who helped me when my back was against the wall. To Tom Walker who shared my experiences in Egypt and whilst serving in the Hertfordshire Constabulary.

To Alex and Joyce Brown and Donald Nelson of the Handsworth No. 1 Residents' Association, also members of the Rotary Club. Joyce's photo is on the wall of Handsworth Community Fire Station, which she helped to found. To John Clark,

Justice of the Peace and Conservative councillor who gave tremendous support to the Lozells Project and has remained my friend ever since.

My good friends Tulsi Dass, Tulsi Thukral, Gurdhev Bagha, Gurmet Suman, Mr Bhange, Santa Singh and Mr Sophal. Sadly Gurdhev Bagha died some years ago. We remain close friends and they were the first to break down the evil of the caste system within Handsworth's community. They were active in encouraging their children to broaden their horizons and seek an equal place in society. To Harbans Singh and Mohinder Mandair, leaders of the Indian groups, continuing to strive for equality and leading by example. To a dear friend Beverly Lindsay, a wonderful personality and consistent leader for the Afro-Caribbean community. Lindsay continually works for the good of her people.

In more recent years, to Basil Clarke MBE, leader of the Lozells Traders Association who grew to be a staunch friend, helping me so much to understand the realities of inner city life in the new millennium. To my colleague Machan Ghattaura, President of the Institute of Asian Businesses, to Om Azad and his family, and my close friend John Eyre, all of whom assist with the work of the Federation.

To Dennis Harbird, former head of Rookery Road Junior School and second chairman of our pioneer Victim Support Scheme. To John Goss OBE, a man who has dedicated his life to the deprived teenagers of Handsworth Wood Boys School, before he transferred in the 1980's to Broadway School. And to Geoff Drake, former head of Hamstead Hall School and District Governor of Rotary, who I was proud to assist as his Sergeant at Arms during his year of office.

To Sidney Caro MBE, a good friend and Liberal Party stalwart. He was central to our Lozells Project. A marvellous man involved in every aspect of community care. He persuaded me to join the Liberals after my retirement and take over from him as Chairman of the All Saints Hospital Patients Committee, where I met and worked for twenty years with my good friend Stan Lamb and his family.

To Ray Hassall, Liberal Democrat city councillor, who master-minded my election campaign in Perry Barr.

To Ken Selvester and Norma, the in-laws of my son Andrew, who have shared my struggle and given so much support to my son, his wife and our grandchildren.

To James Hunte, one who did so much to bring the problems of West Indian families and youth to the notice of the nation. To Said Abdhi and the stalwart councillors and men of the people on the former Birmingham Community Relations Council.

An especial thanks to Guy Cumberpatch and Nishat Rahman of the University of Aston. They did so much to bring to full fruition the Lozells and other projects to help inner city children and youth. Hopefully the city of Birmingham will one day come to fully understand the debt it owes to such men and women.

To Jeff Rooker, formerly an admirable constituency MP and now enjoying well deserved honour in the House of Lords, and Clare Short MP. Clare, as Minister for Overseas Development, carried her good work to a wider front, yet still finds time to be an outstanding constituency representative. Both were so helpful to me during my time at Thornhill Road, and even as political rivals in the 1983 and 1987 general elections.

To Paul Nischal and Jaswant Sohal, stalwart activists on the Soho Road for the benefit of the whole community, and who like me still work daily in Handsworth.

To Gerry Hartman for his creation of the famous Birmingham Bulls American Football team, and to Frank Leadon for keeping them at the highest levels until I took over. An important phase in my life and an equally important chapter in the history of race relations in Birmingham.

A word of encouragement to Jagdish Rai, Lal Harbans and Sharif Akbar, young men and leaders of their community, now striving and working even harder to overcome prejudice in the community in the wake of the World Trade Centre atrocities in the USA. They have achieved much to counteract the effects of more recent inner-city disorder and disturbances, some involving drugs and gun crime.

TO THE MEDIA

I give special thanks to the media, without whose help it would have been impossible to accurately source and convey the spirit of events contained in this project. Some readers may feel that use of media sources is an easy alternative to research. Our press and TV are, however, as much a part of society as you and me. They reflect your attitude and mine as best they can, and will always be part of the eternal debate. And so, a special mention to the following:

To the reporters and staff of the Birmingham Post and Mail, including the Mercury. Especially to journalist Dick Williamson, to Senior Picture Editor Adam Fradgely, and to tireless Post and Mail archivist Anna Burke, without whose skills I could never have assembled our wonderful illustrations.

To BBC Pebble Mill, for their ground-breaking documentary *Shades of Grey*, produced by Roger Casstles and presented by Tony Francis. To the BBC's Ed Doolan, a staunch co-conspirator in getting my message out to the world. To Gloria Hunniford and Jimmy Young who enabled me to speak nationally.

To the makers of *Handsworth Songs*, a film now lost in the archives. Their courageous filming during the eighties of a city in torment is an invaluable source of information for students and historians. Fortunately I still possess a copy.

Thanks too to the national press for recording history so well. To the Daily Mail, the Observer, The Times and Sunday Times and the Daily Express. To Police Review for their help in accurately recalling the traumatic years. To the Wolverhampton Express and Star for their accurate and chilling coverage of the explosion of racism in the late seventies. To the Universe Catholic Newspaper for their gentle flattery.

Finally to my co-author Peter Biddulph and his wife Mary, both of whom cajoled me into making my dream a reality, and to Frances Harrison who produced the final proof read document.

PREFACE

When I first considered writing this book, my aim was simply to tell my story, from early years to modern times. I wanted to pay tribute to those who with me pioneered community policing in Handsworth. I felt that I must place on record what was achieved and has been almost forgotten and ignored. Yet, as it became a more considered project, I sensed that there lay on my shoulders a heavy responsibility to recount honestly the events of those years. Thus I might add just a little to the knowledge of those responsible for today's policing strategies. I have kept over the years all my files and records. They are in order and will be donated to an organisation of my choice following the publication of this book so that students of Police and social policy may learn more of the history of Handsworth.

I was appointed to the Handsworth sub-division of the West Midlands in January 1976 and left in December 1981 in controversial circumstances. I did not retire, as was generally understood and publicly announced. I took early retirement under pressure and with much frustration. Repeated offers, at the height of my achievements, of premature moves to less challenging duties were not acceptable to me. The reasons for moving me might well have seemed justifiable to those responsible, but I sensed intervention and encouragement from government sources unhappy with my criticism of their policing policies.

My style demanded a personal commitment that others, beyond the West Midlands Police Force, by nature of their recruitment and training, their philosophy, ethos and personality, were not ready to accept. This has been highlighted in recent years when some forces have been labelled *institutionally racist*.

Every chief constable in the land today claims to value something he or she calls *community policing*. Yet the McPherson Inquiry[1] concerning Stephen Lawrence, the issue of policing by true consent, the paucity of ethnic recruits among police ranks, recurring inter-racial and anti-Police strife in our deprived inner cities, have all added to the controversy.

Whatever our lip-service to the concept, history continues to show our true nature. The 2001 riots in Burnley, Oldham and Bradford demonstrate that, as in 1981 and 1985, all is not well in our inner cities. The frightening emergence of gun crime and serious assaults makes life hazardous for both Police and public.

Expert reports published in December 2001 and early 2002 confirm that the public are divided and angry. Home Secretary David Blunkett asserts that chief Police officers are out of touch with local people and should take a higher profile. He is impatient with the progress of Police reform, and has added what many feel is insult

---

[1] Stephen Lawrence was murdered on 22 April 1993. Lord McPherson's final report of his Inquiry was published in February 1999.

to injury by appointing an American Police officer from Boston USA to head up the new Home Office Standards Unit with power to monitor and advise forces.

This American officer appears to profess adherence to the tactics that we employed in Handsworth twenty five years ago. During those years he was a member of the US Armed Forces, and was, in all probability, unaware of our strategy. And yet, many recommendations emerging now to improve the situation are identical to the projects we undertook in Handsworth during the seventies and eighties. We are surrounded by ministers, Government officials and senior Police officers who apparently have no knowledge of the pioneering that took place during those decades. The wheel has indeed turned full circle.

I cannot claim sole ownership of all the ideas contained in this book. I discussed and argued with many over the years; Policemen of every rank and from several continents, politicians national and local, university professors, social workers, teachers, community leaders, people in the street, journalists, experts and non-experts, and, of course, local criminals. Most must take credit for showing me how things could be done better. It was out of such day to day learning that I eventually understood the truths of how a multi-racial and deprived area such as Handsworth should be Policed.

The instinct of a nation receiving wave upon wave, a *flood*, as politicians promoting the quick fix will describe them, of immigrants from new sources, runs deep and dangerous. It is primeval. Survival of the race feeds many dictators, most atrocities and wars. It flows through society, from racially biased members of government to racially biased Policemen, from the well-spoken university professor to the man on the omnibus. It must be cautiously researched and gently approached. It is a sinister force, sometimes unseen, always denied. Europe today seemingly marches towards an ever wider multi-national, multi-racial society. Yet even now, within its heart, close by the centre of European Government, we see Nazi marches and salutes, and immigrant women and children consumed by flames of racial hatred. Albanians, Macedonians and Serbs fight endless racial wars but two hundred miles from the fount of Christianity, Rome. Yet I firmly believe that the strategies we used in our tiny society called Handsworth, based as they were on the growth of trust between man and man, race and race, are of value to all of good will.

The solutions we adopted in Handsworth were admired by some, mocked by others. By a few in the political game they were viewed with open hostility. Still, whatever the hurt caused in the past to me and my family, I do not wish to lecture anyone. All I ask is that you approach with an open mind and see the following events as I saw them, from the inside looking out.

David Webb
31st January 2004

ONE: THE FIRST BRICK

A section of house brick soared out of the evening sky and slammed into my head. As the stars cleared a second swooped in and grazed my forehead. A third would follow, but by then I was too far gone to know. The bricks came from the back of the crowd, from the shadows somewhere across the road. Others joined in the throwing. Lives were at risk. A man was shouting: *'GET WEBB!... GET WEBB!..'* My friends, Asians and West Indians all around were grabbing hold, sheltering me. People, white, black, brown, were scattering, panicking. We struggled across the road into the station.

We tried to deploy the Police groups. They had been on standby for three days, hidden away from eyes that looked on any uniform as provocation. It was a hot July evening in the summer of 1981. Riots in Brixton, disorders in Liverpool and running battles in Southall between skinheads and Asian youths; all seeming a foretaste of something more widespread and sinister.

The looters crashed along the Soho Road. All those intent on causing trouble grabbed anything they could carry. Some of the locals joined in. Wheelbarrows were in fashion, commandeered from a local builder's yard. In two minutes, many shop fronts on the main street were smashed, glass tinkling along the pavements. I could hear it from inside the station as a constable patched me up with temporary dressings. My men were around me, looking for guidance. Some were young probationers with children and frightened wives. Some were older, grim-faced, wondering. This was war. Their eyes betrayed them. Had I been wrong all these years? Wrong about Handsworth and the young blacks and Asians and whites? Wrong on how to treat people who were poor, unemployed, of different race and culture? Wrong on how to Police an inner city area?

Shop windows were smashed, the displays looted. The instigators were having a marvellous time. Members of the public were joining in, the great British public. Soon the TV cameras would fly in with those starlings above our Handsworth rooftops to view the carnage and suggest easy solutions.

Within thirty minutes we arrested all the looters we could catch. All too late. Twenty five shops had been looted. Several had been torched, with flames and smoke rising high over a curious city. Fire engines and ambulances joined in the din. We pulled in forty two young men that first night, fifty seven the second night, and nineteen on the Sunday. Only fifty one out of the total of one hundred and eighteen came from Handsworth and the immediate areas. Many had come to our streets to ride the tiger of destruction, have some fun and equip their kitchens and sitting rooms at our expense.

As eight o'clock came on the next morning, wisps of smoke still rose over a shocked suburb and city. Members of the local Police Committee and local community leaders, hastily gathered, were sitting around my living room floor on our deep red carpet. Elsewhere, sleepy-eyed children were pulling on newly looted shoes and clothes, soon to be proudly displayed to school friends. Our house was small and crowded. My wife Bet[1] soothed the atmosphere with coffee and breakfast and chocolate digestives. All were assembled at their request, apologising for their people.

What to do? The Government was dithering, paralysed. As we sat there in the quiet of that July morning, everything life had taught me about people and policing might have been but a deceit. Racial explosions had occurred elsewhere, but those cities had no community policing, at least nothing approaching the depth and complexity of our achievement in Handsworth. Had I been wrong? Were the cynics correct after all? Was true community policing but a myth? Was our only hope the shield and baton, the faceless armoured warrior, the water cannon and rubber bullet and longer sentences and more and bigger prisons?

All eyes were on me, silently wondering. They were worried, confused, fearful. Cities all over Britain with high ethnic populations and social deprivation were watching and waiting. Beyond our quiet street a nation and parts of Europe and America were asking, and would be asking for months to come, perhaps years, *would the earthquake spread wider?* The channels that usually flowed with Home Office advice were silent, at least as far as my station was concerned. Political careers might succeed or fall on how events developed and how I and my tiny force acted and reacted.

The phone chattered with an endless song. Calls from politicians and journalists and experts and researchers; from Britain and Germany, France, Asia, America, even India, Kashmir and Pakistan. TV debates and radio interviews and phone-ins would fill my agenda. My patch would be news around the world for every reason I had struggled to prevent throughout my career. Little could I know then that long before, in the eyes of some in the higher ranks of the Police and government, I had failed. Under the bandages across my forehead, blood was congealed around the swelling cuts. My head still ached. I looked into Bet's worried eyes, took a deep breath, and threw myself, as ever, into the problem. Even as we debated, I sensed that the brick throwers of Soho Road were not the only ones out to *Get Webb.*

***

---

[1] Betty

Twenty-two years later, the events of that hot July evening are now clear to me as a turning point in our understanding of what should be the nature of modern policing in Great Britain. It was then that the truth of what some now know to be the right policy, the only one that finally works, was hung out for public ridicule and challenge.

The morning after the first bricks had been thrown, I went for treatment to the casualty department at Dudley Road Hospital before going home. From that day my blood pressure would increase, my eyesight rapidly deteriorate and hearing problems would begin.

A thousand times, or so it seems, friends have asked me to tell them how it really was, to describe my experiences of policing a community like Handsworth. They know, as I do, that what transpired was a telling commentary on life in a multi-racial society under stress, pockmarked with the lesions of poverty and despair. Yet among those people were and are signs of hope for the future. There, sadly, have been wasted generation after generation of intelligence, strength and potential. Only the resourceful escaped or were able to isolate themselves from the deprivation that imbued every street, every waking moment. The people of Handsworth deserved better.

TWO: POWER OF COMMAND

It is 1948. *The steep gangway has frail wooden steps and thin handrails, straddling the oily water between the troopship Empire Windrush and the walls of Liverpool Dock. It undulates with the rhythmic feet of a line of well dressed athletic men in their twenties and early thirties. All are West Indian, ebony skinned. They descend cautiously. Most wear neat trilby hats; some wear neckties, some flowery bow ties. We cannot tell the colours. This film is in black and white. Their suits appear well pressed. One broad shouldered man looks around him as he descends, curious at this cold grey world. All carry some kind of bag or case. One balances a suitcase on his head, like a porter in a Tarzan film. Is he alone, a family scout?*

A line of neat white dressed ladies follows, bright flowery skirts and coats, white hats, dressed as for a wedding. They have lived on deck across the North Atlantic, with husbands and children, paying £28 a head for admission to the New World, the land of the great white King of the Empire and Commonwealth.

At the front of the slowly descending line is a lady with a young boy-child in the crook of her arm. The child is exhausted, bewildered, dressed as for a first communion, a wide-brimmed hat on his head. The mother looks puzzled, dazed, uncertain with each step. A young sailor emerges from behind the camera, steps crisply up the gangway, grasps the child round the waist, then turns and leads the ladies down to the dock. Was this a charitable act, or just encouragement to the ladies to walk a little faster? The mother makes no reaction. Her eyes are dull, unseeing of the turmoil and bustle of this humble gateway to a promised land. [1]

***

Bet and I were together from our earliest years. In 1950 we became teenage sweethearts, and were engaged in 1954 when I was eighteen, just before I went out to Egypt on National Service. I always felt I was my own boss in the Army, and that suited my temperament nicely. I was developing fast, learning fast, adapting. I was fortunate to obtain rapid promotion to sergeant, serving in the 32nd guards brigade. That's where I learned to shout at people, nicely, of course. I was in charge of training young men coming over to Egypt to learn desert tactics, and how to maintain and use a weapon.[2]

In those days, every man who did National Service went into his local county regiment. Mine was the Bedfordshire and Hertfordshire. Everyone in the regiment was local to me, and I knew most by their first names. The sports we played, the

---

[1] Based on Documentary *Shades of Grey*, BBC 1978.
[2] Fifty years later, in 2003, it has been announced that all 2,000 servicemen who served in Suez are to be awarded the General Service Medal with clasp.

activities we followed, the guard duties, everything we did in Suez we did as local boys. In later years that experience was to stand me in good stead. That's how I learned the power of command, the voice, the sense of discipline, all assisted by an above average physique. It was the beginnings of the skill of man management, how to face down the rebellious, understand the devious, encourage the weakest, how to befriend the one who marches to a different drummer. Under that desert sun, to make big, grown men do things under military discipline, and sometimes to do things they did not like to do, I had to create an aura of command. Otherwise nothing would get done. Once you start like that you have to keep on doing it. It drives you on. It stays with you for the rest of your life.

Back home, Britain was changing. Our nation was recovering from the ravages of the War. The Empire was crumbling around us. India had recently gained its independence[1] and other colonies would soon follow. Our media and governments represented this as some willing donation of freedom and civilisation to thankful nations, and we chose to trust their words. In truth, that freedom was drawn like a tooth from a people who still fondly believed they owned the world, had industries that nations humbly admired, and had a system of government to make compulsory reading for every foreign schoolchild. In the cinemas we and our children watched a weekly diet of Tarzan films and African and Asian sagas. White men were either scheming Europeans (usually Germans), or tall handsome English heroes, shooting elephants, lions, tigers, and advancing armies of jabbering black warriors. And always the black man made a fine porter for the white man's belongings or even the white man himself.

Into our cold, turbulent nation came many by ship, and a few by plane, to create our ethnic policing needs and strategies from the fifties through to the new millennium. Little could I guess that the arrival of the Empire Windrush on that cold Liverpool day would change my life and the lives of all that I would know and love. One day, my path, and the paths of the children and grandchildren of some of those walking that frail gangplank, would meet on the streets of Handsworth, in the mighty workshop we call Birmingham.

---

[1] Independence was finally granted in 1947 after a long and stressful campaign led by Gandhi.

THREE: FINDING MY FEET

Many times in my career friends have asked me why I joined the Police. I always found the question amusing. My grandfather and uncle, both by then sadly passed on, had been Police officers before me. And since I'd spent all my working life in community relations, you would guess that, inspired by a heaven-sent vocation, I would join the Police.

No, here's the real reason. I was just out of the Army, was a fit and active twenty years of age, and after National Service a firm had to take you back into your old job. No interview, no competition. You just turned up and started work. Yet I felt restless. My experience in the Army told me there were other ways of making a living, and my newly acquired skills of command showed me that I might be do well in a different calling. Originally trained as a draughtsman, I was again back in the engineering shop at my old company in Letchworth, Hertfordshire. I worked alongside a friend, Ken Underwood, who was a keen cyclist of national repute, a champion renowned for speed and stamina, hundred mile time trials and all that. He once told me of when he was riding home without lights one winter's night, tearing through the darkness, head down, feeling good, but a danger to man and beast. An old police sergeant on his bike was going the other way and shouted to him to stop, waving him down. Ken thought *'To hell with it. He's never going to catch me'*. So off he went into the darkness, sprinting as fast as he could up and down the hills of Letchworth. He reached home, got off his bike, and was just walking up to the door when the old sergeant arrived puffing and panting on his old iron double cross barred banger. The sergeant, who was over six feet tall, came up behind and collared him for having no lights. Eight miles over the hills, through the dark and damp, and the serg had got his man. From that moment Ken's respect for the Police became as famous as his prowess on the road.

Having worked in the open air in the Army, I got a liking to working outside. In the factory I felt surrounded. I just couldn't settle down. I was living in Letchworth, an industrial new town of around twenty thousand people, and joined the local football team, Letchworth Town. They were a good team in the Spartan League, at that time a top amateur league. A neighbour of mine was a police sergeant and a keen supporter. One Saturday evening we were sharing a pint after a satisfying win over a local team, and he suddenly came out with it:

'Look David, you're a young man still. Why don't you join the Police? It would be a marvellous career for you, coming out of the service with your kind of experience. In the Police you'll have time to play football two or three times a week. You'll get a house rent free, be your own boss. You'll have great time.'

It sounded superb. I swam for the county, was Home Counties ABA middleweight boxing champion, and just loved freedom and activity. My old sergeant was correct. A Police career would guarantee a lifestyle I would enjoy. So I applied to the Hertfordshire Constabulary, was interviewed and started more or less straight away. That's how, in 1955, I joined the Police; simple as that, and I've never regretted it.

At that time, a county police force was very different from an inner city patch. In the county you lived in the Police House surrounded by the community. I call it *the* Police House because it was special place, a fountain of authority among the people, like a vicarage or the house of the local doctor. Wherever you went, you were a member of the community, in or out of uniform. You played your sport against your neighbours, you drank and joked among them. Your wife lived in the community, shopped and shared the gossip. Your children went to school alongside the children of the local villains. You each were part of the community, understood the community. I served in eight different stations across the county, and everywhere we were surrounded by the people I had to police. Another thing about the county was that you didn't stay in the same place for long. They moved us around every two or three years to stop us *going native.* If you transferred from uniform to CID, you had to move. Every promotion, and every change of department, you had to move.

I served as a beat patrol constable, walking the streets and alleys, talking to the children at the school gate, to the teenagers hanging out at the shopping centre. Then I was a traffic patrol officer, handling every kind of crazy situation that a motorist can get himself and other drivers into, chasing down horses, dogs and fugitives across motorways and country lanes. Then I was on Tactical Patrol Group, a kind of Starsky and Hutch team, rushing around the county to put down fights, deal with robberies, fires, hostage situations and family domestic violence. Each police division supplied two or three men with local knowledge, and we worked as a team. The Head was Inspector Gerald Mynott and I was selected, along with a number of other men, as the Chief Constable put it, *'For their abundance of local knowledge.'* We were known locally as *The Big Six*, a group of specially selected Crime Prevention Officers. Indeed, the Hertfordshire Tactical Patrol Group was one of the first in the country. The concept started in Liverpool and was copied by many other forces. We did not have a set programme. We went where the trouble was. We might be in Stevenage or Hitchin for a week, and then St. Albans the next. Each night we were never sure where we would be the following morning. Mobility and flexibility would be the deterrent, and it worked. I also served as detective, and within a few years had crammed in a wealth of experience covering just about the full range of policing responsibilities and skills.

It was the 1950's. The only black sportsmen we saw played cricket for the West Indies, or India, or Pakistan, or ran in the Olympics. The South African Security Services had their own office in South Africa House just off Trafalgar Square in London so they could keep an eye on the anti-apartheid activists.

Meanwhile, as a constable in Hertfordshire, I was on my bike. They gave us all a free bike, big iron things, weighed a ton. So they allowed us to buy our own from a cycle allowance, about two shillings a week. Indeed I've still got that first bike, a fifty years old veteran Raleigh, in my garage. It was knackered when I left Hertfordshire, but I kept it as a memento of the good times. It's nice to see them making a come-back in some Police areas.

Every young probationer and constable went through the county police training centre. They taught us first aid, life saving, every technical and social skill you could imagine. We took all the necessary qualifications:- how to deal with road accidents, handle domestic situations, deliver a baby, prevent conflict, every kind of crisis. We were on our own. Whatever happened we did it, and we had to get it right.

Police radios were a rarity. No luxuries such as blue Police phone boxes. Only the main towns of St Albans and Watford had Police boxes. In the villages we communicated by telephone once every hour at a designated telephone in a shop or someone's house. We had what we called a *via*, going everywhere, working our beats to a particular pattern. We went out at six in the morning and by seven we would be at the village Post Office. Then we were at the butcher's shop by eight, and at nine down on the farm and so on through our shift. Nights were lonelier and available phones fewer. If they wanted you, the phone would ring at the local public kiosk. You would go to the kiosk at an appointed time, the sergeant would tell you where to go, and you'd be off on your bike to an incident. If you got there within half an hour everyone thought it was marvellous.

My local sergeant, Percy Cook, had been in my regiment in the Army. Percy had been a *Chindit* in Burma with the British Forces. A *Chindit,* drawn from white, Indian and Burmese races, was a kind of SAS soldier, operating behind enemy lines. The regimental dress was distinguished by a hat that was a combination of an Australian soldier's hat and a large cockade feather. When the first tranche of Asians came to Letchworth, Percy used to boast that he could communicate with *the natives*. We watched and listened with some amusement as he held conversations which none of us could understand, speaking a combination of pigdin English and sign language.

'Me Percy Cook, me sergeant...'

We used to hide behind the office door in the station rolling with silent laughter as Percy put together a complex statement about some crime or other. Percy admired his interpreter skills. Never did I ever think that when I came to Handsworth I would need just the same skills that Percy demonstrated all those years ago. I travel widely now in my new career and visit India regularly. I find that if I recall how Percy did it and try to imitate him, I can converse with anyone in India at any level of society. *'Me David Webb ...'* The reply is unfailing, *'No problem, Mr Webb.'*

It was at that time that I had my first encounter with Royalty. It was before the days of Police radios. When the Queen and the Royal Family travelled from Buckingham Palace to Sandringham, we were part of the security arrangements. The

Royal Party went through Hertfordshire on the London North Eastern Railway from King's Cross to Sandringham. Every bridge and strategic point had a policeman on watch. He had to report in to headquarters that the train had passed by safely. In the middle of the night the train, with its distinctive purple light on the front and mauve lights on the rear, would thunder past. We would cycle up to the bridge and stand there until the train was gone, then ride on our bikes to the nearest phone kiosk to report in. This might take fifteen minutes or so. God knows what would have happened if something bad had occurred or if our bike had a puncture. I always wonder to this day if Her Majesty was aware that her train was halfway to Sandringham before we constables reached our phone points, and sometimes we never even got there at all.

There were other encounters with the Royals. The Queen Mother, whose family name was *Bowes Lyon*, was loved greatly, especially among those who had braved the wartime Blitz. She would visit her relatives at Bowes Lyon House in Hitchin, where I was a detective constable. Once or twice a year she would stay there, sometimes for days at a time. Tom O'Connor, Eric Clayton and I were assigned to duty, but no luxury for us, no hot soup with the servants. Instead a small wooden hut out the back, near to where the Rolls Royce was parked in the rear garage, was our home. No weapons, no technology, no radios, no heating. The Queen Mother would arrive in the Rolls Royce with her personal detective, also unarmed. We'd wander round to stretch our legs and he'd come out to see us, and give us a fiver each, in those days a week's wages. *'Here chaps, go and get yourselves some fish and chips, and just make sure you keep awake all night. Now we don't want anything going wrong for Her Majesty do we?'* Then he'd go inside to sleep in a comfortable bed, thinking of us sitting quietly eating our chips in our little wooden hut, safeguarding the nation's treasure against thieves and terrorists. Little did he or Her Majesty know that we were comfortably passing the night away in the Roller.

In later years, when at Handsworth, I was to receive a message that would sadden me greatly. Tom, that wonderful man I had known in Letchworth, would die suddenly at the young age of forty six. Tom was an active member of our Wilbury Wanderers football team, and a good family friend to me for so long in my formative years. Whatever he was asked to do, whatever the pressure of work, he always did with a smile. Bet and I would miss him and his friendship greatly.

The Queen herself came one day to Stevenage to officially open the New Town. The ceremony was staged in the Town Centre on top of (and I swear to this day She did not know it) the town centre public toilet. Her way to the ceremony was up a flight of wooden steps to the top of the toilet section, where lay a small square with seating and flower beds. While Her Majesty was mounting the steps to get to the ceremony I had the job of standing beneath to prevent anyone looking upwards as she was passing by. For Policemen and soldiers, when Royalty pass by, it's always a case of salute. In addition, in this case, it was definitely *Eyes Front*. Many times I've been asked *what colour?* It is a secret I will carry to my grave.

In Hertfordshire, it was the tradition that we each lived in Police houses, all together in a row of maybe ten. I used to live next door to the Police sergeant, Fred Darts, an old village type Policeman. He had also been a member of the Bedfordshire and Hertfordshire Regiment during the war. He was a famous Commando, a holder of the Distinguished Conduct Medal, mentioned in the all the books about the Commandos, and one of their biggest heroes. He was a big tough man, but at the same time a real Bedfordshire country boy, skilled in growing great vegetables and glorious flowers. He always reminded me of *Desperate Dan* in the old comics. I used to go down my garden and Fred would be peering through his window, looking out for me.

I thought I knew something about gardening, but I was wrong. As I made a hole to put in a potato, Fred would sneak up behind me in true commando style. *'No boy, you don't put it in like that, you put it in like this...'* And as I cut my grass: *'No boy, you don't cut the grass like that. You cut the grass like this...'* And as I rode my bike: *'No boy, you don't ride it like that. You ride your bike like this...'* Fred and I kept in touch, remained friends for a long time, but now I believe he has passed on.

Bet's Uncle, Horace Thompson (we called him *Tommy*), also lived in Watford. He later retired to the Isle of Wight. *Tommy* was six feet four, a Coldstream Guards Sergeant during the war and the Force Drill Sergeant. He was a lovely man with a charming wife, who spent most of her life in service in the big houses of the South East of England. She was a refined lady, the Downstairs of *Upstairs-Downstairs*. But Tommy was two people. At home with his lovely wife and with friends, he was the soul of discretion, a gentleman of conversation. Yet once a month, as the Police ranks practised their drill and paraded on the square, his voice would carry for miles. His language made the leaves tremble on the trees. The station had a drawerful of complaints and petitions about Tommy and his language.

Tommy gave me some advice when I moved up the ranks to the heights of bike patrol officer: *'Now boy, take your bleepin bike an' go round your bleepin beat. An' they'll give you a bleepin chicken here and a bleepin rabbit there and some bleepin potatoes. So, boy you gotta have a big strong bleepin saddle bag.'* Meeting him on the high street in Watford when his missus was not around was an experience. If we saw him coming, we would head for the nearest quiet corner or the local park before engagement occurred so the public could not hear him. *'Hello David!'* he would bellow. *'Are you bleepin OK?'* It got to a stage that Tommy not only could not get past three words without an expletive, he could not even get past three letters. One of his more famous openers was when he talked about our Antipodean friends: *'Now David, take yer Aus-bleepin-stralians...'*

Tommy and his wife have long since departed to that great Police station in the sky. But there is another story about him that has often been told and deserves telling again. Tommy was station sergeant at Watford. One night a local drunk was brought in, tanked up to the eyeballs, and Tommy installed him safely in the cells. The drunk seemed determined to cause trouble, and kept ringing the emergency call bell. Tommy would open the cell door and ask if he was OK, and he would mumble *'So sorry sergeant, I'll go to sleep now...'* Then five minutes later he was at it again. And so it went on, every five minutes, hour after hour, driving everybody nuts.

At that time a fire arms amnesty was in progress and in an adjoining cell, ready for destruction, was a big pile of rifles. Tommy, at the end of his tether, got together five constables and gave them each an unloaded rifle. He marched the drunk outside and stood him up against a wall. He lined up the smirking constables and roared *'Atteeeenshun!'* Then he turned to the swaying man. *'Look, this is your last warning. If you don't keep quiet we'll shoot you - understood?'* The drunk finally got the message. Next morning he pleaded guilty and was fined As the magistrate made to call the next case, the fellow, much the worse for wear, asked if he could address the court.

'Yes?' said the magistrate.

'Sir, I'm really sorry, really. And I'm so grateful for your mercy and not having me shot last night.'

There was a short, puzzled silence. The magistrate leaned over and muttered to the clerk, *'Poor chap must have had a nightmare...'*

FOUR: FIRST PROMOTION

I rapidly learned that the people protected by my beat expected me to be part of their community, to share their lives and problems. I was still twenty years of age, by modern standards surprisingly young for so much responsibility.

Normally in the Police force we were not always stationed in our own home towns, but I suffered a special domestic situation when my mother was seriously ill, needing assistance from my wife Bet. The other members of my family, my brothers and sisters, would have been too young to cope. So I was allowed for compassionate reasons to move from Watford, which was on one side of the county, back to Letchworth, my home town, and take my family with me. There I was among the friends and neighbours I had known when I was an army sergeant; *all together again* as the old song goes. This time, however, I descended on them as a policeman, following them around, making sure they behaved themselves, just like by the Suez Canal. I could not know this at the time, but all this was making me what I finally became in Handsworth. The style of policing I had to do every day became ingrained into me. It seemed the natural way, it worked, and I was fortunate to understand why. Many times I had to come down hard on people who were my friends, and I was forced to develop skills that enabled me to get them to understand that it was a job that had to be done, and get them to accept the fairness of their punishment or censure. It also worked the other way. People used to send for me rather than any other constable, to go to their house to deal with a problem, because they knew me and my reputation. They knew how I would behave and how I thought, and they wanted me to deal with their problems. That sometimes meant that their children had to be arrested. It was my job.

It is corny to say it and people don't always believe it, but it really was like this; in the old days, as late as the mid fifties, the old-time criminal knew there was a good chance that he would get caught. It was him versus the Policeman, and if he got caught, he put his hands up. You've heard the old saying *Fair Cop,* that's how it used to be. If it was a local crime, committed by local crooks, my clear-up rate as a detective went as high as eighty percent. I knew, sometimes by first name, every local 'personality'. If there had been a burglary the night before, and one of them turned up in the local billiard hall with extra money or cigarettes in his pocket, someone would always get a message to me and a collar was felt. Letchworth was an urban community and the first Garden City. It was the sort of place where a good policeman knew that if he could not solve a crime within a couple of days, it must have been the work of an untraceable criminal passing through.

I kept in touch with football and although a little older, and by now described in the local sports pages as *Portly Webb, seventeen stones and a bit more,* I managed to play on the local team, the Wilbury Wanderers. We used to wander around the football field chasing the ball and occasionally scored a goal or two to win a few medals. The team was run by the chairman of the local magistrates, first name Fred. As a detective I played centre half. My friend Tom O'Connor, an Irishman detective constable, played centre forward. We had a couple of known criminals in the squad. The whole community was represented in a good mix of folks, and it was my first experience of community policing, although in those days we did not see it as that. No person, no criminal, was written off, ever. To me they were all people.

The Court was in the Police station, and held sometimes on a Saturday morning. We would all meet in the Court before we went to a game, and there was Chairman Fred up at the front on the bench. He was getting on a bit and had a habit of slowing down as the cases proceeded. While Fred was up front, we stood at the back giving him the signals to get through the cases quickly, so that we could catch the team bus for the away game. Old Fred's knowledge of the law left something to be desired, and he would deliberately sit next to me on the coach on the way to the game. *'David,'* he would whisper, *' what was it that I sent that young man down for this morning...?'*

As a detective I found that I had more freedom to organise, and we had our interesting moments. Neil Coles, the famous golfer, went to school at St Christopher's in Letchworth. I learned that courses all over the county were getting burgled. Early one winter's morning after a heavy snowfall the assistant professional rang to say there had been a break-in, so I went down to the course and looked around. There, in front of me, was a set of fresh footprints leading from the club house away across the fairways. I followed them half way round the course, and reached the ninth green, covered as it was with snow. In the centre of the green was a pile of human excrement, and right by it, a well used crumpled sheet of paper. So I undid the paper and saw, in clear handwriting, a name and address. I followed the footsteps, taking the paper with me, and went across to where the burglar had got into his van and driven away. Yes, the name on the substitute toilet paper was our man, and he confessed to 'doing' golf clubs all over the county. The court hearing raised a few eyebrows. This was before the days of DNA and carefully managed sampling. *'Good Police work,'* said my sergeant Percy Cook. We used that example to teach young trainee policemen that when looking for evidence, never ignore anything.

It was in Letchworth that I had my first experience in working alongside other races. I had met a few in Egypt, but was isolated, by army routines, from day to day contacts. In Letchworth it was different. The town was small, but it was there that many of the early immigrants who came to Great Britain in 1954 were settled. There were several hundred Asians and West Indians, quite a large ratio in a town of some twenty thousand. They came to work in the great Kryn and Lahy steelworks where, during the war, had been assembled cranes, tracks and tanks. Many experienced workers came down from the steelworks in the North of England. Finally there was the big Hertfordshire Rubber Manufacturing Company.

Letchworth was famous for its government training centre, linked to several huge hostels, holding up to two thousand people. They came from all over England; Latvians, Poles, Italians, Asians, West Indians; all were trained at the Centre. In just a few years after the war, as our industries rebuilt, Letchworth became a bustling multi-national and multi-lingual town. As a young Policeman I came into direct contact with many races, black, brown and white.

Today we hear much talk about crime, race and colour. History will surely find us wanting in our judgmental attitude to race and crime. In the fifties and right up to the seventies, the Asian population and the West Indians were respectable peoples, especially in the county areas. The first Asians coming in the fifties tended to come alone, leaving family at home in India or Pakistan. Old men, young men, shared seven or eight to a house, each possessing a bed roll, which he carried rather as a modern middle class backpacker touring the Himalayas today. The first shift would arrive in the morning, and each store his bed roll in the corner of the workplace. They would work hard and long, with the sole purpose of earning enough money to support parents or wife and family, or eventually go home to start a business. In those early days it was not intended that they would stay in England.

The Afro Caribbeans were seen in a different light. Many had lived in Letchworth for some time, and had been in the West Indian contingents in the Air Force and the Army. They were billeted locally and given government training. Some married local girls, and nobody worried.

One event that stays with me happened one ordinary Saturday morning. As I played football on a Saturday afternoon it was always my habit to avoid trouble in the morning, otherwise I might be delayed by a case and miss my weekly outing on the pitch. So I would drive around and try to pretend I was invisible. As I drove past the big power station the whole place exploded. It turned out later that the switch room had blown up. As I pulled up alongside the devastation there were bodies everywhere, some men dead, some still on fire, screaming for help. I tried and tried, but could not put out the fires. I had to stand there and watch some of them die, twisting in slow agony. Five men perished and many were injured. I felt powerless and guilty, as have many other policemen and firemen at similar disasters.

Perhaps I am fortunate, but I have never felt any animosity, instinctive or otherwise, towards other races. From my childhood days I learned to respect the sincerity and innate kindness of other people. Before the war, in my childhood days, we were poor, had a large family and slept six to a bed. Whenever Mom had another baby, my Aunt, who had six children of her own, would look after us. We learned about true deprivation and sharing first hand.

I had a grandmother who lived some thirty miles from London, and during the wartime bombing, people used to travel each night thirty or so miles to get away from the centre of the city. She had a small home, just two rooms, but used to invite a Jewish family, and put them up in her tiny house. There was some prejudice against

Jews in England even during the war, although people did not know at that stage what had been happening in the concentration camps. That news only emerged at the end of hostilities when Germany and Poland were overrun. The family of Jews were orthodox, and tailors. They would sit and talk for hours with Grandmother. She held no prejudice, and saw them for what they were; folks in need of help. As we came and went throughout the day , we thought nothing of it. I was about nine years old at the time, and my school friends went to school ragged and poor. Yet I went to school in a personally tailored black pin-stripe suit with a waist-coat, and my brother had a brown pin-stripe suit with a waist-coat, all made with gratitude and love. We were probably the best dressed children in England at the time, as good as royalty.

All these events really did not mean much at the time, but, looking back, I can sense something of where my attitudes came from towards people of a different colour and way of life. In Letchworth, in the post-war factories, these people were invited over by our government to do jobs that white people did not want to do. At that time we had more than full employment. Jobs went a-begging, in the foundries, the rubber factory, everywhere. That hot foundry and the smoking rubber factory were places where the white English did not want to work.

The different races were no threat, were not organised, built no temples, no mosques, none of the things that today put the frighteners on the more prejudicial among us. They kept themselves to themselves, met in their own homes, came and went to work. There were no domestic incidents or problems. They sent few children to school. They never got involved in crime. The only problems I ever found as a policeman was that a few of the men liked to have a good drink. After a long day in the foundry, they had a thirst and sometimes would have too much of the white man's medicine. So we would stick them in a cell overnight, give them breakfast, and off they would go straight to the factory for another hard day's work.

I recall one example that upset me as a young officer, which I would not go along with, and was a forerunner of some of the bad things I would find later within the police force. In those days a beat officer in a small town such as Letchworth would go on his rounds with a big saddle-bag on his bike. He needed a big one too. Everyone was his friend. The butcher would give him a leg of pork, the farmer would give him a grouse or a rabbit, and so on all around the beat. It was an enjoyable part of the job of being an old style policeman.

But it could get out of hand. When I first went to Letchworth, the force had just one patrol car, driven by two constables, with a young policeman acting as an observer. For a newly trained constable this was a great experience, riding around in the luxurious depths of a Westminster saloon. One night I got the job and went on patrol with two senior officers. Both were old soldiers with medals and memories. Our patrol area was large, covering the whole of the North of Hertfordshire.

Off we went into the night. After a few miles the driver turned off the regular route, onto a farm track, then into a farmyard. The radio was switched off and we strolled in to meet with the farmer. There we sat in comfort for about an hour, eating cakes and drinking tea. He then handed my colleagues a big parcel. On we went to the next rendezvous and the next big parcel of goodies. And so the whole of the tour of night duty was spent sitting around in comfort and cadging from the community. The huge boot of the Westminster was full. The regulation beat was ignored, all contact with central control severed. We even went over the county border into another area. I had been allocated the job of observer for a week. On the second night, I could take it no longer. I was young, and I could not say too much to those old guys. Well, you can't, can you? Your whole career may depend on it. So I told them: *'Listen lads, this isn't the way I want to do things, I don't want to get involved. This isn't the way I expect to be as a Policeman, so just take me home.'* They dropped me off. I was only four hours into my eight hour tour of duty. That was it. No more luxury, tea and cakes.

Next morning, I went to see the sergeant. I did not want to cause any problems with those old guys, but the things they were doing on that patrol was not my scene. I did not think that Police should behave like that. I asked to be moved to another job, and had a quiet word with the sergeant. I told him: *'Keep your eyes on those two. One day they'll come unstuck.'*

And they did, within about six months. One night the two drove over the county boundary, presumably to collect from a pub, got drunk, and ran off the road down a bank into a village pond. That shiny three litre Westminster, the only car in the Letchworth force, was sitting in a pond in another county, up to its headlights in water and reeds, surrounded by a flock of curious ducks and waterhens. I never found out what their story was but it must have been a good one, as they stayed in the force, but no longer on mobile patrol.

Promotion can come in many guises and sometimes unexpectedly. In those days, in the larger towns like Watford and St Albans, we stood on parade of fifteen or so constables in order of seniority, under the watchful eyes of our eight inspectors. The oldest constable stood at the right end of the line, and the youngest on the left. I was well down the seniority line and if the chief did not give me the worst jobs, they came pretty close. The senior man would have the privilege of the job of observer in the division's only patrol car, next would come the cycle beat constable, last would come the foot patrol officer for the high street. One of the best things around was football duty, and that gave a chance to watch Watford Town, in those days in the Third Division South.

One night I was on my beat, which included the local area called *Cassio Park*, just by the Grand Union Canal. It was my habit to keep in the shadows unseen, and as I walked quietly along by the canal side, a car swished past me and drove into the park. The car seemed somehow familiar. So I waited a little while and then walked up to it, tapped on the window and shone my torch in.

'Good evening sir. Is everything alright?' Two pairs of sheepish eyes blinked back at me from the rear seat. *'Yes, David. Everything's OK.'* Suddenly I was *David*. It was one of the local inspectors with a WPC.

'No problems. Carry on, David. Goodnight.' I completed my rounds and went back to the station. Nothing to report of course. All quiet in Cassio Park. Later, the Inspector's car rolled up to the station, and he disappeared into his office only to reappear at break time about two o'clock in the morning.

'Hello David,' he smiled. *'I've been watching you for a long time. You're coming on very well. How would you like to do football duty?'*

And for the rest of my time in Watford, Saturdays were a pleasure.

FIVE: ANOTHER PROMOTION

The Midlands came into my life in 1966, shortly after the formation of the new West Midlands Constabulary, merging many of the smaller forces into a series of borough forces around Birmingham; Dudley, Wolverhampton, Walsall and Staffordshire County. Experienced people were in demand from as far afield as Northumberland, Wales, Scotland, and like me, from the south of England. I then discovered that there was a chance of promotion to Detective Inspector of the Vice Squad. Never thinking I would be successful, I put in an application. As it turned out I got lucky, and was invited to Brierley Hill Headquarters for an interview with the Deputy Chief Constable Edwin Solomon. Later I heard from him that I was to be offered the job, and told my Chief Constable, who had originally come from Staffordshire himself.

He looked at me quizzically for a moment. *'David, what the **** do you want to go to Staffordshire for? You stay here m'lad. I'll promote you to Inspector soon. Hell, you're the only qualified man in my force. Why drag your family up to that place when you're doing so well?'*

He was right. If I stuck around long enough promotion was certain. It was dead men's shoes, but how long was long enough? I was commander of the renowned Tactical Patrol Group with good prospects. They didn't want to lose me, perhaps could not afford to. Still, here was an offer of promotion from the Midlands. It was a bird in the hand. I rang the Walsall office to fix a start date, booked my three children Andrew, Debbie and Caroline into their new school in Willenhall, and gave my poor wife Bet the job of arranging the furniture van. We were moving to a newly built semi-detached home in a row of police properties in Willenhall, just a mile or two from Handsworth. We had little furniture, so we thought. It took us both a week to pack everything.

We trundled up to Willenhall, busy and proud as sparrows in our new home. Our tiny tots, Andrew, and daughters Debbie and Caroline, moved to the infant school, just around the corner from where we lived. I took some leave during the transfer, and would walk around the town of Walsall, getting a feel for the place. On the appointed morning I polished my uniform to brilliance, marched proudly to the station, walked into the hallway, said good morning to everyone and asked where my desk was.

'Morning Mr. Webb,' said the desk sergeant. *'The Chief Superintendent wants to see you right away.'* He avoided my eyes. Something was wrong. I sat fidgeting on the wooden bench in the hallway fifteen minutes. The call came and I walked in for the first time to meet my new commander, Chief Superintendent Jim Collins. I was soon to discover that he was known affectionately by his men as *'Gentleman Jim'*.

'David, I've got some bad news. The Chief has given the job to Brian Morgan from the Met.'

I went cold, rage welled up in me. What had I done to my career and my family? My job down in Hertfordshire was now promised to someone else. I was trapped.

'OK, what do I do?' I felt like a ticking bomb in its last few seconds.

'In the circumstances, the Chief Constable's decided to give you a job as uniformed Inspector. He's an understanding man. You'll like him when you meet him.'

What a shambles. I was in a strange town, family uprooted, doing a job I hadn't applied or been interviewed for. It was a shock to the system and a test of resolution. Still, there was no going back. I have always been in some ways a fatalist, and over the weeks I rationalised away my fury. I had been promoted after all, and, still only thirty one years of age, lucky to be one of the youngest ever appointed to the rank of inspector. I was still in uniform, but at the next highest rank. It was then that I resolved never to look back in anger. I was stuck and would make the best of it. I did not know it then, but I would soon come to love Walsall and the Midlands and their peoples, and I've never regretted for a moment the way things turned out.

All the same it was unusual. The Chief Constable, without telling his Deputy, Edwin Solomon, had given the job to Brian Morgan of the Metropolitan Police. Brian would in time become a close comrade and friend. He had talent, rising to Assistant Chief Constable for Devon and Cornwall, helping John Alderson, the Chief Constable. He too became a good friend of the distinguished researcher John Brown of the Cranfield Institute. We were to study under John's guidance, spending many a happy day together in library, squash court and bar. Our philosophies of policing were similar, and he and I worked on ideas that later would be singled out for comment and praise by Lord Scarman in his report on the 1981 Brixton riots.

The old Walsall station was in the town centre, covering Walsall, Willenhall, Darlaston and Bloxwich. We were small compared to most borough forces, and I quickly got to know everyone. I was in charge of a group of some forty men. We would do early, late and night shifts in rotation, handling accidents, fires, domestic violence, street fights, burglary. Whatever it was, out we would go on foot or in panda cars. Walsall had been a small Borough Force, akin to a county force in strategy and policing.

If you wanted promotion, you generally had to look elsewhere. Yet if you kept your nose clean and wanted to stay in a particular force for the rest of your life you could, and many of my colleagues did. In spite of the amalgamation, there remained an air of independence, and even four years later we were still using the old Walsall Borough letterheads and paper. Wolverhampton and the others were of like mind. They kept to themselves, and in some ways Walsall remained the small parochial community which it had always been. Not all the old Walsall men welcomed the new senior officers or the changes in name and status, and we newcomers were sometimes given a hard time. They thought we were going to bring new ideas, interfere with their promotion prospects. It became a hard task for the top commanders to bring the forces together.

I have always been a social kind of person, the kind who just has to get active in a social sense, always looking to assist the community in some way. I got an invitation to join the Walsall Round Table. I would later, in 1975, become the Chairman. We did many fund raising events for local charities. We were one of the first organisations to undertake sky diving for charity, and we spent one of our parachuting days raising money to buy a cell separator for the Leukaemia Treatment Department of the Birmingham Children's Hospital. For me, courage under fire was not something I lacked, but the idea of jumping from a plane from two thousand feet after *'A short course of instruction'* was something I preferred to organise rather than perform. Fortunately for me a miracle happened, and Alan Towers of BBC Pebble Mill fame volunteered to take my place. The poor chap broke his leg on landing, but the ensuing publicity raised a ton of money and the machine was duly bought and installed.

In addition to my general responsibilities, and for all my ten years at Walsall, I was the Police Federation Representative, or *the trade union man*. I represented the officers and their problems face to face, argument to argument, at Head Office in Brierley Hill, with Edwin Solomon, by then Chief Constable of the West Midlands following amalgamation of the boroughs. He must have been a forgiving man, asking me on a number of occasions to represent him at awards and other public events. Yet in spite of gaining his confidence, I remained stuck in the ranks.

To my mind, we were moving towards reactive policing, cracking down as the crime occurred or shortly after. I did not always agree. With reactive policing, its all too late.   True, you catch the young criminal, sometimes. Then society takes its revenge, banging him up among veteran criminals. There he will learn the subtleties of a life of crime. If he is not already on drugs he will be surrounded by drugs, get addicted to drugs, learn how to trade drugs. He will form criminal friendships to carry back into society. Once out he will probably not get a job, and will drift in desperation towards former prison friends for the life-cycle to resume. The damage is done and it is hard to turn him back to the straight and narrow. And, while you are cracking down on him, you antagonise his family, his friends and whole sections of the population in his area.

Still, in spite of our more reactive style, I sensed that each emergency had a potential for the positive side of policing. If I was called to a disturbance, I tried to use all my skills to handle the situation in a tactful manner, get the best out of myself and the people involved, including the family of the criminal. So I insisted that my men deal with people in a humane manner. That to me, in my early years of real command, was a beginning of community policing, something of the traditional way.

Police life had its sad side. In 1974 I had the job of visiting some bereaved relatives following the bombing by the IRA of two pubs in the centre of Birmingham. Twenty one people were killed, including three from our area. Many were injured and maimed for life. That kind of job was always the responsibility of the Inspector, and taking the bad news to the next of kin is something you have to do. One of my visits was at five a.m., knocking on the door and waiting while the people got dressed to come down and ask what was going on. I can still see the traumatised faces and hear the sobs in my quieter moments.

Yet life was fun as well. We used to play snooker in our refreshment breaks, and I developed a good relationship with my men. Although I was over thirty years of age, I was still a good soccer player. The station was short of four or five players, so I made a come-back and recruited, with some arm twisting, the remainder. In 1971 we were featured in the Walsall Observer as winning six out of nine games with thirty four goals against seventeen. On those fast-fading photos, we were a tough bunch, reminiscent of the kind of people we locked up on a daily basis. From then on we won the annual force championship trophy eight years in a row. While still on the theme of football, I recall having to stand in court and prosecute the England goal keeper Peter Shilton, and outline the evidence against him for driving at over one hundred miles an hour in our section of motorway. We collared him at the Gailey roundabout.

I played squash even at a relatively advanced age. If someone disagreed with me, I used to love driving my point home with a well timed smash. Not to the corner as you might expect. My aim was more of a disciplinary one, and I would aim at the nether regions. Diabolical! They would have a big round love bite across their backside for days. The two chief superintendents now[1] in charge of Handsworth and West Bromwich were two of my young officers. The first thing they said when I sponsored them in joining the Rotary Club was that they would never again play squash with me. Both have now developed into fine officers with a great sense of community spirit, and both have served as Presidents of the Handsworth Rotary. At the time, however, they were rubbing their bruises and complaining that I never played such a thing as a friendly game. I don't think they minded. Well, not that much.

There were some interesting characters too. One of the more famous ones, regrettably now dead, as many of them are now, was the lead Detective in the Birmingham Six bombing arrests. George Reade was my next door neighbour, and our wives were great friends. George became famous within the Force for his activities. In later years, MP Chris Mullin and his friend the lawyer Ivan Geffen, would come after George as part of their investigations preceding the appeal of the Birmingham Six.[2]

---

[1] 2001 - Geoffrey Reece and Bruce Gilbert
[2] All six were freed on appeal and compensated in 1991

George was a great detective, and would get up to all sorts of tricks. Our houses shared a garage, side by side, and each garage had metal overhead doors. His aim when turning into his garage was none too sure, and he would occasionally dent my garage door with his front bumper. I repaired it the first few times but gave up after that. After a year of George's attentions it resembled a ploughed field.

As the Police Federation man, I would confront Chief Constable Edwin Solomon every month over some issue or other. One day we nervously went by appointment to defend the actions of two officers. This time I and they were in the wrong and I was the bad guy. The officers, a sergeant and a PC, had attended a burglary in the early hours in Walsall by the old town square. Meantime, the Council had changed the town centre into a one-way affair, and the information had been slow in percolating through our system. The two had driven to the incident against the traffic flow and ended their chase in a collision. Charged with careless driving and damaging a Police vehicle, they were in serious trouble, and careers and pensions were at stake.

Edwin was a loveable fellow in the morning, but after a 'good' lunch could be somewhat unpredictable. We arrived there at ten sharp for the morning appointment, but things were delayed for various reasons and we had to see him after lunch. I feared our case would suffer the kiss of death. At three on the dot we trundled sheepishly into his office. I opened our account, explaining away as best I could the offence that the two had committed; how these fine upstanding officers had many years of good service to the public, unblemished records, dependant wives and children etc. Suddenly, like a judge, Edwin held up his hand to stop me mid-sentence: *'That bloody Borough Council! When I was Chief Constable in Walsall they wouldn't have messed things up like this. I don't agree with this at all. Clear off!'*

What to do? We scurried out and I asked his secretary: *'Look, I don't know if he's decided if my members are guilty or not. You'd better go back in and ask him what his verdict is. The careers of my members depend on it.'*

So in she went and asked him what the verdict was. Edwin looked at her, puzzled. *'What verdict...?'* The two were speechless but off the hook. What a day...

I eventually moved to the Prosecutions Department. I would go to court each day, acting as the prosecuting advocate. All this time I was learning fast, beginning to understand the spirit that drives a Police force, how to look after a diverse bunch of characters, including some strong personalities. As Federation Representative, working with men in all sorts of disciplinary trouble, it teaches you the foibles of human nature, how to read and understand highly complex situations, and how to react and decide. We were dealing situations affecting men's careers and families, so every excuse in the book came my way, every evasive strategy, every technique of lying. I learned every possible method of sanction plus a few that I invented myself.

In 1967 I was one of a select group sent to the Police Staff College at Bramshill, and on several training courses which offered an opportunity for promotion to the ranks of Chief Inspector and Chief Superintendent. Yet, by 1975, I was highly frustrated. Eight years had passed at inspector rank without further promotion. I was disappointed with life and myself. I had been interviewed by a series of selection boards and was becoming known to most of them. By then I knew all the questions and what was behind them. I began to sense that my Federation activities might be the problem, creating resentment and undercurrents of jealousy. As Police Federation Secretary, I had to confront the Chief Constable, and we would argue strongly. Not good for anyone's career. I finally reached the stage whereby I was supervising and conducting prosecutions from the Prosecutions Department at Walsall, and coping with Federation work as well. It was all too much and the strain began to show. So in the autumn of 1975 I decided to end my work with the Federation.

I was unpopular with some of the hierarchy, plus the Chief Constable of West Midlands. However, the changes continued, and the force was once again reorganised and amalgamated with Birmingham City to become the new West Midlands Police Force. The Chief Constable of the new Force, Phillip Knights, later Lord Knights, must have seen and heard enough to suggest that my experience would be useful elsewhere. One week after leaving the Federation I was in my office getting some papers ready for a court case. The door opened and there smiled my friend Superintendent Ray Morris. *'Congratulations David. You've been promoted to Chief Inspector. You're going to Handsworth.'*

SIX: HANDSWORTH - FIRST CONTACT

*'**Imagine young West Indians**, perhaps born in the early sixties, their parents come to England, leaving them behind with aunts or grandparents in a little village. Having their schooling in a poor Victorian barn of a place, coming over here at the end of the sixties, joining their fathers and mothers. No longer perhaps feeling at home. Their parents may have another family, may have parted, Mom and Dad are working.*

They go to school and mix with children like themselves, very much at a disadvantage, feeling at a loss, continually at a disadvantage. They come onto the labour market just at the worst time, a time of high unemployment, particularly for young people.

Soon they get involved with the Police, perhaps some act of minor delinquency. The Police come round. The parents themselves get het up and reject their children. And this act of rejection is very common in many ways. And so, leaving their parents, they shack up with others of their kind, in squats or communes. On the one hand searching for purpose, searching for identity; on the other hand involved more and more in criminality, acts of violence against the old and defenceless.

It's a scenario. And the question is, how do we stop it, how do we contain it? How do we prevent more children coming at risk? This is a problem, I think, for the families, the community, the statutory authorities, for the employers. It is the beginning, I believe, of understanding in Handsworth.'[1]

***

January 1976 was a raw, cold month. I did not even know at that time where Handsworth was. Rumours among the ranks said it was a bed of nails for even experienced policemen. Some people who had been there before me had suffered a hard time, and did not stay long. The place was said to be difficult for senior officers to cope with because of the multi racial situation, and the problems were getting worse each year.

I was a Chief Inspector, deputy to Superintendent Gerry Finch, and above him, Chief Superintendent Joe Matthews. Both wonderful men who taught me a lot. Gerry in particular had already started to develop his own ways of relating with the locals.

The media were taking a close interest. I cannot recall when the term *Angry Suburb* was first used, but looking back now it definitely seems to fit those first few

---

[1] *Shades of Grey*, BBC 1978, words of introduction spoken by John Brown to interviewer Tony Francis.

months. There was, though, no sending to Handsworth as somewhere you imprison a man as some kind of punishment for a chief's displeasure, although some might have thought so at the time. Still, I was over the moon, and happy to be moving on. My life was progressing again, and here was a chance to do something different. Even the role of Deputy Sub-Divisional Commander was a position of true authority. I felt I could start to make things happen. It had always been clear to me what kind of policeman I wanted to be. Whatever needed to be done, I believed that I was capable of doing it. I was confident, I had the personality and the experience, and now here was the opportunity. Whether others were pleased to see me arrive might be a different story. I would find out in time. Underneath it all, I knew that when in command, you can never please everyone, so I did not try.

One of the first things that struck me was the resentment that the residents showed towards the Police. When I was out on the streets talking to shopkeepers, the ordinary people, I could feel it. Handsworth was littered with abandoned and empty houses. Owners had moved to other areas, had escaped to the suburbs. Their former homes were worthless and deteriorating. Several houses owned by Birmingham City Council lay empty and boarded up with corrugated tin sheets, with insufficient money to repair and re-let them, or maybe the Committee system had just not got round to doing the work. Many houses (we called them *squats)* had been taken over by groups of *rastas*. There were two types. True *Rastafarians* were mostly confused souls, deeply sincere, believing in the Ethiopian religious tradition and smoking peace-bringing marijuana as part of their rituals. Others were groups of young black men and girls who had run away from home, or been rejected by parents. They were aged between sixteen and twenty four, calling themselves *Dreads* from the custom of growing hair long in plaited dreadlocks. Both groups were either involved with or on the edge of minor crime. Both groups hated the Police. They were the *Rastamen*, and we were the soldiers of *Babylon*, enslavers of an oppressed black nation. An arrest in any one of those squats was a hostile, sometimes violent confrontation between People and State.

Most reported crimes were theft, burglary, drugs; the basic bread and butter of people on the fringes of society surviving in the only way they knew how. Many were not at that time entitled to benefits since they had run away from home and parents were searching for them. Many were young girls, some with babies, some on drugs. Every single day was the same sad list of crimes and arrests, all expensive in time and manpower.

***

These young men are Dreads. *They wear their hair in long plaited dreadlocks. The leader is eighteen, mature for his years, streetwise. His jeans are worn and shiny, his running shoes scuffed. A tight gold chain around his neck peeps*

34

through the vee of a black woolly sweater. A large black woollen hat with a thick red stripe is folded back to encircle his head. Into the red stripe is woven a white stripe. It has the appearance of a crown. A round pleasant face has a thick lipped fetching smile that reveals strong teeth. Long lashed unsmiling eyes are deep brown, with large hypnotic pupils. He glances away from us, left, right, downward, a hint of cynicism, distrust, self doubt. Somewhere are rejected - or rejecting- parents. His compatriots are young athletic black men, each a potential for explosion, yet relaxed and good natured among friends.

Our leader speaks: 'When am walkin on the streets at night, y'know, they jus come an stop me, y'know, they'll come out and ask me, they say 'Why d'ya wear ya hat?'. So I say 'To keep my head warm.' So this gets em aggravated, so they start pickin on me and askin, where am going, where am comin from, wass ma name, where do I live, an if you don't answer you find yeself in the back of the car.'

His head rocks from side to side on its axis. He swallows, uncertain. Still, his friends have caught the signals. Above a murmur of approval, a voice mutters 'True...'

'Have you been in trouble with the Law?'

'Only once...' He smiles. His friends know everything. His lips form a beginning. 'B...' He hesitates. 'But...' Again he stops. 'But... Ah... You see... Ah was not... Ah wasn't guilty.' [1]

***

Around this time, Phillip Knights started to take an interest in my ideas. At that early stage they were not formed into a coherent philosophy, yet, within the old Victorian Thornhill Road Station, I was already starting to challenge the usual routines, by questioning assumptions, by pressing for change on a number of fronts, and, looking back on it now, probably causing a few problems for those around and above me. In spite of the dangers faced each day by constables walking the streets, I suspected that if we could establish a beginning of confidence with the members of the public, then things would start to happen and trust would show its face. So I promoted the idea that foot patrols might be effective in crime prevention, rather than using those same men in a reactive situation after a crime had been committed.

For the centre of Birmingham, where groups of young men and women would congregate in shopping centres, Phillip Knights decided to commit a greater part of his forces to foot patrols. He had observed a shock fourteen percent rise in crime in the West Midlands, and stated openly that the rapidly lengthening dole queues were adding to the problem. That did not go down well with the Government. The use of the Special Patrol Group had generally effectively contained the problem, but it

---

[1] Shades of Grey, 1978

seemed to him that more uniformed foot patrols would be a significant improvement. Our problems were big enough within Handsworth. Unfortunately Great Britain had a habit of occasionally adding to our working day with its own, much larger problems, and we then were in the centre of a whirlpool of troubled souls and events on a scale that today seems difficult to imagine.

In Spring 1976 Robert Relf, a fifty-one year old man living in Leamington, put his house on the market and advertised it as saleable only to white English people. A national outcry ensued from black and Asian representatives, and Relf was convicted under current race relations laws and committed to Winson Green Prison. West Midlands Police were approached by representatives of the National Front, at that time calling for the immediate repatriation of all non-white English people and the complete cessation of all immigration. They intended to march in the area of Winson Green Prison to protest at the jailing of Relf. At that time it was impossible for us to ban a peaceful demonstration, whatever we might think of the views of the marchers. For some days they had mounted a small peaceful demonstration at the gates of the prison, but we were moving rapidly towards some form of confrontation with organisations opposing the Front. The prison was just outside Handsworth and many of our men would be involved in policing the event and damping down trouble.

Things were moving fast and we had little time to prepare. On Friday 15th May we reviewed the situation, and understood that the small demonstration would become a crowd of some two thousand. They in turn would be opposed by members of the Anti-Fascist Committee, the Indian Workers Association, the Bangladeshi Association, the local Polytechnic Students Union, the Birmingham University Union and elements of Rastafarian groups living locally. The National Front had agreed with us a route for the march, but we knew for sure that things would become confused and that people would be injured. Breakaway groups would charge down side streets and smash up shops and attack people. Any lone Policewoman directing people and traffic away from the main trouble area would become a target. We knew also that we would have a flood of arrests, and three police stations prepared their cells for an influx of angry demonstrators. We had a list of seven premises that might be targetted for attack, among them our own Thornhill Road Station. So, in addition to protecting the prison and the various peaceful demonstration groups and members of the public, we would have to find a way or protecting our own buildings and office staff.

Members of the public rarely understand that our nation expects men and women as young as twenty, as part of their daily job, to go into a real battle, where strong young men will target them from a short distance with house bricks, slabs of concrete, iron spikes and petrol bombs. It makes playing in the rugby front row for England seem like a picnic. Looking back, it is quaint how small things remain in memory. Among our instructions to assemble for an event that would leave young men and women constables injured, perhaps seriously, perhaps even killed, was one tiny promise: *'Packed lunches and tea will be provided for all personnel on duty.'*

Next day, Saturday 16th May, the march started peacefully in Foundry Road opposite the prison. That day too saw my first encounter with James Hunte, a man who would in time emerge as a significant personality in the history of Handsworth. He was with a large contingent of young rastas and West Indian youths, not causing trouble at the time. He was at the helm of the demonstration, and at the beginning of an interesting career.

Before long, the crowd lining the route exploded with a hail of stones and other missiles. A triple line of constables tried to keep the two sides apart, but inevitably we ourselves became the target as *protectors of the fascists*. It was a right old battle. We had to mount a rescue operation to evacuate several families from neighbouring houses under a hail of bricks. At that time we had no riot shields, so we invaded all the local gardens and yards and commandeered as many dustbin lids as we could muster. Sadly there were never enough to protect our men. Ambulances ferried the injured, including several young constables, to the local Dudley Road Hospital for treatment. Most had flesh wounds requiring stitches. One sergeant caught a house brick plumb centre of his forehead, and one of my constables was hit on the leg by a large lump of concrete. No one was killed, but that was more by luck than anything else. The constable reflected later: *'They just let us have it with everything they could lay their hands on. We just had to stay there and take it.'*

Twenty eight people were arrested. It was not a small number, if you remember that we were mainly occupied in keeping ourselves out of hospital. The list of injuries to all of the police forces present was terrifying. We were 'C' division, with eight injured and three off work as a result. Three other divisions had supplied officers for the Winson Green patrol, and in total, fifty two men and women were injured of whom sixteen were off work as a result. When we hear of people making claims for compensation today for sometimes quite minor things, we should remind ourselves of the kind of commitment those police men and women gave at every demonstration. Out of our division's eight injured, here are a few examples:

PC1 - Bruising to chest and right ankle - reported for duty next day.

PC2 - Cut to right hand, bruising to left knee - reported for duty next day.

PC3 - Bruising to back and left knee - reported for duty next day.

Other divisions were just as affected:

Cut to lip.

Injured knee.

Laceration to right leg.

Bruised neck, back, chest and eyes.

Bruised stomach.

And so on for fifty two men and women. Each had then to go out next day and face the public from where had emerged many of their assailants. It takes a special kind of person to do that day after day, demonstration after demonstration, and a special kind of wife or husband. One surreal photograph taken as the first bricks flew was in Foundry Road. Behind the attackers, across an entire wall of a two storey building, was a poster featuring Ian Botham and other members of the England Cricket Team enjoying a post-game victory drink - *Ansells Bittermen - You can't beat 'em.*

While all this had been brewing in the previous week, the Home Secretary had Relf quietly shipped north to Stafford jail, and fifty or so National Front supporters followed the prison convoy to mount a demonstration there. That particular demonstration went peacefully, much to the relief of the people of Stafford. And, while our battle of Winson Green had been raging, Relf, suffering from the effects of a hunger strike in protest at his imprisonment, was being treated and cared for by a Nigerian doctor with skin as black as ebony.

SEVEN: AN ODDBALL GETS THE MESSAGE

His eyes *are quick and smiling. 'In the force, you get good policemen and bad policemen. And as the majority of the Police are white, you know, they might not like black people, you know, and as they're learning all the time about black youths mugging old women and all of that. So that sort of brings up prejudice against...' He punches the word out, 'us.'*

The interviewer searches wider. 'Are things between you and the Police getting better or worse?'

'I'd say worse.'

'Since when?'

'Since they killed that policeman. [1] *I feel that, you know, all black people have been convicted for it. That night, you know, they got everybody, all the black people, anybody they could, even far away from the scene of the crime. Since then, everything has got worse.'* [2]

* * *

Some weeks before the Winson Green affair, we were trying to involve the public in the old Thornhill Road Station. The idea came up of an *open house*. I cannot remember where it came from or whether it was totally new, but it proved to be an amazing success, so much so that it gave me ideas on what might be possible if we could only trust the local people.

On Sunday 17th May 1976, the very day after and only a mile from the battlefield of Winson Green, children of all races came to see us, sucking ice lollies and gobstoppers from a local sweetshop. They and their parents came mostly via the correct way, that is at the front entrance, but gangs of them came in by the tradesmen's entrance at the rear, skidding to a halt on their chopper bikes. A troop of Brownies, the 23rd Birmingham Pack, accompanied by Brown Owl Mrs Eileen Gibbons, marched in as disciplined as a troop of excited Brownies can be, and one of my men was charged with the duty of showing the children around the Black Maria. Many of the constables on duty still had bruises from the previous day's battles, and after what had happened just along the road, the enjoyment by the people of *all things Police* took us by surprise. It was standing room only in the main office as groups queued to be shown around. We counted three hundred and fifty visitors that day. One young man, a six year old Ian Hunter, just loved his short ride on a patrol

---

[1] On Thursday 17th July 1975 twenty year old constable Christopher Green was stabbed to death in the West Midlands.

[2] *Shades of Grey,* BBC 1978

motorcycle. He was grinning from ear to ear and proclaimed *'That was great'*. His father Cyril was born in Jamaica and was manager of a nearby pub, *The Frighted Horse*. Cyril agreed: *'Its been a most unusual afternoon.'*

That same rainbow day, a Birmingham magistrate who lived in Handsworth wrote to the Birmingham Evening Mail that, in his view, a small part of our area had been taken over by International Socialists and Black Power. He feared that anyone who was a known objector to Black Power would be singled out and attacked by gangs of young men on the rampage. He recounted conversations with his friends among the Asian shopkeepers, who had a history of stability in their lives and families. They included the original white and West Indian residents of Handsworth, now growing older, unable to move for financial reasons.

'These people are afraid to open their doors. The local church leaders are dismayed about the situation. Yet when we raise these matters with the local Police, everyone thinks we are exaggerating and being hysterical.'

Things were not helped by occasional visits from Rudy Narayan, a local gentleman lawyer. Rudy was frequently in trouble with the Bar Council and was eventually struck off, to be later reinstated. Rudy talked to the Sun Newspaper, at that time undergoing one of its many shudders of indignation about society. Rudy explained to the reporter the purpose of a newly formed national Black People's Mobilisation Committee:

'The Committee has very specific powers. Simply, whenever an incident happens it is our job to get coachloads and carloads of people from all over the area within 24 hours to join in. The inhibitions in the minds of black youth have been released. They are now free to express their grievances in a physical way. My role is to get a sense of urgency into the situation and get people on to the streets whenever we need them. We are not planning conflict with the Police, but there may be situations where the Police are involved...'

Sometimes the rastas and Dreads would simply take over a house that happened to be empty for a few days while undergoing repair. We were drawn into one complex problem that proved impossible to resolve. And yet, no other organisation existed in our local society with the power and means to deal with it. The local Hestia Housing Association had upgraded a house with the intention of installing needy people from their priority list. Unfortunately they left the house unguarded and three couples moved in, then refused to move, even when bailiffs were called. The matter was eventually resolved by legal evictions.

In those large empty houses, resident young girls became a special kind of problem. I was frequently badgered by worried parents who wanted my men to go in and, as the parents saw it, rescue their daughters. Unfortunately the young ladies were in many cases just as determined as the young men, tough and evasive, as streetwise as they come. They would attack my officers as fiercely as the young men. Most of the parents had come over in 1948, bringing strong family values. Now, twenty years later, their children were out of control, out of reach, out of understanding.

The young men in the squats would defend themselves in considerable numbers. Every time we were called to any trouble, a mugging, a blues party, suspected drugs involvement, a crowd would quickly form and we would have to send a group of ten or fifteen men to arrest just one person. Then those who wanted to make trouble would find an excuse; crowds would gather outside the station and demonstrate. It was like that almost every day. We were continually under siege. My men could not do the kind of policing that I was used to elsewhere. They did not have time to go out on day patrols because there was frequent conflict and paperwork resulting from incidents the previous night. M colleagues told me that our situation was not unique. Similar problems were arising in other inner city areas with large numbers of black and Asian people.

We had a number of young inexperienced policemen, and all our officers lived outside Handsworth. They had none of the rapport I was fortunate to have down in Letchworth. I feared that Handsworth was breeding a generation of policeman who would never know the satisfaction of meeting the local population, getting to befriend the local councillor, be welcome in a school. A generation of policemen who would, as a result of their battles with ethnic groups and individuals, develop prejudices that later in their career would inevitably lead to an abuse of power against some racial minority.

To add to this, we had not just a West Indian population which was highly disadvantaged, we had every race imaginable. In one street we counted twenty four different nationalities and racial sub-groups. There were older Caribbean families, salt of the earth, highly religious, strict Christians, who had come over in 1948; the younger West Indians, many of them rastas; we had Indians, Pakistanis, Bangladeshis, all with their own castes. The Indian families were notable for their belief in their children, with high expectations and an industrious, shop keeper and business ethos. And we had Irish, Polish, Chinese, Vietnamese, and somewhere in there, white English families. All had different ambitions, life-styles, traditions, cultures, languages and expectations. Yet, from the outside, as Radio One disk jockey Tommy Vance called us on an interview I did with him a few years later, we had been viewed simply as *The Black Suburb*.

As always, you cannot judge a book by its cover. One series of meetings involved the local Rastafarian Sect, and taught me that things were not as black and white as they seemed. The local Parish Anglican Vicar, Father Charles, convened a meeting and invited us to send along a representative to meet with the Sect. They wanted, among other things, to explain in a non-confrontational situation something of the history and background of their religion. About a hundred people were present, predominantly West Indian and mainly Rastafarians, but others present included John Plummer of the International Socialist Movement, Ted Ratnaraji from the Race

41

Relations Commission, Bill Assam, the local Community Relations Field Officer and a number of people from the City's Social Services. Lloyd Blake, Chairman of the local West Indian Federation Association, chaired the meeting, and we were addressed by Claudius Haughton, Chairman of the Sect, a Finfe Gabriel who was Chaplain to the Sect and, up from London, the Secretary of the Ethiopian Orthodox Church, a Mr Mahitana Sellassie, a charming gentleman.

We in the Police felt that the format of the meeting, with so many outsiders present, did not allow us to explore in depth issues which we felt were important, so we persuaded the Sect's representatives to meet us in a more informal and private setting. At first, they were reluctant, fearing that such a meeting would discredit them among their followers, but were persuaded.

Haughton explained the realities as he saw it. He had been told by his local Rastafarian followers, all of whom knew the situation on the streets first hand, that there were in fact only one hundred true members of the movement in the whole of Birmingham. All were concerned that there was a local minority of West Indian youths responsible for much of the crime, with their hair plaited in locks and wearing woollen hats bearing the colours of the Ethiopian Flag. These youths, he maintained, were bringing the Movement into disrepute, but attempts were being made to recruit them officially into the Movement and dissuade them from their habits of crime. We were so impressed with the sincerity and clarity of approach, that we saw it as a useful way of developing community understanding to a higher level. I remember that they had asked for the initial meeting and had co-operated all along. It was an impressive attitude, bearing in mind the spate of allegations of Police brutality, some sadly true, that were current on the streets.

A local magazine conducted a revealing interview with a young true Rastafarian called Denis, who lived in a house owned by the Midland Area Improvement Association, a local housing group with the aim of assisting the deprived and unemployed find somewhere to live. The kitchen was sparse and clean, and Denis was cooking a meal of salt fish in dough with curry flavouring. He explained that his mother thought he was crazy, but now that he had a job as a shaper in a machine factory, she did not seem to mind so much. His parents were ardent Pentecostals and were puzzled by his life-style. Denis had high dreadlocks, but used a typical woolly hat to keep his hair hidden away from work mates and policemen on the streets. Denis and his friends were bitterly resentful at the way that some local papers portrayed them in a hysterically distorted picture of crime and laziness: *'None of those who write about us have been to see us, so how do they know what's happening?'*

Another brandished a headline *STREETS OF TERROR*, and in his anger slipped into Jamaican dialect *'Dem write dat shit in paper 'bout us, right, it seen by bosses, right, you go job, man, dey see you knots (dreadlocks), no job.'*

One of his friends, Prince, commented on the continual harassment, and how he and his friends would judge those who they felt were responsible: *'Everyone have to face their own judgement... In the meantime I just have to live my life as well as I can. That's why Jesus came to Earth...'* It affected me deeply. Whether or not they were speaking the truth, and I had no reason to doubt it, I had a duty to understand the problems of these people. They had just as much right to fair policing as any other citizen. It was not my job to find them work, nor to run the city or the country, but it was for me and my colleagues to ensure that as far as we humanly could we would protect them as much as any other ethnic or religious group.

It was around that time that I got to know James Hunte a little more closely. James, originally from Barbados, had grown to be a leader of a large association of West Indian members and was an active defender of West Indian rights. It would take a while for me to get close enough to understand James as a person. At the time, he was under attack from other members of his organisation, and allegations of all kinds were flying thick and fast within Handsworth and in the local and national newspapers.

He was a tall, slightly shy man, pleasant to talk to when he was not protecting his members from *white oppression*. He always seemed to me to be on the defensive, even when among friends. His hair style varied from pleasantly curly up to a startling great crown of fuzzy back-combed hair. He ran his organisations, including one called West Midlands Community Growth and Support, from his end-of-terrace house in the centre of Handsworth, becoming too easily involved, it seemed to me, in controversy. One row was about the famous phrase *Send them home and pay their fare*. James received a number of approaches from young blacks, disillusioned with life in a Handsworth squat, and wanting to go home to Jamaica. *The Times* reporter followed up the story, interviewing one sixteen year old: *'Sure man, I want to go home, there's nothin' here for me. I can't take any more of this Police harassment.'* The headline rumbled *'BACK TO CARIBBEAN' PLAN STARTS A STORM*. Above was a large, badly lit photo of James standing in a fly-postered alley, wearing a check, ominously English gentleman sports jacket, hands casually in pockets and on his head a large woollen hat *a la Rasta*. James' involvement was not a good move, and aroused great opposition and some personal invective from other organisations representing West Indian groups. Some were simply out to recruit more paying members, but that was not the point. It gave them a great opportunity to portray him as supporting what they described as pro-National Front propaganda.

Early in 1976 there had been allegations of what might be described as a lack of financial control in the affairs of the West Midlands Community Growth and Support organisation, and a group from within the organisation had attempted to oust James from power. The allegations centred on a number of Birmingham City Council and other grants which the opposing group said had never appeared in the Association's accounts. An emergency meeting held in the Rialto club in Soho Road to discuss the allegations broke into disarray, with a fight in front of the chairman's table. A formal investigation later proved that the grants had never existed and that Hunte had in fact paid for some of the expenses out of his own pocket. So he was cleared, but I always felt that the episode had damaged him somewhat in the public eye.[1]

I would not describe James as one of my closest friends, but he was a likeable and well meaning man and we got on well together as colleagues in adversity. Above all, he was a survivor and a leader, and I felt I could trust him to deliver on communicating to his people and supporters the fact that we in the Police were not interested in oppressing anyone, that we had a job to do to protect against street disorder in the interests of the whole community. Those in the Chief Constable's office at times questioned the wisdom of getting too close to him. Still, James, in spite of his many faults and some criticism of him from his own people, retained considerable credibility. He saw the whole picture and could get things done.

There was high and growing unemployment, mostly among young black men. The housing stock was crumbling before our eyes. Local schools were unable to get the best teachers, and low expectation was leading to low achievement. We were creating a young population who would become virtually unemployable. The words *location, location, location* applied just as much to the young man or woman seeking a job as they did to property. If your address ended with the word *Handsworth*, you stood no chance whatever of an interview. There was always the potential for violence and explosion. The newspapers frequently named us *The Angry Suburb*. From the outside looking in, every prejudice that every politician wanted to exploit was proved so easily, and the view came at me regularly in letters and comments. A typical letter to me said: *'The blacks have turned Handsworth into an un-policeable run-down town. They give us nothing but trouble, and we white English are having to pay for it.'*

We were part of a confused, downward, self compounding spiral, and the Thornhill Road Station and its beleaguered force were in the eye of the storm. We felt it every hour of every day, under attack physically and mentally, some fearful of coming to work, afraid for the emotional state of their wives and families. This was a community many at Thornhill Road felt they could never be part of, a natural enemy. Meanwhile, the politicians and the media watched every move we made.

Each morning, as I sat in my office, the clerk would put on my desk the list of incidents from the previous night. There before me lay the true reality of Handsworth's bad name. Whereas a typical police arrest would involve one, perhaps two policemen, there were vivid accounts of having to send four or five constables, of mini riots, racial confrontations with whole groups and families, all to arrest just one

---

[1] *Fights disrupt question time*, Birmingham Post 15th November 1976

44

individual. It was expensive, hard, thankless work, but it seemed to me that it really did not have to be like that.

'Blow me!' I said to myself one afternoon. Yes, I really did say that and remember the moment clearly. This was not the sort of policing that I had been brought up on, where a single policeman could walk the streets in safety; could go into the schools and make friends, gain respect. It was defensive and reactive policing at its worst. I began to feel as if I was in one of the one of the worst areas of New York.

The first real change in my approach was more or less forced on me. It was 1976. The summer had been one of the longest and hottest on record, and pavements would shimmer late into the evenings from the heat of the day. On the morning of Wednesday 8th September, we arrested a West Indian youth for an offence of robbery on a seventy six year old lady, who had sustained injuries, including a broken leg. This was the kind of episode that in less civilised times might create a lynch mob. The young man would later plead guilty, and get a substantial term in prison. Extreme violence had been used towards the arresting officers by other youths and girls, and one young man and three girls were in custody. At around 2.00 pm about fifty people gathered and lined up at the front of the station, demanding the release of the girls. The crowd was mainly black people, men, women, children, standing on the pavement and encircling the front entrance. They looked under that summer sky like some crowd enjoying a Sunday afternoon get together. There was at that point no violence, just some occasional loud protest that what we were doing was wrong. We feared very much that we could, by the end of the day, have a riot on our hands, so we called for reinforcements to be assembled out of sight and a Special Patrol Group to be in reserve.

I lined up my men in front of the building as a precaution. There we stood, a line of policemen, a crowd of black protesters, all facing each other. *'Release them!'* shouted the crowd, over and over again. Then some of the crowd started to throw things, and a few bricks came through the windows of the Station. The first salvo stopped, but another small crowd assembled on the opposite side of the road, armed menacingly with bricks and sticks gathered from some unoccupied houses some fifty yards away. So I went downstairs to talk to the main group and whoever would step forward as a leader. We were each lined up, small armies ready for battle. I stepped forward, and their leader took a short step forward, just like in a Western. As I was talking to him, I saw, more felt than saw, a hostility that was to him and the young people around him fully justified. Those people were hurting deeply about a grievance they could not find words to express.

The strange thing was that the hostility was not against any one individual, certainly not to me as a person or as a policeman. The hostility was against something much bigger, against the structure of something out there that we might call society and its ignorance and misunderstanding of their condition and grievances.

They were saying things about the arrest and the robbery and goings-on inside the station that I knew to be untrue, and adding grievances about employment and the Government. I was determined to play it by the book and tell them the realities of life. I cannot recall my exact words but the following is pretty close:

'Look, the people inside are being treated properly, they are being questioned properly, represented by solicitors and other legal representatives. They will be treated fairly inside my station, I will make sure of it. They will get proper bail when they've been questioned. You have no reason to demonstrate out here. It will make no difference to me or anyone else, and will not change what is going on in my station. If you want to stand outside you can, but just behave yourselves. When your friends come out, and they'll be out soon, ask them how they were treated. If they were not treated properly, then you can come up to my office, see me personally, and tell me how you feel.'

They accepted it. I did not feel in any danger, but I had broken the confrontational rules of Handsworth. This kind of talk from a policeman shocked them. I had reasoned with them, and was astonished that they reacted positively. It was the beginnings of an understanding that would prove crucial to everything that happened afterwards. Yet what astonished me more was the reaction of some of my colleagues and a few of the men under my command. They did not like it. They believed that the way to deal with the situation was to bring in thirty or forty police from outside in big armoured vans, get out the shields and batons, arrest the lot and stick fifty of them in the cells. I calculated that if we did that, we would end up with not just fifty, but a thousand outside the Station. So what would we do then? Arrest a thousand people? The whole thing was to me just stupid, a farce, everything that policing should not be.

That night I reflected on the day's events. *Every time we arrest somebody, especially a black person, are we to go through this?* There had to be a better way, the way I had been taught and seen to work in my early years. From that day on, I was determined to bring that better way to my new patch. Nobody was going to stop me. I knew in my heart that it was right for these people and all those out there looking to me for protection and support. It was also right that the men in my Station should be able to look forward to safer tours of duty, and their wives and families to peaceful nights. However, at that early stage I was not the man in charge. I was subject to the command of Superintendent Gerry Finch, and he must by then have been wondering what kind of oddball he had been lumbered with.

EIGHT: AN UNDERSTANDING BEGINS

The Victorian chapel stands strong among these poor streets, a statement of authority founded when a Queen ruled nations of every creed, every language, every colour. Square classical windows and an arched doorway that dare not hint a Papist gothic curve now welcome, behind grey walls hidden by patched white paint, a few children's children of one of those conquered nations. How the builder would marvel at the new song springing within his handiwork.

The Pentecostal pastor, a big, proud, black-hatted woman, shakes like an earthquake as she slaps great hands together in song, white collar and bib struggling for purchase around her shoulders. She rolls with the beat, leans back and raises her head high, strong teeth gleaming as she roars out a hymn of hope and resolve.

Behind her a guitar band thumps along in ragged rhythm, aided by rattling tambourines and a hundred clapping hands, some on the downbeat, others less sophisticated on the up. Men in Sunday best grey and brown suits, ladies in cloth coats and furs, and at the front, exposed in the forward pew, sits a young mother. Beside her leans a toddler, eyes wide in wonderment, hands flailing in early ritual fumblings. She cradles a sleeping child enfolded in white blankets on one arm, and with the other grasps a huge tambourine which she slams against her thigh in rhythmic trust in the Lord.[1]

***

Gerry was an excellent Superintendent, working under difficult circumstances, trying in his own way to effectively police a traumatised people. High unemployment all around, inter-racial tensions, poor and failing schools, deteriorating housing, little or no local industries. Still even in that unhelpful context he had laid a few foundations.

Some commentators have given me all the credit for developing the concept of Community Policing Handsworth style, yet it was people like Gerry who helped me get the thing started, at least in its basic form. I have always tried to give him full recognition for what he did. Community policing had been done elsewhere, but not of the type and intensity that was to prove necessary in Handsworth.

I was delighted to be promoted and Gerry treated me well. He said: *'David, this is your patch, you are in charge, now go out and get the job done.'* I would like this book to be seen in part as a tribute to him, the Divisional Chief Superintendent

---

[1] *Shades of Grey,* BBC 1978.

Joe Matthews, his deputy Bob Snee, deputy David O'Dowd, now Sir David O'Dowd, Chief of Her Majesty's Inspectors of Constabulary, and all those who understood what we were trying to do. Shortly after my arrival, Gerry was promoted to Chief Superintendent and left Handsworth for a new job. I will always remember Gerry, even though I have not seen him since those early days.

Gerry did not find it easy. He had been a Guardsman. Some said that his military upbringing and bearing did not help in situations requiring a softer touch. I took him out several times as his Chief Inspector to social functions to meet community leaders from the West Indian and Asian groups. I helped him a much as I could, calling on the experience of my early years in Letchworth. He understood the problems, but it was not force policy or practise at that time to do the things I had in mind. I was already Chairman of the Round Table, and had many contacts in the West Indian, Asian and white English communities. Several channels emerged through which I might be able to get things moving. These were early thoughts, the beginnings of what was to prove a radical, difficult philosophy. Then I got lucky.

John Brown popped his head around my office door one morning in May 1977. He and I would develop a deep and lasting friendship, sadly cut short by his untimely death. Growing national and international awareness of our problems in Handsworth fired the interest of Chief Constable Phillip Knights and Anthony Wilson, Secretary of the Barrow and Geraldine E. Cadbury Trust. They invited John to undertake a study of policing in the area in and immediately around Handsworth, focus on Police-West Indian relations, and, if possible, suggest ways of change and improvement. [1]

John was a studious and quiet man, gentle and slow to speak, with a highly perceptive and at times combative mind. History will judge him well as one who understood the heady chemistry of race relations, crime, policing policy and the true needs of a society schooled by a reactive media to gut instinct policing and quick fixes to complex social issues. His well-lived-in frame had visited a number of Caribbean islands and several police forces in Britain.

He set himself four main tasks. First, he aimed his main proposals at the causes of conflict rather than the symptoms. This was to be misinterpreted by a hostile press and not a few academics when his report was published later in the year. Second, he sought ways to improve the quality of 'contact' policing, that is, the daily face to face encounters between the policeman or woman on foot and the child in school, the citizen on the sidewalk, and the potential criminal in the street. Third, and this was to emerge as his most relevant area of study, he examined the role of the Police in relation to the various social agencies and local community resources. These he identified as the local community group leaders, the various federations and support groups run by and on behalf of the West Indian peoples, the Asian temples

---

[1] *Shades of Grey* - A Cranfield Institute Study 1977

and mosques and their leaders and clergy. All of these initiatives he felt would point to the value of preventive strategies, ways of offering youth at risk *'...alternatives through improved employment, work experience, educational, cultural and recreational opportunities.'*

It was summer 1977. Britain was moving towards a political climate where Government employment policy would later be summed up by a senior minister[1] and close confident of a Prime Minister at a Party Conference with: *'When my father looked for work in the thirties, he got on his bike...'*

John's views, albeit based on first hand research, interviews and evidence, were discounted, misrepresented, and attacked. Two prominent academics Professors John Rex and Thomlinson, were to comment that Brown's recommendations *'... can only have the effect of directing the Police ... to use violence against an easily recognised minority, whilst possibly failing to actively prevent the growth of crime ...'* A strange interpretation indeed, which I invite you to consider as we move on to look at the kinds of things John examined and recommended.

His first analysis was a study of the geography of Handsworth, the ethnic and age mix, social factors and crime statistics. He exposed the fact that the majority of typical crime in the area (there were few rich bankers and, therefore, little fraud and money laundering) was against the person and personal property. In a telling paragraph that would later haunt him in many distorted guises, he found that in my Sub-Division C, robberies, thefts from the person, burglary, wounding and assaults were by a group of about two hundred youths of West Indian origin or descent, many calling themselves Rastafarians or *'Dreads'*. Almost all were unemployed. He estimated an overall unemployment rate of twenty five percent of all West Indian youth in the locality. In addition to being responsible for high crime rates, these youngsters were seen as semi-hero *Robin Hoods*, with a corrosive influence on local West Indian children on the fringes of the culture, thus adding to a further decay of law and order.

On the police front, he proved that, to achieve better foot patrolling, our Handsworth Sub-Division needed nearly twenty percent more strength in uniformed officers. Constables most responsible for personal contact policing, the type that brought the public and police together in confrontations, were characterised by their youth and lack of experience. He concluded that the emphasis needed to shift from car to foot patrolling. Over-emphasis of the reactive role of panda car patrols only served to make the police more remote from the public that we were supposed to serve.

We had at that time fifteen permanent beat officers (PBOs), who spent so much time with other duties such as football matches that it hampered their ability to develop relationships with their communities. We had overt, sometimes intense,

---

[1] Rt. Honourable Norman Tebbitt.

conflict between CID officers and young West Indians. Arrests in squats caused most injuries to policemen, yet there was a deep and sincere fear on the part of the West Indian youths that if caught, they would be beaten up. Both sides expected trouble, whatever and whenever the contact. All allegations of police brutality should, he maintained, be the subject of independent research. On the other hand, he found that CID officers faced intense pressures, often with threats of violence to themselves and their families, and this would at times impair their judgement and reactions to youngsters. To complicate matters, older West Indians, the original Caribbean immigrants to Handsworth from the fifties, were pressing for firmer police action against the Dreads.

An important comment was that few West Indian social groups in Handsworth had either major community significance, or a developed capacity for effective community action. One local need, he felt, was the setting up of a forum or inter-agency dialogue, specifically relating to youth problems in Handsworth. He highlighted the effect of national economic decisions on local conditions and attitudes, jobs, investment and educational achievement. Finally he suggested avenues for further research to look in more depth at critical aspects of some of the problems that he had identified.

What he demonstrated above all was the importance of valuing people for what they are, members of a complex society. He was allowed to go where and when he liked. He wandered down alleyways, met with *Dreads* in their squats, asked searching and sometimes risky questions, went out with constables on foot patrol, sat in the rear of a patrol car chasing down criminals, witnessed arrests and fights, sat in on interviews in the Station, witnessed exploding violence in the cells. Nothing was hidden or kept from him. Indeed, he gained so much trust that he was able to interview, within the C1 Divisional Force, some of my most vehement critics. When I later read his first study, *Shades of Grey*, and his follow-up analysis, *Handsworth Revisited*, it was uncanny to read the words of underlying criticism from those who had co-operated fully with me at the time.

John took a deep interest in the histories of those young black immigrants and children of immigrants. He found the West Indian lads among the most poorly equipped for employment. Many he spoke to had suffered a schooling split between widely differing education systems in the West Indies and in Britain, and it showed in their poor records of attainment and self-expectation. Many had broken or separated families, many had been rejected by their parents, or had themselves rejected, with inner conflict and bitterness, their parents. Deprived and out of work amid English society, they saw themselves as victims of a white racist nation, whose army of defence was the white and racist police force of Handsworth and the world beyond.

The Permanent Beat Officers we deployed to do 'contact' policing saw the problems and the chemistry of conflict first hand. A perceptive PBO commented:

'I can see the problem of the Dreads who live in the squats. No one wants to know them. Many of their parents won't have anything to do with them. Once they get into trouble two or three times, that's it. So they find places in the squats. There's five main Rasta squats on my beat now, maybe fifty children in all. Numbers are never firm, they're always coming and going ... but the pattern's growing. More children in trouble, more houses left vacant as the locals move out. And when they settle, then they're on the lookout for easy cash and food. So you find a rash of shoplifting, break-ins, burglary, robbery all round about, usually committed when cash or supplies run low...'

One telling interview was of a young woman PC, out on foot patrol, always operating on or near the main roads, and never on her own after 6.00 p.m. *'They've said they'll take a WPC, gangbang her and return the bits to Thornhill Road ... I've been followed by groups of Rastas out on patrol, and involved in incidents that really frighten me. And the Policeman I'm, well, almost engaged to, he wants me out, at least from this kind of job in this kind of area...'*

Yet in the same interview, the WPC showed that her job enabled her to see a different side of Handsworth, and gave me hope that these people should never be written off. *'One the one hand I'm moaning about the problems here. But I wouldn't work anywhere else... Out on the beat, like 10 beat, that's my favourite, there's this tremendous mix: West Indian, Asian, English, Irish... And you see that the blacks there are not all the same. You need to see that, because in this job, you sometimes get to feel that there's not good and bad, just bad. And that isn't true"*

It would be wrong of me to repeat all of John's analysis, and I would recommend that the reader take the opportunity to study it first hand. There are though several issues that seem important to me in the context of my own story. He interviewed an experienced constable out on foot patrol, his beat covering some thirty streets in an area of dilapidation and decline.

'Yes, it can be depressing, especially when you've been away, say on holiday for a while, and come back and see it again. Everywhere you look, there's problems - lack of play space, youth clubs, places to meet. Everything's run down ... I'd like to spend more time with the people, especially the juveniles. It takes time to build up relationships with them, especially those in trouble. Most of the juveniles in trouble come from unstable or disturbed homes. You've got to show that you're willing to talk, and listen to them. Some of the Rastas, even, they're very intelligent, a pleasure to talk to... But mostly there's too little time. The beat's too big. I'm only scratching the surface.'

The complexity and sheer impossibility of resolving issues as they happened, rather than through the longer term development of preventive systems, was perfectly illustrated in a despairing letter posted to one of my PBO's by a group of residents living next to a squat. For those who might react with *'Clear 'em out and lock em up'*, I invite you to imagine the letter as a question to be discussed and answered as part of a test in social management, and how you would really in truth handle it with its myriad of possible outcomes.

'Dear Sir,

Please could you do anything to help our neighbours and myself who are being driven out of our minds with worry. There are these squatters at no. 17 who are making a thorough nuisance of themselves with radiogrammes blaring as loud as can be from morning till evening all the windows wide open, then coming into the main road intimidating anyone who would dare to say anything to them. They lean out of the windows watching every move so that we are afraid to leave our own houses empty, we are afraid to come down our own road where many of us have lived all our lives, We get treated to displays of limbo dancing in the road.

Surely we don't have to put up with this behaviour, even though we are told nothing can be done to get them out. We have phoned the Police on numerous occasions but without results because of course these lads are crafty. After causing a real rumpus in the road they then keep quiet for a short period before starting up again. Then invariably they are hanging out of the bedroom windows so naturally can see the panda arriving.

Please, can you help us as we are all really very desperate. Everyone is talking about selling up but it is not always convenient to move and after all why should we because of half a dozen wayward youths? I am not giving my exact address as if a panda car should call on us we are afraid of the consequences.'

Many Asian shopkeepers had their own demands, constantly asking me to get stuck into the young West Indian muggers stealing gold chains from their wives and daughters. They were not at all unhappy for me to arrest every black person who appeared on the street, criminal or not.

One of the hardest internal tasks I faced was to break down in some way the resistance of the CID towards my ideas. To be fair to them, they faced, as John Brown found when he interviewed them all, a sub culture of recurrent crime, a hard core, seemingly impossible to change. Every incident they attended or investigated, they would face the same crimes, the same young faces, sometimes vicious and uncaring. It was hard for a detective to resist the natural human instinct for retribution. When referring to an old man's injuries sustained in a robbery by a group of young West Indian lads, one CID officer said:

'I saw him in hospital. Grand old bloke. Still conscious, chatting up the nurses. And I saw his leg. His knee-cap all shattered. The leg almost in two pieces. You could have put your fist in the hole between the pieces. And when I saw the children who did it, (just) so high, the youngest 11, I didn't believe that children that size could have done it.'

In June 1977 I was promoted again, this time to command as Superintendent, and suddenly I was in control, with all the responsibility and stress and disruption to my life that went with it. What to do? I could not choose the country or the society, could not change Government policy or create jobs, could not reverse the decades of neglect of Handsworth and all its insidious effects. There we were, an exposed Sub-Division and a despairing jumble of a society, locked together in an unholy marriage for better, for worse.

But I wasn't disheartened. Above my desk hung a big wooden spoon, that once belonged to my father who lovingly passed it down to me. I, equally lovingly, named it on a sign that no-one entering my office could miss, *The World's Greatest Stirrer*.

NINE: ANGRY SUBURB

Overnight snow *has dusted the fields and pavements with a blue sheen that crunches beneath the feet. Straggly limes, notched into the pavements, lean at random angles, black against a grey sky.*

'There are, of course, a lot of complaints by the West Indians against police harassment?'

The young constable replies: 'Yes...'

'Does that happen?'

'It does, I must admit, it does. But I feel its... put down to the inexperience of younger policemen. They're brought into Handsworth, given a fairly difficult job to do, looking after the population of Handsworth, which is basically coloureds, West Indians, who are, a lot of them, trouble makers.'

His cheeks and nose glow red in the sharp air. The snow is falling again, flecking his dark uniform with confetti that slowly fades to icy droplets. The interviewer persists. 'What sort of harassment are we talking about?'

'Happenings in the street, like, you're called to deal with an incident, and you have a young policeman there. He's just inexperienced, doesn't know how to deal with things calmly. Somebody starts shouting and he shouts back, then a slanging match begins.' [1]

***

Some time in the future, in 1985, someone was to write in the Police Review, a national magazine for the Force, that life in Handsworth was good, that it was a nice place to live. But what he failed to see was that we were truly the *angry suburb*. While we were doing all those nice things in Handsworth Park, and with residents' associations and representative groups, we did it against a background of a constant barrage of crime, dissension, violence and abuse.

Here are a couple of examples of how bad it could get. After one of our panda cars had been damaged in an attack by a young West Indian, two of my officers chased him to a house run by the local housing association. The officers had to break down the door to get in and then were attacked by a crowd. We sent reinforcements who, in turn, had to force their way in to rescue the first two policemen. It was a surprise to me that no one had been killed. Seven people were charged.

---

[1] *Shades of Grey.* BBC 1978.

Another incident occurred outside a club when an abusive melee refused to move on, and the road exploded with a rain of bricks and paving slabs from a crowd of around seventy people. The affair lasted only a couple of minutes, but several of my men were injured. One was struck in the back by a paving stone, and a sliver of concrete was embedded in his spine, later to be removed by surgery. One had cuts and bruises to his right elbow, another was struck behind the right ear by a large stone. A woman PC was cut along her leg by a broken bottle. Two other officers were injured. All were off duty for several days as a result of their injuries.

Our powder keg of a police patch could be susceptible to trouble from around the world as well as just the home grown issues, and our tiny area on the edge of Europe was sometimes the focus. On 15th August 1977 the National Front held a meeting in a school in Boulton Road in Ladywood on the edge of Handsworth. An Anthony Reed-Herbert spoke to a crowd of about one hundred and twenty people, maintaining that *'All the other political parties are combining in a great conspiracy to destroy the foundation of British life. We are pledged to destroy all immigration to this country.'*[1]

Again, as with the battle of Winson Green, there were demonstrations and then violent attacks by Socialist Workers Groups, but this time even more vicious and dangerous. The mob advanced down the main Soho Road, and Thornhill Road Station came under attack. Superintendent Bob Snee and I came under a hail of petrol bombs and missiles. We called up reinforcements. One of my constables, Selwyn Bowen, was driving a van full of policemen coming to our aid when an attack came in from both sides. Selwyn was temporarily blinded by splinters of glass from a shattered windscreen. The crowd forced the van door open and more well-aimed bricks hit him in the ribs and back of the head. Sue Bailey, one of my women sergeants, used her body as a shield to protect him, standing in front of the van and facing down the crowd as bricks flew past her head. About fifty women officers and three hundred and fifty men protected the Station. Eventually the rioters dispersed, but it was at a time of their choosing. If they had been better organised, they could have burned us to the ground.

Sue, who was 5 feet six inches tall, explained that she had been terrified: *'There was a large crowd of jeering youths. I faced them and I think I would have been more afraid if I had had five minutes to think about it.'*

I was furious with the world and myself for having to put a woman in a situation of such risk. I was quoted in the local papers: *'For WPCs to be involved was bloody ridiculous... In a situation like that to have women in the front line linking arms in a cordon was impracticable and dangerous. Physically they wouldn't be able to cope... But they wanted to be treated like the men...'*

---

[1] Compiled from Police reports and national and local press coverage.

I imagine that I was quoted accurately. Looking at it now I should have said it differently. In front of me as I spoke to the reporter, I remember vividly a police helmet that was crushed up like a paper hat. I do not know to whom it belonged. I still believe that women should not be put in that kind of situation; not a popular view with feminists. My daughter Debbie is a policewoman with twenty four years service, and she knows my views. Women are as good as men in most situations, and where it comes to intuition and human understanding are far ahead. Yet front line duties in situations of physical risk are not the place for a woman, and never will be as far as I am concerned.

Michael Heseltine was as angry as I was, speaking on the streets of nearby Ladywood twenty-four hours later. *'The failure of the Labour Government to support our forces of law and order is an appalling comment on them. The Government is paralysed and unable to support the brave men and women who are upholding not only the law, but also the basic liberties of our citizens. The Left is now on the march...'*

Two days later, the Labour Government's Michael Foot toured our damaged streets. He did not bother to visit us in Thornhill Road Station. Meanwhile, the National Front announced plans to march in October through the streets of Manchester, perhaps hoping to trigger the same kind of mayhem as in Handsworth.

The events also caused a furore nationally, and the issue of rubber bullets and tear gas was put forward as one way of controlling demonstrations and riots. Interestingly Chief Constable Phillip Knights hit back strongly. *'It was twelve months ago, at the Winson Green riots, that I realised that we should have to issue shields if it happened again. But if we get to the stage where we have to arm the Police with tear gas and rubber bullets, you can all be alarmed.'* In support of the back-lash, various politicians, local and national, reeled off the usual panaceas - *'Birch the hooligans!'* and *'Meet violence with violence!'*

These kinds of events came thick and fast. It took all of my powers as a man-manager to maintain morale as well as adequate staffing rotas. In August 1977 a chilling list placed on my desk revealed that in the first six months of that year, thirty one people had been arrested for assaults on police officers, and thirty five male constables and two women constables were recorded as injured, almost twenty percent of our total sub-divisional manpower of around two hundred. Two constables had been repeatedly injured, on four separate days, with each injury followed by a spell of leave to recover. I often wondered how the local law-abiding population felt about life in Handsworth.

That year the Institute of Race Relations took up the cudgels in submitted evidence to the Royal Commission of Criminal Procedure. [1] They said that from their research among ethnic communities the Police were seen as an occupying force. Black people, especially young men, were automatically viewed as criminals,

---

[1] *Black people persecuted by Police,* Daily Mail 1977, actual date unknown.

muggers and illegal immigrants. The Police in general were said to reflect the *institutional racism* in British society. This same phrase was to emerge more than twenty years later in Lord McPherson's report on the Stephen Lawrence murder investigation, and has taken on a special meaning.

The reply, by Jim Jardine, Chairman of the Police Federation, was sadly predictable. Even though the Institute's evidence was based on first hand interviews with ethnic groups extending over six months, he dismissed it all as *'A lot of rubbish... I am very annoyed...the Police treat black people exactly the same as they treat white people.'* Whether right or wrong, the evidence deserved more inspection and serious discussion than that. Even if entirely wrong, should not the *perception* by the ethnic population require some action and investigation?

The national Daily Mail took a similar line. Under a leader headline *THE POLICE AND THE BLACKS* it called the evidence *A shameful travesty of the truth.*, and commented: *This malevolent report of the Institute which, it is interesting to recall, six years ago lurched so far to the left that even the British Council of Churches withdrew its financial support... can only sabotage efforts to improve the climate of race relations.*

In August 1977 we were honoured by an approach from the distinguished correspondent of *Le Monde,* Mlle Nicole Bernheim. She visited Notting Hill in London, Thornhill Road Station, and Walsall, meeting myself and Joe Matthews, and a host of Rastafarians and Asians, seeking answers on issues of race, crime and culture. Nicole received short shrift from some of our citizens: *'For all our efforts, having tried to make contact with the black Rastafarian leaders, we were told in reply that they did not want to talk with 'a representative of dirty French colonialism'.*[1]

---

[1] *Dirty French colonialism,* Le Monde, 30th August 1977

TEN: THE PROJECT

'I was jus walkin up the road, an I saw this Police car parked on a yellow line'.

Jacky is a lovely girl, perhaps eighteen, high forehead, long slender nose, proud jutting lips and curling chin. A high yellow and blue headscarf draws her features higher, prouder. She gazes through the brightness of the window away to the vistas of her memory.

'An I said to the Policeman, 'You're not supposed to be parked on a double yellow line.' So I carried on walking up Leyton Road an then he jus followed me slowly with his car. An he was calling me 'Black bastard' an 'We should all go back to our own country' an all this an that, but I took no notice an I carried on walkin up the road.

So then he called me an says 'Come here, you.'

So I went down an I says to him, 'Its no good arguing with you, 'cause you always win in the end.'

An he says, 'That's right you black bastard.'

So I carried on walking, an then I started to run, an as soon as I reached my gate, he just turned around an he blocked me, so I ran in my house an told my dad.

An then my pregnant sister come downstairs, because he was pushin down the door, an he came in and started to push her out of the way. So I started to defend my sister, you know, I only gave him, say, one scratch an a kick. An he jus came with the handcuffs an about six panda cars an three meat wagons outside my house, to come for little me.

I mean, I didn't do nothin wrong. I just told him that he'd parked on a double yellow line. An I was in court for that.'[1]

***

As Superintendent, all was on my shoulders. Confronted with every policing problem it was possible to conceive, all within an area three miles square, I had a choice. I could sit there bemused, plod along in the old way, react to each problem as it came along. Or I could analyse what the problems were, how they related to each other, cause and effect, seek ways of breaking the cycle of despair and conflict.

My priority soon became clear; get out into the people and take my men with me; visit and speak to every community group in Handsworth, to the temples, the schools, the churches, the community leaders, the teachers, the residents' associations, the old age pensioners. *We will go out on all days, all times suitable for the people,*

---

[1] *Shades of Grey,* BBC 1978.

get feedback as to what is going wrong, build up two way contact, and create the
beginnings of confidence in us, and what the nation expects of us.

But I had under me two hundred and fifty men and women from all sorts of backgrounds, many with ideas of their own, doing things in their own way with no understanding of the overall direction of events. It would be hard for them, their instincts conditioned by years of pressure from politicians and the media, and violent attacks by local criminals and teenagers. Among them, I knew for sure, were a few racist policemen, violent policemen, liars who would break the law to keep the law. If I went too far one way, I would lose the confidence of my Force. They would see me as taking a soft option with trouble makers. Yet, if I went too far the other way, I would lose the confidence of the community and its leaders. I would have to manage all sides of the equation, walk the tightrope.

Talking to the young West Indians was a special challenge. Whatever I said to them, I knew, would quickly get back into the community. So, I would tell them the truth about themselves and about us, so when they told their friends what I had said, it would fit with their actual, not mythical, experience. To deny that there was harassment and some violence would be stupid. I knew that some children had been brutalised by a few of my men. I also knew that some youngsters used a local mythology of violence by my constables, to build their reputations among their Rastafarian and Dread friends. Perhaps, even for them, the truth would slowly re-focus their minds, suggest that after all there was some credibility on the part of the Handsworth Force. We would build slowly, prove the existence of a few good policemen, then a few more.

One of the things I studied, to the extent that it became at times my central focus, was the fascinating web of society that kept all these people together, gave them identity as citizens. Among them were natural leaders and naturally forming groups. Our policing tasks were quite basic, keep the peace, protect life and property, prevent and detect crime. To achieve those three aims, we had to influence the sequence of cause and effect, use whatever leadership tools Handsworth offered. We at Thornhill Road Station were not elected politicians, but no rules existed to prevent us from going to council meetings, nor to meetings of residents' associations. We could meet the leaders of ethnic groups, explain our policies, admit that we had done things wrong, find ways of developing trust and co-operation. We could do this month after month, day after day, hour after hour, and slowly but surely things would come our way.

I too would have to become involved on the streets, take risks. Thus I might truly understand what my officers were experiencing, the hate, the pressure, the cynicism. I knew that if I did that, some routine administrative tasks would slide down the agenda and my popularity with my superiors would suffer. Yet I could not just sit back when there was trouble on the streets and my men were being shelled with bricks and sticks and say, *'Sorry, I've got this report to write. I'll come and sort it out tomorrow.'* If there was a big march coming up with a potential for trouble it was not sufficient to sit at my desk and rely on written reports from my officers. I had to check things for myself, get a feel for the upcoming event, keep relationships with the organisers in good shape, do my planning, ensure things went smoothly, be there on the day to supervise. Eventually it would get to the stage when my phone at home would ring at all hours of the day and night. My urge to solve the apparently insoluble drew me on like a vision.

James Hunte's West Indian Community Growth and Support, organised as it was, provided a focus that fairly indicated the feelings and aspirations of many young blacks, especially the unemployed and disadvantaged. It could and frequently did serve as an irritant to the Police and other parts of the British structure. On one occasion James and members of the Association invaded a meeting of the Selly Oak (South Birmingham) Health Authority to protest over the alleged wrongful disciplining of a staff nurse. There were times I felt he would pick an administrative 'fight' with me in public, so that his members would see that he was really on their side. They were punches I was content to slip.

As well as the Association, we had the West Indian Lodge of Mechanics and the local West Indian churches. The city as a whole had a Community Relations Council, with representatives coming from Handsworth and areas close by. The place in Handsworth where the older, original West Indian immigrants would meet was lovingly named *The Faith and Confidence Fellowship Social Club*, with around five hundred members. Grey haired first generation immigrants would enjoy a friendly drink, cards or dominoes. I was fascinated by the interplay of that uniquely West Indian laughter, unaffected and loud. The clack of dominoes filled the smoky room, as what had started thirty minutes earlier as a friendly contest took on the tension of an international incident. Then all would explode into raucous laughter, cries of triumph and despair and calls for another round of drinks. The views of that older generation about their descendants on the streets had an uncanny parallel to those I heard and saw around me in the British white media:

'These youth, they don't wan' to work. And they no more Rasta than fly... True Rastas are good quiet people. These lads is hooligans, man, just hooligans. A disgrace to us all. They should take a shipload of them to mid-Atlantic, just sink them all there.' [1]

I commissioned an analysis of all the white resident groups throughout Handsworth, and was amazed at how many there were and how in touch they were with what was happening in their area, right down to such things as a leaking tap causing problems in a side street. We divided Handsworth for this purpose into seventeen areas, covered by a total of seventeen formal Residents' Associations or informal groups. We made sure that we had good relations with all of them, sending

---

[1] *Shades of Grey*, BBC 1978.

along to some a Superintendent, a Chief Inspector and a Sergeant, all at a time convenient for the residents, and mostly late into the evenings.

To add to all these, we met regularly with the Sikh Temple Committee, Rastafarian Church Leaders and members, the combined West Indian Churches, executives of the Cadbury Trust, all highly active in assisting the poor and deprived. And we were represented at local school associations and parent groups, the Council for Racial Equality, and the inevitable forum for local businessmen, the Round Table.

Handsworth Number One Resident's Association with its four hundred members represented the good folks from nine surrounding streets. I instructed my constables to attend every meeting, and report what we had done to improve things since the previous meeting. The Committee Secretary was English, the Chairman West Indian. The Association had a youth section, including some West Indian members, under a West Indian Secretary and an English Chairman.

Sadly, I never felt that the local politicians, that is, the MPs and councillors, were able to influence things to a high degree. I could do nothing about that. We were the Police, with limited powers of social interference. Yet it was imperative we get out among the people, and do things that policemen had never done before. There were dangers with this approach, but I estimated that the gains would outweigh the losses. I made it plain from then on at every opportunity, in the canteen, in the office, in my briefings, everywhere, even on the squash court.

In 1977 the birthday of the Guru Ravidass, born six centuries before, was celebrated in a big way throughout India and Britain. Our local Sikh community focused their festivities on the Temple of the Shri Guru Ravidass Bhawan in Union Row, Handsworth. The Asian community had many members who were part of the Ravidass religion. For years I had regarded the Ravidass movement as an accurate reflection of the culture, wishes and aspirations of many Asians. Superintendent Jones, Inspector Keith Newell, Sergeant Bradley and I were invited as special guests. We were highly honoured and privileged to be there. Superintendent Jones[1] and I were invited to address the believers in the Temple. As far as I can tell, that was a unique invitation to non-believers from a different race.

The temple was filled with prayer, poetry and singing from early morning into evening, and a procession of three thousand people walked, sang and danced across the city to the Digbeth Civic Hall, so often the focus of National Front meetings. Only nine hundred and fifty admission tickets were allowed, while the remaining crowds stayed outside to enjoy themselves with yet more song, music and dance. What a contrast from so much that occurred in what was, during those years, a rather shabby quarter of Birmingham! We made allowance for any prisoners arrested in the event of protests or missile throwing, but in the end all was unnecessary. Our sole problem was a well attended football game at Birmingham City FC just a mile or so

---

[1] Superintendent Jones had succeeded Supt. Finch as commander of the sub-division, but was promoted to Deputy Divisional Commander at Walsall after a very brief stay in Handsworth.

from the procession route, but all was timed to avoid the arrival and departure of the fans.

The day ended with a reception and meal at the Grand Hotel on Colmore Row. The Deputy Lord Mayor, several local MPs, and the Chief Constable were invited. Crowds and parked coaches lined the streets, much to the disgruntlement of passers by. The peaceable and law-abiding members of the Ravidass honoured their God with respect and pride. Sadly, within but a few months, other groups happy to call themselves pure white British would create a different kind of procession.

Matters of more earthly importance were at hand with a visit from the Chairman Designate of the Commission for Racial Equality, David Lane. He visited just about every representative group in Handsworth. From the Hindu temple he was driven to the Sikh temple, from there to the Birmingham Central Mosque, from there to the Punjab Christian Society, from there for lunch with a local general practitioner, to the YMCA, and finally to a reception of over seventy people at the Strathallan Hotel. A busy day indeed. A tiny indicator of the resource problems that we and most forces suffered from was a note on our operational plan for the day: *'Because of operational commitments in other parts of the city, no personal radios will be available. All officers will make themselves conversant with the location of public and private telephones.'*

At that time yet another idea began to form in my mind. My beat officers were learning fast, and attitudes were changing. Their new role was making them more acceptable to young and old, more easily trusted. Soon we would have to further, develop a wider attack on misunderstanding. It was frustrating to be surrounded by a Chief Constable, his deputies and assistants, chief Superintendents, a CID and a force of junior constables, and see, day after day, evidence of lack of sympathy with others working with similar aims, namely social workers and probation officers.

Looking back on it now, the only way that I can describe the attitude of some of my colleagues towards those professions was, that the police attitude generally was to view with scorn the activities of the so-called 'soft option' brigade. Some of the senior police in Handsworth had been there for more than fifteen years. They were imbued, soaked through and through, with the belief there was nothing to be gained in talking to social workers or probation people. Many around me believed that the job of a social worker was to find excuses for the criminal, waste time and money, and keep young thugs out of jail. Not all my colleagues were of this view, but sufficient were around, and in senior enough positions, to ensure that any contacts with social workers and probation officers were discouraged. So I began to examine, quietly, how we could arrange for our younger constables to undertake secondments, sit in with social workers as they talked to clients, meet with probation officers trying to assist young former criminals to find self esteem and a job, go into the homes of criminals and meet their parents and brothers and sisters, observe for themselves the causes of crime, see the reality of poverty and unemployment.

This divergence of understanding was natural. A probation officer or social worker would automatically try to empathise with and protect the confidence of their client. He or she was employed to assist, with advice on benefits, a house, care for a young child, reconciliation with parents, a fair prosecution in court. The sole job of the Police and the CID was seen as the winning of a prosecution and, in the eyes of many, including the accused, *cracking down hard on crime.*

It was much later that the importance of collaboration on a common agenda came home to all, from constable to Chief Constable, from social worker to probation officer to headmaster to pupil. I will come back to this in the following chapters. It proved to be a powerful achievement.

All this was total pioneering. There were no handbooks of instruction, no recorded guidance, no training courses, no letters from chief constables telling us *This is the way we should do it.* No policeman in England had to my knowledge ever been faced with a situation of such complexity. I was on my own, feeling my way, analysing as best I could, making up the rules as I went along, taking risks, relying on my instincts and force of personality to see me through.

At times there was resistance. On 18th October 1977, I sent a memo to Chief Superintendent Joe Matthews proposing that I attend a meeting with city councillors and community representatives to advise how the Police might participate in a new community project, later to become known as *The Lozells Project.* Anticipating some reluctance at headquarters, I asked in writing for authority to attend. Luckily for me and the Project, the permission came direct from the Chief Constable: *'With reference to the Lozells Project I do not think we should appear to be 'pouring cold water'. We must be whole hearted and co-operative on the next move if not a bit more so.'*

So, in December 1978, Chief Constable Phillip Knights took the entire package[1] to a meeting with the chief officers of the West Midlands Education Service and the Probation and Social Services. Also present were representatives of what was called *The Birmingham Inner City Partnership Project*, part of a long overdue Government sponsored movement to try to regenerate inner city areas around the country. The proposal would grow into *The Lozells Project.* The aim was to reduce crime and vandalism, develop closer links with the local community, and encourage local people to join with us to solve the community's problems. Little did we know that this would reach the ears of the Heavyweight Champion of the World, Mohammed Ali.

At the same time, I wrote to all those who, I hoped, might be willing to give of their time on a management committee to run a building central to the project, the Wallace Lawler Centre. The head of the Centre was Sidney Caro, a well-known local member of the Liberal Party ,and a close and good friend. We had initially discussed various options and he arranged for us to use the place. It was great. For the first time

---

[1] In an unusual fit of foresight, I kept all of the papers for the Lozells and other initiatives. This account, and those in other chapters, are drawn directly from minutes and correspondence.

since I arrived at Handsworth, we could work formally, face to face, with other statutory agencies within a building to suit our purpose, and to which the public would be welcomed. We had the blessing of the Government and the City of Birmingham, and I had the blessing of my Chief Constable. We had some fifty thousand pounds a year of funding, and premises to go with it. All I had to do was to ensure a continuing change of culture among my own men and women.

Chief Superintendent Joe Matthews set up and chaired the overall Steering Committee. I negotiated the use of premises at the Centre, and chaired a Project Committee which obtained funding for mini-buses, appointed support staff and installed furniture. We started several activities, with a social services play scheme, a *St Paul's Community Workshop,* run by the probation service, for youngsters convicted for car stealing, and an education service school toybank. A warden was appointed, an ex-teacher Mike Dobson, and before long we were off and running. I will not bore you with the full list of activities, but would ask you to envisage a typical day, all taking place, upstairs and downstairs, within the same building and on the playground area. People of all ages, races and backgrounds rubbing shoulders in the corridors and on the stairs, meeting in the canteen, and across coffee tables. Among them social workers, probation officers, education staff, and policemen in and out of uniform.

11.00 - 15.30 Lucas Industries Retirement Club - Art Class - 12 to 16 adults.

13.00 - 15.00 Unemployed club - pool, darts, snooker - 16 to 25 youths.

16.15 - 18.30 Youth Club Junior section - table tennis, pool, darts, table football, five-a-side football, 7-a-side netball. Staffed mainly by police from C Division with voluntary assistance - 40 to 85 youths.

19.30 - 21.45 Youth Club Senior section - table tennis, pool, darts, small games, table football, snooker. Staffed mainly by police with voluntary assistance and sessional staff from the Aston and Handsworth Institute - 45 to 120 young people, ratio of 40% female to 60% male.

For those readers who may still believe that the main job of a senior policeman is to crack down on crime, this is how we shared our priorities for the young: Lozells Project expenditure and Wallace Lawler Centre was the responsibility of Superintendent O'Dowd (David O'Dowd, later Chief Constable of Northamptonshire and Her Majesty's Inspector of Constabulary). Transport, youth club and Holte School Camp were allocated to Chief Superintendent Joe Matthews. The Intermediate age treatment programme, St Paul's Community Workshop for young offenders, Handsworth football tournament, and Lozells Junior and Infant School, were all part my job.

In addition, we had special advisory sessions on unemployment and how to get out of it, careers guidance and job opportunities clubs. We organised swimming clubs and dancing classes. My Permanent Beat Officers were all at the forefront, and I insisted that they attend sessions on a rota basis. I wanted them to all meet young black men in a non-confrontational situation, to talk to them, and exchange words well away from the street setting. In this way when both races next met on the street, one in uniform, one wearing dreadlocks and a woolly hat, much of the suspicion and tension would be gone. Things looked to be running well, creating human understanding, heading off future crime and violence. To our critics, however, there was no way to demonstrate our success in reducing crime and the potential for crime, because, of course, you cannot demonstrate cause and effect for a non-event.

John Brown commented in flattering terms:

'What is apparent in the Handsworth context is the extent to which police functions relate to those of other statutory and voluntary services. All confront ... common problems. No service can work effectively in isolation, nor through purely reactive policies. The sub-divisional commander, Superintendent Webb, therefore wisely puts primary emphasis on linking police tasks with those of other agencies and upon activating community backing and preventive resources. In such ways he seeks to create a climate of collaboration and trust for his men to work in.'

A local barrister Rudy Narayan, now dead, used to write in the *Voice*, a local newspaper for black people. Rudy would defend most of the black and Asian cases in the area. If I remember correctly, he came originally from Guyana. He was disbarred and re-instated by the legal establishment four or five times. Still, he represented many people in his time, and like it or not, I and my people needed his help from time to time. Rudy was a nuisance to us, a thorn in our side, fighting us hard in the courts, case after case, sometimes in highly devious ways. I worked hard on changing Rudy, taking him around with me, into the pubs, into the houses and then he began to understand. Eventually, under a *nom de plume,* he showed through his writings that he sympathised with much of what I was trying to do. He could never of course admit it to his members or clients. He sadly died of a heart attack in 1999.

One forum I was particularly interested in developing was the *Black Youth in Handsworth Consultative Group.* In August 1976 we had formed what we called simply a Police Liaison Committee, attended by black voluntary and full time community workers. This led one year later to a highly unusual gathering, including the community workers, myself and three sergeants, and more than fifty black youngsters, many from the *Two hundred Dreads* later to be vilified in the local and national press as being responsible for all the crime in Handsworth. Amazingly, we had a most attentive audience. They watched two films, *The Policeman,* and *Your Police and You.* A structured and polite discussion followed about the films, the duties imposed by the nation upon the Police, the grievances of the young black men, the law concerning powers of arrest, stop and search, and the big one, allegations of police brutality towards young blacks.

We discussed a real event, an arrest of a young West Indian for stealing property. The young black man who challenged us in this was careful to explain that his criticisms were not directed at police action of arrest, but the method which had been followed. That gave us a valuable chance to explain to them the problems we ourselves faced. We had to send large numbers to an arrest because, whatever the rights or wrongs of any event, our young men and women were being violently attacked. For the first time, many of the young black men who had come to the meeting intent on showing us that we were the true pigs, learned that around seventy of our young officers had been injured within recent months, going home battered and troubled to wives and children. It was then that those present began to understand that there were two sides to the policing issue.

So, all these groups, activities, meetings, became our supporting cavalry. We would need them frequently to help calm their members in times of tension. On a single day that year we had the phenomenon of three separate marches, all originating in the same area of Handsworth, all with different aims and potentially violent outcomes. The Birmingham Trades Council marched in one direction, the Committee against Racism and Fascism marched in another, and the National Front Party of Great Britain in yet another. Each ended with large public meetings and ferocious speeches by the organisers. All in all, around five thousand demonstrators for one cause or another were on the streets, plus any number of potentially hostile spectators of every racial mix. Amazingly, only four persons were arrested for public order offences.

Chief Inspector Harry Udall was in charge of the CID. Contrary to popular belief, I never interfered with his tasks or laid down guidelines. Harry and I got on well together and we never clashed. We both knew what the other was trying to achieve, yet there were things I had set my mind to that I knew would benefit Handsworth. So Harry and his people knew that whilst I was in charge they would have to accommodate me and my ways. Still, there was resistance from some in the CID which expressed itself by various means. There was also resistance from some uniformed officers who were not Permanent Beat Officers. They would never say anything. They would just do something, and life became interesting.

James Hunte, as well as being a local community leader of the West Indian people, was a local councillor. James and I disagreed over many things, and he had gained his reputation among his followers from his skill at tweaking the tail of the white man, and mine. On the matter of community policing, however, we were in absolute agreement, working on many joint ventures, later to include the *Handsworth Festival*, and *The Mohammed Ali Centre*, visited and opened by the Great Man himself.

John Brown interviewed Hunte at length, describing him as *The leader of a West Indian self-help club.* Hunte's starting position was that he felt it totally futile to even discuss the matter of co-operation with the local police. We were the agents of a capitalist society whose racism had infected and enslaved the whole Caribbean. As the interview proceeded it emerged, slowly, that in fact I had met James several times to discuss the arrangements for the African Liberation Day celebrations, including a march for Freedom, followed by a big rally in Handsworth Park. Yet even then Hunte seemed confused and negative.

'Its a waste of time... Even if he (Webb) has good intentions, he can't do anything. It's impossible because of the racism of all the coppers.'

Hunte felt that National Front influence was gaining ground fast within the police service generally. He admitted, however, to John Brown that he had reached agreement with me on a deliberately low level of policing of the march itself, and the following celebrations.

South Africa, too, intruded onto our agenda. Handsworth would prove to be a main centre of United Kingdom resistance against the activities of the South African government. Nelson Mandela was in jail on Robben Island, but at that time forgotten by much of the world. Hundreds were expected to walk, some with motives and agendas well beyond the original intentions of the organisers. James Hunte and I faced the problem of how to steward and control the day so that it would not become a cause of friction or violence between the races. After reflection, I decided that the police ought not to take the lead in controlling the day. I felt that the community itself should accept responsibility for something that a certain section of the community was doing. It would strengthen community bonds. I feared that if we were there in force, marching alongside the protesting group, some idiots would see it as an excuse to taunt us, thus destroying to some extent good police and community relations.

In my private discussions with Hunte I explained the problems we could both face if things got out of hand. I told him firmly, *'Look, you can steward it. I will arrange a very minor presence. You can wave your banners and shout your slogans, but I don't want all the good work we have done to build good community relations being destroyed in any way.'*

A couple of days later, all the community leaders met at James Hunte's house to work out their plans and organise the event. James was a councillor with Birmingham City Council, and a member of the Police Authority. He and seven others were gathered together to work out what was best for Handsworth and Africa Day.

The news must have leaked out among my Force. Unfortunately for Hunte and the councillors and community leaders, some of them had parked their cars facing the wrong direction, in a thirty mile an hour zone, without lights. It was, of course, an offence. Still, there were that same evening thousands of cars parked in similar fashion all over the Midlands and few were given a second look. Two of my constables rolled up in a panda car, and ticketed every vehicle on the street outside James' house with a fixed penalty notice. Nowhere else, just that street. I was furious. The two constables were making a point, and targeting a group who were trying to help me with community policing.

I did not interfere. To do so would give credence to the view that I was soft on the coloured population. I explained to the community leaders that there was nothing that I could do, and the fines would have to be paid. It was the law.

The two officers explained: *'We did not know who they were, Sir. It was sheer coincidence that we were there at that particular time, Sir.'*

So I said: *'Good, well done, lads. Thank you. You knew there was something going on?'*

'No Sir.'

'You knew that you might upset the apple cart with the Africa Liberation Day march?'

'No Sir.'

'OK that's it. End of the story.'

So it was, as far as the two were concerned. They soon developed a liking for a sub-division other than Handsworth.

Hunte would never knew the full story of that evening ticketing. As regards our plans for Africa Day, in his and the public eye, there would be minimum policing, and some said openly that I was taking risks, that I was following the soft option. As commanding officer I would be at the head of the procession with the organisers. An inspector, a sergeant and ten constables would walk alongside. That was all the public and the marchers would see. Yet on the day, behind the scenes we secretly deployed one hundred and twenty senior and rank constables, two Special Patrol hit squads, riot shields, mobile vans, and a number of dog handlers. Three stations across the west of the City were primed to receive prisoners. We also allowed for some hot heads who seemed intent on trouble. Crude propaganda leaflets were circulating, that tied us and the government together as supporters of Apartheid. One in particular linked us with police operations in London with what was described as *OPERATION NIGGER HUNT* in which the white girl friend of some black youths had, so it was said, been stripped naked and left in a cell for several hours. *ORGANISE AGAINST POLICE BRUTALITY AND STATE ATTACKS* the leaflets shouted. *DEMONSTRATE! - VICTORY TO FREEDOM FIGHTERS! - BLACK WORKERS TO POWER! - BRITAIN, SOWETO, ONE STRUGGLE!* We also knew from our intelligence that a local known agitator G had a group of Rastafarian youths engaged in making weapons, including catapults, for use against the accompanying constables. So we took no chances.

The celebrations extended over three days and the event was a success from start to finish. West Indians came from all over the country and joined in the cultural events, held at Handsworth Park. The final day saw a peaceful march of about a thousand people, towards an evening of music and dancing. Everywhere were leaflets, preaching about the *Fascist Police* and what we were doing to the black races. The starry sky echoed with spine-chilling speeches, but the night ended in a carnival atmosphere on the green grass of the Park. There were films, black poetry, plays and sketches, dance groups, paintings and photographic exhibitions and a concert featuring the group *Aswad*. All suggested to me that there was more potential for good in Handsworth's people than I or the nation had ever imagined. That march was not only fun. It did much to channel and reinforce opinion against the South African government. Next day James Hunte and his people took on the job of clearing up the litter.

ELEVEN: BED OF NAILS

My Force contained mostly young inexperienced policemen. Many had not chosen to come there, *a bed of nails* as they saw it. What I was saying and doing was strange, alien to everything they expected from a career in the Police, alien to much of the media's *Starsky & Hutch* solution to every street crime. Whatever the Police do is public, and subject to criticism. In that sense it is political, even though in law policemen have no political role whatever, nor are they elected. The true role of the policeman is to be the servant of the people. Whenever a crime or demonstration occurred, the Government and party conference line was to crack down on it. No excuses, *'hit 'em hard'*, *'lock 'em up'*, crime is controlled, problem solved, standing ovation, vote of confidence in the Home Secretary. Life and people, however, are never as straightforward as that. A criminal does not disappear. He comes back at you, sometimes worse than before, especially the young apprentice.

A major problem that we never discussed openly was the fear factor. When humans, and Policemen, are afraid, they are unpredictable. The fear in the hearts and minds of wives and children goes even deeper and can influence a policeman's reactions for the worse. If I could bring Handsworth to a level where my men could walk around without being harassed or beaten up, it would be better for them and their families. Things could still go wrong I knew, but I also knew that things could be better, so much better. This was not just new for Handsworth. When national reactions and media interest started to roll in through various channels, I soon realised that many saw it as new for Britain.

Another thing I did at that time, which to some would seem contrary to what they saw as my *softly softly* approach, was to raid every club in the neighbourhood. There were six clubs in Handsworth, each causing serious problems. All kinds of things were going on. Strip clubs, gambling joints, blues clubs. Drugs were being bought, sold and used, heavily. With these came the background crimes of territorial disputes, and the foundation of even more serious crime in the future.

Meanwhile the Great British Public driving in and out of Birmingham each day and night down the main Soho Road, which links Birmingham's Centre with the West, could see it all. Men, and a few women, were hanging about in groups, spilling out of the clubs, fighting and milling about, rather similar to our towns and city centres now, except that it is today the white races that are notorious for such. People would write letters to me and the newspapers, *'Why is all this happening? Why don't the Police do something about it? Why don't you lock them all up?'* etc.

So I went to each of the club owners. *'Look,'* I said, *'I'm not having this in my patch. You will run your club properly, and I do not want your customers out on the street. I want them inside the club. And if there is trouble I want it sorted out inside. You should be ashamed of the way the public see your area, saying what a ramshackle place it is. Is this how you want to be seen? I'm telling you now. I will stop you, close you down if it continues.'*

At first they took no notice, so I warned them again. In those days you could get a fine of two thousand pounds, and a club could lose its licence. Still it did not work for the bad owners, so I raided them one at a time and stood the owners up in court for all to see. From then on, right to the day of my leaving Handsworth, I did not have a single instance of serious trouble in any of the clubs. Two of the people involved were a Levi and Mrs Knights at the Monte Carlo Club. A Bernard Whyte ran another club on the opposite side of the road. All heeded my initial warnings, are still in business and we remain friends to this day.

The public houses were also a centre for trouble. If we heard of any drugs changing hands in a pub, and we got good intelligence as the locals began to trust us, I would warn the owner. Then I discovered that the owner was being threatened by local traders and was more afraid of them than of me. So I would tell each pub owner to pass on a warning in my name, tell the dealers that I had been to the pub, and if I found out that any drugs were around the place, I would raid it. Everyone we caught would be in court, the pub would lose its licence and the place closed down. It worked. The pubs soon began to clean up their act, and the traders moved to other areas.

In 1985 I was to be accused by the Chairman of the Police Federation of being pro-cannabis and taking a soft line on drugs. He claimed that the public really had wanted me to hit the users hard. Things, however, are never that simple. Drug traders often have better intelligence than the Police. Many times, when huge police raids are made, smashing places up, searching and arresting everybody, creating future enemies, few if any drugs are discovered. Thus it may help at this point to refer to the famous *stop and search* blitz in London, that, many agreed later, was one of the trigger events leading to the Brixton street riots of 1981.

Operation Swamp, carried out between the 6th and the 11th of April, was an attempt to search every suspicious person on the streets of Brixton, and arrest all drug dealers, carriers, burglars and robbers. The Metropolitan Police believed, on good intelligence, so they thought, that this was the way to frighten the criminal, to prove to the public that the Police were in control, and, in the process, catch many criminals in the act. *Everyone knew* that the streets were teeming with young black men possessing criminal intent and drugs, stolen goods, and some with offensive weapons in their pockets. The street crime figures proved it, didn't they?

The results were revealing. Over six days the operation required the services of one hundred and twelve overworked police officers, and an enormous amount of overtime. Out of nine hundred and forty three 'stops', just over half were black people. Two thirds were under twenty one years of age. One hundred and eighteen arrests were made leading to seventy five charges. The seventy five charges included one robbery, one attempted burglary, and twenty charges of theft or attempted theft.

In short, a highly expensive operation over six days had produced twenty-two significant charges, but along the way had required the stopping, searching and inconveniencing of over eight hundred and sixty eight innocent people. The question was, what would the majority of those people do, especially the young innocent black folk, when they next saw a crime in progress? Would they call the Police and trust them to act fairly? Within days there would be serious and expensive street riots. Would they support the Police or the rioters? I think we can guess the answer.

Operation Swamp would occur four years after I arrived in Handsworth. The few among those in command who thought as I did were already aware of the negative effects of such policies. If we cracked down on everyone, if we charged in wielding batons on every disturbance, if we raided every *squat* to search for drugs or stolen goods, yes, we would catch a few criminals. We also knew, however, that there was a more important goal that could lead to a better society. As well as arresting the criminal, it was my job to find a way to get the good folk in Handsworth to be on our side. We had a duty to persuade parents and teachers, brothers and sisters, to influence the school child, to deter the potential teenage criminal, and, if he or she could not be deterred, then to help us catch the criminal. Furthermore, we had to find a way to counteract the adulation that some young black criminals received as *Robin Hoods* in their territory. In other words to achieve *policing by consent*.

On the other hand, I never discouraged or prevented any CID man or constable from arresting someone caught in possession of drugs. The law had to be firmly enforced. We did not seek out the minor user, as the trade-off was not worth it. There is a relevance to the recurring debate today. While I was doing these things in the late 1970's and being criticised for it, some members of the Shadow Cabinet and Government junior ministers, as we now know, were smoking cannabis in London. A be-sweatered President Clinton, while a respected Rhodes Scholar at Oxford University, held and smelled but *did not inhale*. The debate is running as I write.[1] There must be a better way. Every aspect should be examined and put in its proper context. If cannabis is proved, in its totality of cause and effect, to be harmful to society, then we must discourage its use. Many other drugs are more destructive, and I feel contempt and anger for those who profit from the trade.

Meanwhile, my Rastas and most of my young black street children were smoking cannabis. I did not then regard cannabis as I did other drugs, and most of the rastas were good, sincere people.

---

[1] July 2001

72

TWELVE: ROOTS OF RACISM

A foundation for my strategy had to be a good understanding of the nature of racism. In the preface to this book I explore something of its origins and strength. At that time in Birmingham and cities across the United Kingdom such as Leicester, Burnley, Oldham, Bradford, Liverpool, Bristol, and of course London, a major component was the gathering of large immigrant populations in one particular area.

How did we indigenous British see these folks? They congregated in areas of old poor housing, seemingly a part and cause of the decline. The West Indians had their churches, wonderful centres of song and religious expression, and clubs. The Asians, of which there are many different races, had temples and mosques, and their *Gudwaras* (Sikh temples). All sent children to schools, sometimes in large groups, competing for places against our own children. The shops were different, Asian, West Indian, Chinese, Turkish and many others. The smells were different. Haberdashers sold strange and colourful Asian silks and satins. Jewellers displayed wonderfully crafted gold and diamond adornments. Local industries special to the immigrants sprang up, bringing the same rules that were followed in the homeland and sometimes contrary to British industrial traditions and laws. Their music was happy and sad, strange, seemingly out of tune, always alien. These new peoples would organise, make demands, sometimes act in most un-English, most unreasonable ways. They were neglectful, some of them, of the Queen's English. Finally, they competed for our jobs and it seemed worse in the 70's and 80's than it had ever been.

It is then that the outsider is seen as a threat, usually by people with no first hand knowledge. This perception is sometimes more strongly expressed from rural and urban areas of the country, by people who have never seen or been in contact with immigrants, have never sat down and had a meal with them, never been to school with them, have no knowledge of their lifestyle or aspirations, have never talked, never listened, never laughed, never touched.

Some among the British public felt, and still feel, from deep within, that their treasured way of life is threatened, that the lives of their children and grandchildren will be changed for the worse. Enoch Powell was right in some ways. An influx of immigrants can cause trouble. He was, though, out of order in expressing it the way he did. So, we have to ask, why and from where does the trouble come? We should also consider how racism can be manipulated by people intent on political aims, by fringe political and other organisers and instigators, on both sides of the racial divide..

I am one of few people in the country fortunate to have known the situation first hand. I know what it was like in the fifties, how the newcomers had to live, what their aspirations were and what were their ideals, and I know how it is now.

Immigrants are now among the top professionals in the country, their children go to university and top schools, with unashamed British and English aspirations. They present our TV news, write our newspapers, lead our industries, make our laws. Their children go to India, Pakistan and the West Indies to visit relatives, and then return. Some tell me they are glad to get back to England. They have lost their identification with the homeland of their parents and grandparents. Our lifestyles are the same. The only difference for many is the colour of our skin. These people are not going to go home, not go away. The idea of rewards for going home would never work and never did. History, too, reminds us that in the sixth century, after the departure of the Romans, our nation was invaded by a white alien race called the *Anglo-Saxons*.

My force had a high proportion of young probationers. How did they see the racial mix that lived and worked all around them? How did they feel when faced with a sea of hostile black and later, brown, faces?

There are racially motivated policemen throughout the nation's Police. Their prejudice is rooted in the section of society they come from. I sensed then that racism among the public and in the Police was as strong as it had ever been. My young constables would day after day come face to face with young black men of the same age. Young men with no qualifications or work and no apparent interest in obtaining either, standing in groups on street corners or outside clubs and squats, all hostile, questioning, demanding, challenging. At times the banter would contain humour, and the teenagers would tease terribly with their street patois, unintelligible to the white man. At others, whenever the constable had reason to believe that the law was about to be or had been broken, ranks would close and faces harden. In other words, normal human reactions in a situation of confrontation.

Throughout our society racism is common. There are racist doctors, racist lawyers, racist members of Parliament, even racist members of the National Health Service. Policemen are what we would expect them to be, members of the public, normal human beings with a suspicion of those who are *different*. We cannot pretend that policemen could be anything else. If we try to do so, then we drive a wedge between the Police and public. We must start from the point that we are all members of the same species, have natural instincts that reject those who are *different*. We must then devise skills and techniques to overcome those fears.

Meanwhile, while undertaking a measure of social engineering without precedent, we cannot allow ourselves to tolerate racist attitudes or actions anywhere, particularly amongst the Police. The Police are in a unique position, with power and authority over all communities. And they can misuse that authority if they choose. So, among the men and women on my force, I made it clear that if something did happen that revealed, among our officers, racism in any form, we would try to create a culture in which colleagues would forget comrade loyalties, would *blow the whistle* and ensure that the racist actions were identified and disciplined. If it proved necessary, then the racist policeman would be driven out of the Police themselves.

A policeman is like any other member of the public, yet he or she has to do the dirty work on behalf of the public. It is easy, dealing day after day with a hostile flotsam and jetsam of black faces, to believe that most young black men are inherently bad. It is but a short step to then believe that a young black man is bad *because* he is black. As I look back I am convinced that this assumption was behind much of the media coverage at the time and in the minds of many men around me. We see it today in the intermittent controversy about *black street crime*, and I will return to it later with examples of the kind of uninformed assumptions that a society can make when racial issues are at the heart of the debate.

We received some criticisms from the media; yet most, especially those who spent sufficient time in Handsworth to allow them to understand how the place ticked, were helpful. We hid nothing from the press. We answered every question as best we could.

It was in December 1977 that John Brown went public on his findings in his study *Shades of Grey*. The reactions of press and public were wide ranging. Derek Humphrey of the Sunday Times produced a thoughtful feature, taking the trouble to visit Handsworth and interview some of these alleged young black thugs for himself; a group of four homeless Rastas in a self-help project, seeing how they survived amongst an area almost devoid of employment. He had been there some seven years before and was struck by the deterioration since his last visit. He was most impressed by the humility of the young black men that he visited, and their anger against the uninformed racism of the local and national press.

The local Birmingham Post rumbled *TERROR GANGS SHOCK* with an opening sweep of *'A HARD core of 200 young West Indians are bringing terror to a three-mile area of a Birmingham suburb, says a report out today.'* The Sunday Telegraph led the national field on December 4th with *'200 CRIMES A MONTH BY GANG OF MUGGERS'*. The Guardian followed the next day with *'Last year around 400 crimes a month were committed in Handsworth by more than 200 West Indians.'* The Daily Mail's reporter Keith Colling went further, increasing the number of crimes by over ten percent, and then mistakenly attributing them all to black West Indians. Columnist Frederick Whitehead wrote in the Birmingham Post: *'The tree-lined street where I used to live in Handsworth, Birmingham, is now an alley of putrefaction. Many of its houses are postules of profanity, its gutters gather the jetsam of decay and the faces of the alien people who live there are a fretwork of sullen resignation.'*

Sadly relations with the Barrow and Geraldine S. Cadbury Trust were to take a dive. For whatever reason, the Trust exploded with anger. *'Disastrous,'* commented the Secretary, Anthony Wilson. *'It was never the Trust's intention in sponsoring the report that it should have been anything other than a document to assist the Police as they revised their own policy... This is not the same as saying that only the Police should see it.'* On the matter of *200 young thugs terrorising the putrefying streets of Handsworth* Anthony Wilson felt the national coverage had been exploitative and at times deliberately so: *'This report... is not a picture of a society where there is no kind of social control. There are only 200 young people involved in crime...'* John's recommendation for the drafting into my force of a further twenty experienced constables to act as PBOs had, he felt, been deliberately distorted nationally as a way of confronting the street criminals. John's recommendation had of course been the exact opposite - that of finding a way of developing face to face contacts with young blacks and school children and parents to indicate to them that there were better ways of venting their frustrations.

A saddened John Brown later confessed to me his bitterness at the lack of interest shown nationally and locally to the main part of his report, the *Why* of Handsworth. I always sensed that from then on he was deeply troubled. On the wisdom of his releasing the report to the press, he felt it was a matter of debate: *'It seems futile to discuss it.* Of the national press articles he said, *'It is not what the report said, but what was made of it by a number of interested parties. I can only assume that the media has some kind of interest in polarising the issue'*.

John may at times have suspected that he had failed to deliver the message in a way that society might understand, but his report found much favour with the Chief Constable, Phillip Knights, who had initially asked him to visit Handsworth to undertake the research. Within months, Knights arranged for the addition of several younger experienced officers to my Permanent Beat Officer strength. We reshaped our beats and the supervisory structure, and increased the overall strength of the Permanent Beat Officers from sixteen in mid 1977 to one sergeant and twenty one constables. In addition, I was allowed and supported in my efforts, to give more status and importance to the role of the permanent beat officer.

Most Police stations around Birmingham were old Victorian places. Thornhill Station was among them and had been the old Staffordshire County Police Station and Police Court combined. It is still there after more than a hundred years. From the outside it was a proud, grey-haired old place. We changed the inside a lot, converting it into an effective workplace. We kept it spotless and the civilian cleaners did a great job. They just loved the pristine Victorian wall and floor tiles, the woodwork, the ceilings and the great stylish doors. I still have the clock they gave me when I retired, and a photo taken of me in my office with some of my staff today stands proudly alongside wedding photos. You can see the comfort and the good situation we had there. Yes, I have many fond memories of the old place at Thornhill Road. Only recently, after thirty years loyal and devoted service, my typist Ann retired. May she and her husband have a long and happy life together.

When *Her Majesty's Inspector of Constabulary* arrives, it is a big affair. The staff car rolls up to the station front entrance, in comes Her Majesty's Delegate, and you and your staff are effectively on trial. The commander of the station has to strut around introducing everyone and demonstrating the efficiency of himself and his staff. This Inspection was different. The visitor was my old Chief Constable in

Hertfordshire, and he had a lot to talk about and a morning to fill. So instead of marching around inspecting me and my men, he sat chatting in my office as my secretary Ann brought in biscuits and cup after large cup of tea.

Outside, carved in dark millstone grit into the fabric of the building, above the main entrance of the station, was a huge Staffordshire knot, with the words *Police Court*, and the year the place was built, 1890 or thereabouts. Her Majesty's Inspector was a former Staffordshire man, so at the end of the inspection, thinking he would like that kind of thing, I took him outside to proudly show off our Staffordshire knot. When we got outside it was gone.

'Where's my Staffordshire knot?' I demanded loudly.

An upstairs window opened and a junior constable mumbled down: *'Sir, we thought you would want it removed because you would not want Her Majesty's Inspectorate to think he was in the wrong area.'* It had disappeared overnight, with me totally unaware of the disappearance.. So much for my efficient station. We laughed so much we nearly wet ourselves.

Recent events [1] have again sadly demonstrated that the Great British Public, whether racist or not, cannot always tell the difference between an Indian, a Pakistani, or a Bangladeshi, or an Arab. Furthermore they know even less about the respective religions, beliefs and aspirations.

I'm mindful of an old joke about a Jew and a Chinaman, both complete strangers, sitting side by side in a pub. Suddenly the Jew turns around and smacks the Chinaman right on the chin, and the man flies across the floor to land in a heap. The dazed man gets up and dusts himself down.

'My friend, what did you do that for?'

The Jew looks at him furiously. *'That was for Pearl Harbour.'*

'But I'm nothing to do with Pearl Harbour. I'm Chinese, not Japanese.'

'You've got black hair, buck teeth and slitty eyes. What's the difference?'

The Chinaman sits down and thinks for a few seconds, then turns and clouts the Jew, sending him spinning across the floor. The Jew picks himself up, dusts himself down and speaks.

'OK, OK, I knocked you off your stool, now we're quits.'

'No,' says the Chinaman. *'That's for the Titanic.'*

'But the Titanic hit an iceberg,' stammers the Jew.

'Iceberg, Goldberg, it's all the same to me.'

---

[1] *Islamic extremists steered four loaded passenger aircraft on the World Trade Centre in New York, the Pentagon, and (probably) Camp David, 11th September 2001. Widespread aggression and some attacks occurred against people of various Eastern races in the following weeks.*

THIRTEEN: STORMY WEATHER

1978 was a horrible year. We were surrounded by conflicting philosophies and confused demands, by stormbringers visiting discontent on our streets as proof of a march to some great victory. Into our traumatised suburb poured wild propaganda and ideas, simple facts presented and re-presented, twisted inside out to prove opposites. Each added its own insidious chemistry and I began, like a naturalist, to collect specimens. I often wondered at the psychology of those preaching this kind of stuff. If they did not believe it and were intent on stirring our tiny society into rebellion, when demonstrations occurred they would be at the rear, urging the faithful onward into battle. If they did believe it, what disasters and death might they bring in confrontation with the Police?

If a man really believes, he can justify any action, feel happy in attacking those who are *different*. It can range from the near beheading of a white policeman in London's Broadwater Farm Riots in August 1975 to the neutering, hanging and burning of blacks in Mississippi, from the throwing of bricks through a kitchen window, to the burning of children. In May 2001 the police in Coventry investigated a suspected arson attack on the house of an Asian family, Hindu I believe. The attacker poured petrol or something similar through the letter box of a terrace house and within seconds the upstairs rooms were filled with smoke. The mother went back in to rescue her children and perished. The father, a simple and humble man, appeared on television shocked, stunned and alone.

As for my specimens? Among the mildest is:

'Government and Police have long smelt the growing anger of rebellion, from black and white unemployed youth, from the black community, from workers in a struggle for jobs and wages. Their response has been to train up and equip a Police Force capable of containing any trouble, that is, brutally crushing all resistance, through organised intimidation, harassment and violence ... snatch squads, Special Branch, police raids, mass arrests, CS gas and other new methods of maintaining law and order.'

Another referred to G R, at that time in custody in Thornhill Road Station, and called on all to picket the main Birmingham Law Courts where he was being tried. A conspiracy was under way, a campaign to repress the black man. *'In Handsworth the centre of this campaign is Thornhill Road Station. It is from there that the thugs in blue are sent out on daily patrols to harass and beat us up on our streets, in our shops and homes. It is Thornhill Road that sent out gangs to beat up, arrest and frame brothers A W and GR... The floors and walls of this station are stained with the blood of those held and beaten up...'*

On the subject of an arrest of another West Indian man, the following appeared in *Pioneer News*, a local political magazine:

'On Thursday March 22nd 1978, the pigs from Thornhill Road Police, armed with batons, dogs, guns, riot shields and members of the Special Patrol Group moved in on a house on the corner of Hutlow Road and Westminster Road. There were at least 60 to 70 pigs in this military type operation for the arrest of one black youth.

This brother and several people in the house were kept under siege for quite some time. The presence of people outside the house hampered the pigs in such a way that the pigs started to threaten them. Eventually one of the local stooges James Hunte arrived on the scene and with the help of the youth's mother persuaded him to give himself up

Although released from Thornhill Road that night, he was rearrested a few days later and given a vicious beating resulting in a broken arm. He was taken to Winson Green Prison and refused a doctor even though he complained of severe pains.

Nearly two weeks later, brother EB was ... confronted by five pigs from Ladywood Station. They burst in and after some questioning proceeded to batter him unconscious. While one of the pigs was throttling him he asked the brother if he could breathe. E waved his arm indicating that he couldn't so the pig pressed even harder on E's throat. He was then dragged into the Police car outside and beaten up all the way to the station, being kicked several times in the testicles. Brother EB told me that he literally saw death...'

In June the *Workers Weekly* recounted the death in custody of a Major Singh, who had committed suicide while in a cell at Winson Green Prison. It required a special meeting with five representatives of the Sikh Temple, three relatives, three prison officers, two representatives of the Birmingham Community Relations Council, a chief cuperintendent, myself and three other senior officers to resolve the following allegations and reassure the relatives to their satisfaction that the entire article was nothing more than propaganda. The relatives had known nothing of the allegations and their grief was compounded by the following:

'On June 1st Major Singh of Handsworth, Birmingham, died in Winson Green Prison, murdered by police and prison warders. After a fight in Soho Road he was arrested on May 6th and severely beaten up by the police, with several of them stamping on his back. When his relations were eventually allowed to see him on May 9th he was in a serious condition. However, all requests for bail were rejected and applications for him to be taken to hospital were refused. He appeared in court on May 16th and May 31st, on both occasions it being obvious that he had been subjected to serious mistreatment. police still refused him medical attention, and he died on June 1st, after many beatings and other tortures. The 'official' announcement was that he had hanged himself with sheets. This is typical fascist type concoction spread by the state authorities to cover up that it is they who are responsible for this racist murder...

A further example of this racism of the Police is that as soon as Major Singh was arrested they were trying to make out that he was an illegal immigrant and he was held in custody on that excuse, whilst since his death they have refused the right of the family to see Major Singh's body.

The people of Handsworth will not forget this crime. They will add it to the long list of crimes committed by police and prison authorities in Birmingham and strengthen their determination even more to FIGHT BACK AGAINST ALL GOVERNMENT AND NAZI ORGANISED RACIAL ATTACKS.'

The white races, too, were represented, but not in such frequency or ferocity. A small pinkish leaflet circulating in 1978 opened:

'All three parties, having systematically refused to consult us about coloured immigrations, are compelling Britain to accept unwanted multi-racialism and the continuing invasion by people of alien cultures. WE WANT NONE OF IT... The Race Relations Industry must be prevented from re-writing British History with our money and for the benefit of coloured immigrants.

Our Laws are being bent and disregarded in order to accommodate the illegal immigrants and alien customs... Home Office regulations are so ineffectual that every year tens of thousands of immigrants enter Britain illegally, while British passports and British nationality are granted regularly to known anti-establishment agitators...

Schools are grossly overcrowded because of the high illegal immigrant birth rate and hundreds of our children cannot be properly educated... British mothers are compelled to have their babies at home whilst immigrant mothers occupy hospital maternity beds... WE DEMAND HUMAN RIGHTS FOR WHITES.'

Meanwhile a few miles to the west, in Wolverhampton, racial conflict[1] was adding its own contribution. Reporters Gerry Anderson and West Indian Torrance Mendez examined the local situation. The Police Federation, which represents the views of rank and file policemen throughout the nation, had recently concluded its conference in Blackpool. Conservative MP Eldon Griffiths, addressing the conference, forecast a chilling future for our major cities. *'The 1980's will see no-go areas which police would enter only when armed. Major cities will face racial conflict surrounded by wastelands dominated by muggers and vandals.'*

On January 9th 1978, at a football game between Exeter and Wolverhampton Wanderers, youths in the stands wore Ku Klux Klan hoods. January 27th saw a black versus white rampage along Wolverhampton's George Street. February 4th witnessed an anti-racist march through town and on 25th February a public mock kangaroo court put the Police on trial. On March 2nd, the Ku Klux Klan leader himself arrived from the USA to claim that he had established a *den* in Wolverhampton. Another anti-

---

[1] *Wolverhampton: must we allow the image of hostility and bitterness blur the reality?* Wolverhampton Express and Star 23rd May 1978.

racist march was followed by a shotgun shooting of two West Indian youths. A local self-employed building worker was interviewed:

'Give me a gun and pass the ammunition. I don't want to just get rid of the blacks. I want rid of the Chinese, the Poles, the Dutch and the Irish and all the other bastards who are sucking this country dry. I love England. I fought for her in Aden, and I'm not having these b****s f***g my country up.'

People were worried. The Roman Catholic Auxiliary Bishop of Birmingham feared that the problem would escalate. *'Unemployment is the real problem for all the young people. It means that they have a lot of free time on their hands, and that is the root of the problem... The other thing that has contributed to the problem is the National Front which is a disturbing element.'* We too were concerned. An explosion in Wolverhampton would spread across the West Midlands like a plague.

Pride of place in my collection goes to something that has always made me ponder. Was it propaganda by the National Front? Or was it true 'black' propaganda by some group hoping to stir up black resentment so as to harness the effect against the white policeman? It features at its head two crude but identical drawings. One is said to be an ape, the other a negro, and each has a series of arrows pointing to parts of its body. Each being is half crouching, half seated on some form of bench, legs akimbo, leaning forward, arms swinging low to the ground. The use of the American spelling of *color* and the American 'Z' is interesting. Reading clockwise the arrows indicate:

'(Hair) - animal wool. (Head) - dolicocephalic mellon shaped head. (Brain) - small. (Smell) - animal. (Arms) - long. (Color) - black ape. (Legs) - weak lower limbs. (Hands) - big. (Toes) - prehensile toe. (Calf) - small high calf. (Heel) - protruding. (Feet) - large. (Shin) - round ape shape. (Legs) - short. (Thumb) - short ape. (Pelvis) - forward slanting. (Lips) - Prognathous ape jaw. (Skull) - ape groove in skull.'

Below these pictures is a headline:

'SCIENTISTS SAY NEGRO STILL IN APE STAGE - RACES POSITIVELY NOT EQUAL.

(1)   The negro's head above shows the archaic form. The front of the negro's skull is much smaller than the white man's, thus giving the negro less room for the higher faculties, such as affection, self control, will power, reason, judgement, apperception, orientation and a feeling for the relationship of personality to environment.

(2)   The negro's eyeball is tinged with yellow as is the ape's. The jaw protrudes so that the facial angle of the negro is 70 degrees as is the ape's. The white man's facial angle is 72 degrees.

Etc etc, ad nauseam. The pamphlet ends: *'MONGRELIZATION OF THE RACES WOULD DESTROY WHITE CIVILIZATION'* [1]

---

[1] The term *Mongrel Nation* was used by Peter Townend, a United Kingdom MP opposing all further immigration in the June 2001 election campaign.

February 1978 saw a National Front march and meeting in nearby Digbeth, and many of our Handsworth force were jointly allocated to crowd control duties. Opposing the Front were an estimated four to five thousand demonstrators, anti fascist groups, Socialist Workers Party people, and several small groups of black and Asian men and women from our Handsworth area and other parts of the West Midlands. Chief Constable Phillip Knights and several of us watched as it developed. Local reporters easily identified the ringleader of the demonstrators:

'Communist singled out as leader of hooligan mob'.

On a highly charged and confused day, and having identified the leader who was waving a red flag (also at that time the theme song of the Labour Party), the reporter moved to the following statement[1] about the protesters:

'POSSESSION OF THE STREETS IS THE KEY TO POWER IN THE STATE: This headline was a favourite slogan of Hitler's infamous SA (from Sturmabteilungen, meaning "Storm Troopers') the brown shirted masses of the Nazi movement. It is a grim irony that those who, as these pictures show, flocked onto the streets of Digbeth, Birmingham on Saturday are anti-nazis in every sense of the word.

Yet they were using exactly the same kind of tactics, giving expression to a spirit of intransigence and intolerance that is dangerous beyond belief. It is now a matter of history how the activities of the SA rabble paved the way to the extinction of all political freedom in Germany and to racial intolerance on an official and terrifying scale.

But Hitler held these people in deep contempt. 'Such elements are unusable in times of peace, but in turbulent periods it is quite different', he said. 'Fundamentally they are just outgrown children. With what blind obedience they followed me."

Photos showed white and black united against the Police, with posters proclaiming, *'BEWARE ! THE POLICE ARE THE REAL MUGGERS...FIGHT BACK WITH FLAME..'* Our instigator, waving his red flag, was featured riding on the shoulders of a black West Indian youth.

Inside the Digbeth Civic Hall John Tyndall, chairman of the National Front, thundered: *'If anyone is going to be smashed it will not be the National Front. We are going to need our young people to be physically fit as well as equipped with the right arguments and ideas. Bright youngsters are being held back in multi-racial classes by the stupidest, and we know who the stupidest are, don't we?'*

While all this was going on our thin blue line, behind slender plastic riot shields, was trying to keep order and separation between the competing crowds. As there were few about outside the Hall, the only available target was the phalanx of blue uniforms and helmets. In several short but vicious spells of battering and missiles, twenty two officers were injured, including three women, and one constable had a fractured skull. We arrested thirty three people. One young woman constable, on traffic duty some way from the centre of the demonstration, was unluckily spotted

---

[1] *Communist singled out as leader of hooligan mob,* Birmingham Post 20th February 1978

by a breakaway group of demonstrators. They started to throw bricks. One knocked her hat off. Another hit her on the forehead. She took refuge in a local cafe, but the owner was unfortunately singled out for a similar treatment, and all his windows were smashed before constables could intervene and restore order.

Simple solutions followed. Perhaps the Birmingham Lord Mayor, Councillor Freda Cocks, had my policing policies in mind as she roared: *'Birch the Digbeth thugs... The do-gooders have had their way for long enough. I think its time magistrates were given the power to order the birch in extreme cases. Let's be a bit old fashioned and give these hooligans a thump up their backsides.'*

Elsewhere in England, Enoch Powell rode the storm to advantage, proposing to repatriate up to one hundred thousand immigrants each year for the next twenty years. Mrs Thatcher was not amused. Meanwhile the white-haired Ted Heath was attacking her from her back-benches, aided by a former minister Peter Walker who said:

'Immense permanent damage could come from the Tories stirring up an anti immigrant line... Mr Powell and the National Front will continually outbid us in preying on the fears and prejudices of people... I've no doubt that it will get a lot of votes - but I have no doubt that it will mean total disaster for the country.'

Mrs Thatcher attempted the middle road: *'We will demand a stricter entry policy for the relatives and dependants of immigrants already here.'*

Like all senior officers around the country, I was troubled and frustrated at times by the way that the legal system and sentencing policies made control of crime even more difficult. This was especially true of the typical Handsworth crime of mugging and street robbery, for which bail would be normally granted.

As an example, while out on bail, some of our young citizens had a tendency to commit more crime, producing a legal overlap difficult to contain. A report that dropped onto my desk in January 1978 typified the problem. Five young men were on bail, for committing a series of robberies along the Birchfield, Lozells and Soho roads. They were suspected of many other offences. We believed that while out on bail they were continuing to offend. Three other young men were believed to be planning several other robberies in partnership with the first five on our list.

Another three were on bail for robbery of a taxi driver and use of a knife in Broughton Road. A further four had robbed a taxi driver at knife point in Lozells Road, again all were on bail. Another youngster had been involved with the above people in a series of robberies in Soho Road. Yet another three were on bail for robbery in Handsworth and conspiracy to rob in Stafford, some twenty miles to the north. Finally, thirteen more men were on bail for various kinds of robberies in other parts. So, we had a web of several dozen crimes and suspected crimes shared between a relatively small group of thirty one young men.

Even though my prosecuting constables and legal advisers pointed out the risks of further offences to the magistrates, bail was still granted. Meanwhile, whilst still out on bail, twelve of the thirty one were re-arrested for further crimes. My problem was not to identify and arrest, indeed, we were experts at that; but how to find some way to break the cycle among those young men already on a criminal career? Not just for them, but for their younger brothers and sisters, and their friends among the children in the schools, I had to find ways of deterring them from a similar future. Unless I acted, the alternative was to stand around for five or six years, wait for them to grow up, commit their first minor crimes, and then arrest them. Thus, a policy of despair that would be corrosive to Handsworth, those children and their families.

An example of the confusion and despair prevalent in the streets occurred in February that year, when Dennis Howell MP sent me a series of letters on behalf of some of his constituents in the Lozells area. Several muggings had taken place and the local residents had asked to meet him to protest that we should be doing more to counteract the problem. To Dennis' chagrin, only six people attended the meeting, whether out of apathy or despair was never clear.

I did some research and was shocked to find that in the previous twelve months, Handsworth had suffered one hundred and thirty seven robberies, and one hundred and forty eight thefts from the person. This was far higher than the eighty two recorded in neighbouring Lozells. Those robberies in our patch had involved culprits identified as four hundred and twenty West Indians, two Asians, twenty whites, and forty two not known. Meanwhile, out there in the community, the only time the people would see a policeman was when something went wrong. A policeman had become a head seen through the windows of a passing panda car, or an anonymous face in a row of grim anonymous faces arriving in a van to arrest a suspect or to break up a fight outside a local pub. I used to ask people, even community leaders: *'Who is your local police officer? When did you last see a policeman other than going down the road in a police car? Do you know any policemen socially? Have you ever seen a policeman socially?'* The answer was always a firm yet puzzled *'No.'* Clearly we were not seen as a part of Handsworth society. We were aliens in our own community.

It was around this time that I met a BBC documentary producer Roger Casstles, based at Pebble Mill Studios in Edgbaston. He was interested in the work of John Brown and our policing methods, and was convinced that our story should be told to a wider audience. With reporter Tony Francis, the camera crew recorded a series of interviews and events that will, I believe, be seen by historians as a rich reminder of Handsworth throughout the '70s and '80s. *Shades of Grey* was to receive the coveted Pye Colour Television 'Best Regional Programme' later that year, the first time the BBC won the award, and was chosen from a record number of twenty six entries. Roger, born in Biddulph in Staffordshire, was to become a close friend.

British Broadcasting Corporation
Broadcasting Centre, Pebble Mill Road,

Birmingham
1st March 1978
Dear David,

I would like once again to express my thanks for all the co-operation afforded to us while filming Shades of Grey, both by your staff at Thornhill Road Station, and particularly yourself. Although the final result was perhaps a little less than we might have hoped for, the reaction to the film has been favourable, and I should like to think that the programme may help in some small way towards the future.

Please extend my thanks to all your officers - I trust we will meet again under less frenetic circumstances some time in the future!

Yours sincerely,
Roger Casstles,
Producer

***

There is a range of human skills that are essential to community policing; the voice, the mannerisms, the look of authority. If you cannot influence things by force of personality, the public and the criminal will break you. To run a large and powerful organisation requires special qualities, and there were others across the police ranks of Britain who helped me to understand those qualities. I was privileged to meet on a number of occasions John Alderson, Chief Constable of Devon and Cornwall, and we found a great deal of common ground. As for what we were developing in Handsworth, officers from other forces visited from all over the UK to see what was going on, and they loved it. As they studied our methods, it became clear to many that we were using techniques that were outside the usual activities of the Police, as they and their supervisors, and even the Home Secretary, understood them.

John Rex, at that time a professor at Warwick University said that what I was doing was not community policing. I did not agree, and every attempt to solve a policing problem in an ethnic area since that time has proved my point. The only person who can succeed at community policing within the traditional structure of British society is the police superintendent with the backing of his force. No one else is better placed. The Police are the only authoritative service present twenty four hours a day, seven days a week. All society professions, other than medical or nursing, go home at night and at weekends. The Police are the only people with the job of continuous patrolling of streets and the people. Social Services cannot do it. The Probation Service cannot do it. The Education Department cannot do it. Local MPs and councillors cannot do it. If we had elected neighbourhood mayors with authority and resources, it might be possible. We must remember that the aim is peaceful streets and crime free towns, and community policing is the best way, not the perfect way, to achieve this. If the Police, because of political resistance or inertia, do not want to take the lead, then community policing falls into disuse and society drifts into an uncertain future.

It takes years to achieve true community policing within a policing zone. A commander has to retain experienced constables and detectives long enough for them to have a positive impact, to become known and trusted. Over the years the people will get to know just how far they can go with you, and you with them. Only then can you bring about major change and make a real difference to peoples' day to day lives. Why? Well, it seemed so obvious to me. If you only ever met your son or your daughter, wife or neighbour when things go wrong, then problems would never get solved. Thus, when the infant in the school builds trust with the local constable, that child will be much less likely to throw a brick at that constable, whatever may be the perceived provocation. And he will grow to understand that to do any kind of crime is a bad thing, whatever his peer group may tell him.

Then the residents of an area will start to ask their local policeman for advice on all kinds of problems, even social ones. Even though it is not that policeman's job to sort the problem, he can advise on who to contact, or even himself contact the person via the force network, so that something can be done. And he can come back next week to the residents' meeting and be ready to say what he has done about the problem. Feedback will come naturally. Multiply that feedback by eighteen or twenty local bobbies, and soon you will assemble a library of knowledge that will help you head off further problems. Remember that in those days, as now, eighty percent of police work does not involve actual crimes. The local policeman, the beat officer, is mostly concerned with social and related issues.

I had a good blend of young and older officers, but some were seriously inexperienced. I needed older heads in the key role of community policeman. The problem with some of the younger constables was that they could get themselves into trouble easily. To get to grips with it I needed to train my officers to understand how I would want them to deal with situations. At that time standard Police handbooks did not equip them for it, so I tried to devise my own compensation for that lack of training. It raised a few eyebrows, but I stuck at it.

At that time we were attempting to recruit more ethnic minority trainee police men and women. It was difficult to break through the barriers. Phillip Knights set up a five man squad of coloured officers with the job of recruiting from the ethnic population groups. They approached thirty seven immigrant clubs and associations in the West Midlands region, with its population of several millions. Sadly only eight replied, and visits by one of our coloured recruiting officers failed to produce a single success. Over the previous twelve months the whole of the West Midlands area had managed to recruit one coloured woman and three coloured men. True, in the first half of 1978 we had sixty coloured applicants, but most were unable to meet the educational or physical requirements. With all the anti-police propaganda and hostility on the streets from West Indians from the ages of twelve to thirty, policing was a job you applied for if you had a vocation to be something as rare as a celibate priest or an ancient mariner.

FOURTEEN: SIGNS OF HOPE

The policeman is kneeling, eye to eye with the children, white, West Indian, Asian. They shuffle around him like ducklings, glancing puzzled at the young blonde haired journalist, at the camera crew, then turn to face the policeman again.

'So, you remember,' he warns. 'Be careful, don't forget the Green Cross code when you cross the road'

They laugh with innocent enjoyment. 'Yes mister...'

The policeman turns to the journalist. 'The average age of most of these children is perhaps five or six years. So obviously they'll be, or the biggest part of them will be, in Handsworth in the next ten years, leaving school and searching for jobs. And if, for instance, they get into trouble after they've left school, then at least I've done my part in trying to get across to them that crime doesn't pay, in the long run. I talk to them as children and hope that it sticks in their minds as they grow older.'

'How has your job changed in the last few years? Has it become more dangerous?'

'No, I don't think it's become more dangerous. Now I've been given a job to do, whereby I've got an area to cover. I've got to know people living in the area. I've got to know all the criminals and the good people, and I've been taken into their confidence. As a beat man, all their troubles come through me. People know me as a policeman now, whereas the general panda driver, they only see him when trouble arises.'[1]

***

A brief ray of sunshine occurred in 1978 when we looked around for ways to get our policemen more involved with the community through the medium of sport; the leaders, the parents, the children, the teenagers, the young unemployed, the schools, the school children, the teachers. Sitting there in our midst, between Church Lane and the Soho Road, green and beautiful, was Handsworth Park. In the middle was a lovely cricket field out of use and in bad condition, but, amazingly, the cricket pavilion still stood. People were afraid to go there for fear of being mugged. The local West Indians came to ask for my support in getting the field back into shape. They and the local Asians had featured some highly talented cricketers, merging to call themselves the *Continental and Rangers Club*. Our aim was to get the public coming in to watch on Saturdays and Sundays, and our friends also had ideas for a

---

[1] *Shades of Grey*, BBC 1978

bowls lawn for the older residents. The Park might once again be used as a place where all members of the public could come along and enjoy themselves. I managed to persuade the Parks Department to restore the wicket. Then our local police cricket team took on the Unity Social Club's West Indians in a game arranged by PC David Hutchinson and parks patrol officer Milton Coddrington. We were soundly defeated, skittled out for fifty eight runs against eighty eight, but it was fun. Our aim was eventually to get the younger West Indians involved, and we would, in time, make good progress.

Football too had potential as a healing game. I sensed signs of a momentum for good. I happened to mention the possibility of some kind of activity for the youngsters in one of my many meetings with Anthony Wilson of the Cadbury Trust. Anthony promised funding for equipment to support a football league for all the local schools, and before long it duly arrived. Sergeant Ted Schuck, PC Harte and other PBO's would assist the local teachers in organising and refereeing the games. Twelve schools were invited to Handsworth Park and twelve turned out. We divided the league into two sections so that at the end we would have two finalists competing for a two-foot high silver trophy, and ran the competition throughout August. We issued a detailed press release, and invited reporters and photographers to come along. The winners were the lads of William Cowper School who beat Lozells Juniors in an exciting final. Everyone, the headmasters, the PBOs, all of us in the station felt we had done a great job. Letters of congratulation from teachers and parents flooded in.

More than one hundred and fifty children had played in the tournament, a further two hundred brothers and sisters had supported them. In addition, the parents and uncles and aunts of two hundred and fifty families had come along to join in. Yet whereas the Digbeth National Front demonstration had filled the entire front and middle pages of local and national papers over several days, our tournament achieved, in the Birmingham Post, one six inch by eight inch photograph and below that, an explanation of forty seven words.

In March the annual celebration of the birthday of the Guru Ravidass saw the ever colourful procession from the Sikh temple in Union Row over to the City Centre, with drums and music, dancing and singing. No problems, no trouble, no arrests. Later in the year we were honoured by a visit from Mrs Indira Gandhi, Prime Minister of India between 1966 to 1977. She was still the leader of the Indian Congress Party and would, in 1980, be again Prime Minister. In 1984, two of her bodyguards would assassinate her, in revenge for damage caused to the Golden Temple, the revered shrine of the Sikh religion, while her forces ejected an army of Sikh militants earlier that year. Her cortege started at the Guru Ravidass temple, then moved to the local Holyhead Cinema, where she gave an address to the crowd. We expected the visit to cause much disturbance due to the troubles back home in India, and recent skirmishes between Sikhs and police in London. Fortunately all went smoothly. We policed the event heavily, and apart from half a dozen arrests effected as Mrs Gandhi entered the cinema, the large crowds remained peaceful and went home happy. I felt we were lucky to get away with it. We were dealing with enormous prejudices spanning two continents and things could have gone badly wrong.

Indeed, Mrs Gandhi was so impressed with our local community spirit, that she came over to talk with me privately. As we parted, she gripped my hand firmly, and fixed me with those dark Asian eyes, irresistible to prime ministers and police superintendents. *'This has been a wonderful day, just wonderful. I would like it very much if you and your wife could find time to visit our home when you next come to India.'*

It is tempting after all these years to see things in a rosy light, but I only have to browse through one of my files and all comes back in stark reality. Two of my young officers had to be rescued from a crowd of hostile Rastas after attempting to arrest a man for damaging the panda car in which they had been sitting. They were on patrol and had parked up near some traffic lights. There was no trouble at the time and no apparent danger. Suddenly a hostile crowd of young Rastas gathered round the car, raining blows and kicking at it from all directions. The constables chased one man into a local house and were then attacked by the occupants. We had to send reinforcements to rescue them. It was a week before they recovered from their cuts and bruises.

More trouble happened when a large group of youths attacked some of my officers. We had to break down the door to get into the house, and the whole place erupted into a pitched battle. Seven young men were in the dock, one on a charge of grievous bodily harm and assaulting a policemen. *Shocking* I hear, *Lock them up and throw away the key*. Yes, perhaps, but it was not sufficient to just mouth simple solutions. It was our job also to attack the roots of crime, get to the potential criminals before that all important *first blooding*.

A further problem was that few of my men, and virtually none of the other reputed leaders of the community lived, the teachers, the social workers, the Council officers, society's managers, lived in the area. It is not a natural thing to do. They preferred to live where the wife liked to live, feel safe at night, walk the children to a good school, get a good price on the house when it was sold. So it was hard for them to really understood our policing area and its problems. Most would drive in, do a day's work, and then drive home, relieved to get away. Consequently they failed to feel as the local people felt, see the world through local eyes. My young constables, too, lived outside the area and did not have the in-depth knowledge of customs or family traditions. The local people were, in reverse, just as suspicious of the in-comers, seeing them as an impotent and untrustworthy middle class; as policemen who, in spite of all the talk, were unable to change things for the better.

This remained a major issue and I had to find ways around it. I'm not sure how well I really succeeded, because the necessary housing and removal expenses and other financial and social compensations to members of the Force nationally were not available. Also, to bring about a change in policy on these matters would require an understanding city council and national government.

A typical expression of public perception of what made for effective policing in those years, was a two page feature by Fenton Bresler of the national Daily Mail. In November 1978 he visited the West Midlands Police Headquarters, interviewed Deputy Chief Constable Maurice Buck, visited several stations, and talked at length to a newly appointed beat constable. His piece was headlined *'The loneliest man in town. - Exactly one week a policeman and he's the only walking barrier to crime in the heart of Birmingham.'* Fenton then was offered the opportunity to 'play at policing' and he went at it with a relish: *'... Some no doubt do it out of a sense of duty. But there is also a more mundane reason than that - its exciting. I felt a thrill myself as our F Division Zulu car zoomed round a roundabout during a chase after a stolen car on the Spaghetti Junction in the early hours of the morning...'*

Back in the real world I decided to take my concepts to a new level. It occurred to me that what we were trying to serve in Handsworth was a patchwork of tiny *villages*, similar in basic structure to those I had known early in my career. Sure, the languages and colours were different, there were more poor people, the housing generally was of a lower standard, yet the problems were basically the same. So, I decided to organise my policing area into smaller zones, make each of my foot soldiers the Village Policeman for his patch. He would get in there and know everything there is to know about his village. His hours and shifts would be adjusted to what was necessary to achieve our aims.

In the Police, as everywhere, there were glamorous jobs and less glamorous jobs. Young men and women anxious for promotion and good mortgages naturally aspired to move to the more glamorous areas. All wanted to be detectives. The least glamorous job of all was to walk around on foot, to be a *PC Plod*. How many times have we seen the TV hero superintendent warn his detective that if he makes that mistake again he will be *back on the beat in a flash*. For me the reverse was true. I had to convince the authorities that the job of the beat officer in Handsworth was not the lowest job, it was the highest job, the key to policing by consent. It was from the demeanour, and actions, and attitude and conversations of those young constables that the public would build its impression of our Handsworth Force. That impression would bring with it an attitude to us, the State, the Government and the rest of society.

I wanted those men to be the best, the most experienced. I wanted them to be skilled at meeting with local community associations, with local organisations, to go into the schools, talk with the young, to relate to the club owners, the shop keepers, the young men on the street corners, the Rastas in the squats. Furthermore I wanted them to be skilled at mingling with youngsters progressing on our local Duke of Edinburgh Award scheme and with their parents. In short, my beat constables should feel at home with every part of our community. I said to myself: *They will have their beat, will stay on their beat, will become known and know everybody. Everything that is happening in their village will become known to the sergeant back in the station. The sergeant will ensure that their duties are arranged to fit with their responsibilities, so that if there is a meeting of their resident's association in the evening, they will be scheduled and expected to go there and report to the residents on what they have done since the last meeting. They will listen, relate and understand, prove to those at the meeting that the Police are there to protect and assist, show by our actions that the Police are the servants of the people, not their masters. And they will meet and talk to the parents of young children at home and at a time convenient to the parents.*

Out of my force of some two hundred officers, I looked and tested, watched and interviewed, until I found the twenty whom I felt confident that I could train and trust and send out on foot, alone, day and night, to their separate 'villages'. These were my *Permanent Beat Officers* (PBOs). Something more was needed. It was good for the PBOs to go onto the streets and meet the adults, but criminal tendencies start well before adulthood. I had to get the message into the schools as well, to enable them the PBOs to understand the feelings and problems of the school children.

My officers would be more than just visitors into the schools. We had to become a proactive part of the curriculum, invest officer time at all levels into re-educating the youngsters in the first two years of their secondary education, correcting those insidious bad influences that surrounded them in society. At the same time, I had to get as many of my force as possible to meet not just with pupils, but their teachers and parents, with social workers and probation officers responsible for their care and after-care when in trouble. I did not know it then but what I was proposing was radical, too radical for some, but in the Handsworth context just simple logic. All these ideas were later to come together as an organised philosophy we called *The Handsworth Experiment*.

As the idea took shape I realised that someone very special would be required to lead my chosen team into the schools and to persuade the CID and constables that we had to change our relationships with those professions which effectively were trying to do what we were trying to do, but on a different path. Luckily, right under my nose was the ideal person, described by one observer as '*A great smiling, booming barrel of a man, as much at odds with his uniform as in tune with his new role; as much at home in European history as in a Brummie pub; a lovely man in the opinion of many in Handsworth; and a fine, natural teacher.*' [1] Sergeant Ted Schuck was big man in every sense, with an infectious laugh and a philosophy to go with it. He had worked in Handsworth from 1975, first as a Patrol Sergeant, then a Station Sergeant. He had witnessed and been involved in a lot of 'hard', reactive policing, and

---

[1] John Brown, *Shades of Grey* and *Handsworth Revisited*.

understood how young constables under fire would feel. In spite of it all he had kept, unlike some in the force, his pleasantness, some would say his Christian approach, to people of all classes, all religions, all races.

So I sent for Ted and we sat down together in my office. That meeting was important for many reasons. Unusually for me, I closed the office door, much to the curiosity of the corridor people. I wanted to go over the whole range of the why's and wherefore's of Handsworth, the causes and effects of youth crime as I saw them, the inter-relationship between social conditions and the attitudes of the growing school children and future criminality, and why I felt he would be the man to lead it all. He listened intently for about half an hour, then his face broke into an enormous smile. *'Sir, it'll be a big job and quite a change for me, but if you think I can do it, then I will.'*

His first annual report to me showed that it had been a wise decision. We had agreed that his main emphasis would be to get the message into the schools, junior and secondary, right throughout the school experience of those young children of every race and class. Ted laid down his guidelines thus: *'In planning school activities, three important factors must always be considered by the Police. Firstly, we are not school teachers. Secondly, whatever degree of activity we are considering at any school, we must have the full support of the headmaster and his staff, and the cardinal rule on this must always be that we go into the school on his invitation. Thirdly, we must also consider that over-activity at any particular school can do damage toour image in certain circumstances.'*

That year, my PBOs talked with eight thousand pupils in their schools, and eleven hundred children of all ages visited Thornhill Road Station. We had free ranging discussions with them and their teachers in the station corridors. They walked freely around the station and saw everything, including the cells. Sixth form debating societies discussed policing issues and we were severely challenged at times by uninhibited future leaders of society. We organised Law and Order weeks in the junior schools. These grew to become major projects, with programmes of written and art work on policing. Our beat officers gave presentations, and we laid on visits by horse, dog and car patrols, and showed films on all sorts of social and police-connected subjects. Our evenings too were busy, and we met parents, teachers and pupils, formally and informally. It saddened me at times to look at those smiling, enthusiastic children, and know that the press and many around the country were implicitly condemning them as work shy blacks, future criminals, a burden to society. We were the *angry suburb,* the *black suburb,* the place you did not want mentioned on your job application if you were leaving school.

The increased role of my PBOs raised some eyebrows. One, PC Tony O'Loughlan, became involved with the school outings and took a group swimming each Wednesday. Then he would get the same children to come and meet him in the Station and show them around. He later commented: *'It's not policing the old-*

fashioned way. But to deal properly with youth, you have to get to know them, especially with immigrant groups suspicious of the Police and authority. If you can get on friendly relations with them, you're half way there. The children learn to trust you, and often this influences the parents. I know that if I go to any of their houses, I'll get a good reception. If a kid's misbehaving, I can go and see the parents, sort things out before they develop.'

Tony was to be given a BBC Nationwide Golden Helmet Award for his community work, having been nominated by the children at St Mary's Church of England School. I believe that the BBC made a special exception for him. They had ended the award series, but in the circumstances, brought it back for just one more programme. This to me meant more than any award I could mention. It was proof that what I was trying to do was the right thing, especially for the young, the potential leaders of the future.

We were to take this school programme to further heights but for the time being, there were some reservations. A few had criticisms, about the insufficient training I was giving to prepare my constables for the local patrols, about the personal stress, particularly when groups of young West Indians would sexually tease, sometime harass, young women constables. Most accepted that our aims were good and sincere and it began to take effect. By the time they had completed their training and had got to know their beats, they were convinced that what we were doing was right for the people of Handsworth. Older policemen among my force reacted in mixed ways. Some loved my approach; to them it was not, in essence, new. It was something they had always understood, remembering their early years and how the village policing tradition had worked well. They were happy to get their own patch, their own duties, be their own boss, work to a timetable that suited the needs of their population, become respected and trusted, be the *Chief Constable* of their area.

Meanwhile, our Handsworth methods were getting national prominence. We were saying things radical beyond measure for some. It was at that stage that I raised the concept of the village *team*. One detective was assigned to link with each PBO, so that both would get to know the patch in depth. Any crime that was committed within their zone was studied and acted on by the two acting as a team. This was totally new, a breaking down of barriers. Then, as the intelligence started to come in, I appointed a collator. He received the reports from each of the beat officers, and assembled and assessed the information. In turn, other CID officers started to benefit with intelligence on criminals and potential criminals.

Those local beat officers were not spies. We must not forget that the vast majority of the population of each beat area longed to be free of the robberies, and drugs and any kind of crime. They just wanted a peaceful area where their children would be secure, and people could work safely and go out at night without being mugged. So they were happy to join in the new policy and give information to their local bobby. If a criminal or drug dealer moved into an area, we knew about it pretty quickly and in advance of any illegal activity.

I maintain to this day that nobody knows an area better than the PC on the beat. He knows the good and the bad, the old and the young. He knows the lads most likely to commit crime, and he knows who to ask when a crime had been committed. He knows the families, can read their body language, watch for unusual goings on, feel the pulse of his area. He is an invaluable source of information to the detective, and if they work together effectively many types of crime can be controlled and reduced.

I held regular meetings with all levels in my Force, and cannot remember any bad experiences. I watched my men closely for any signs of resentment against these new ideas. All was so contrary to many of the concepts instilled into them during their training, and for some it was a hard transition. If any did object or became restless, I would gently move them on to duties that would not interfere with my concept of community policing. All who were willing to be part of my community policing structure understood that they were seen by me as someone special.

The schools were equally delighted that working Policemen should visit and talk to the children. With the help of the Duke of Edinburgh Award organisers, we introduced the concept of Police Subjects into the award curriculum. A constable would visit the schools to teach about the role of the Police in society in terms the children could understand. That Little League Football programme for the older boys was supplemented by Little League Netball for the girls. We started our own youth club and recruited and trained a group of youth club leaders. Within our highly successful *Lozells Project,* we introduced an arrangement whereby social workers, probation officers, teachers, Police and Social services were formally asked to work together at the Wallace Lawler Centre, exchange information views and solutions and lead and teach the young about their future duty to society. Finally we started taking groups of up to thirty children, including young minor criminals or potential criminals, to outdoor adventure camps. While on such camps they could learn to interrelate, work as a team, regain self esteem and respect for others, and, perhaps for the first time in their sad lives, believe that they could be better citizens.[1]

The very first camp we arranged started with a bang. The lead team included a sergeant and a social worker, and the social worker's wallet was stolen by one of the juveniles, a regular offender. Late that night the sergeant phoned me to say that *'the wheels had come off'* and asking what he should do about it. It took a day of persuasion, by the sergeant and I, to convince the disgruntled social worker not to prosecute the boy and remove him from the camp and his friends. The two spent the

---

[1] See also the Youth Justice Board report of August 2001 on *Splash Schemes,* in which 30,000 youngsters went in 2000 to camps and other activities in the school holidays. Teenage crime fell by between 18 and 36 percent.

remainder of the week working together to warn the young man, and bring him to some semblance of self awareness as to his likely future, if he did not change.

In September 1978 I sent some of my officers to a rather unusual exercise in barrier breaking. Acting Chief Inspector Hawkesford and Sergeant Schuck attended a ceremony at the Sikh Temple in Birmingham's Soho Road, where they met with leaders of the various religions, Catholics, Protestants, Muslims, Jews and others. They shared a traditional Sikh meal, were shown around the temple and discussed aspects of the Orthodox Sikh religion. Following this, a selection was made of a privileged group, of some twenty persons, including Hawkesford and Schuck, to meet and ask questions of the *Sant*, who was the head of that particular sect in the British Isles. Although many of the questions did not concern directly law and order, the *Sant* asked if there was anything he could do to assist us, by use of his contacts and influence within his own community. His sect live to a very strict religious code, representing the highest aspects of Sikh religion, and accordingly, their views are also respected by other denominations of a more numerous nature, such as the Ravidass and Valmic communities.

By this time my intentions were clear to most people in Handsworth, and many letters flooded in, some vehemently critical, most supportive. One in particular saddened me, being in some ways supportive, and yet the gentleman's final lines indicated that I had many miles to go before we could achieve real peace and safety on our streets.

'23rd October 1978

To Mr Webb, Thornhill Police Station

Dear Sir,

I feel I must write and place on record my appreciation for the wonderful attention and help I have received since your station took over the area from Lozells Road station many years ago. Your officers have been most helpful, courteous and very dignified on the many occasions when my premises suffered a 'break-in', customers being mugged and in many other ways whereas I am full aware that your staff are stretched to the limit.

I sincerely trust that in this area you will eventually overcome the many problems you are faced with. Once again thank you so much. I was forced to close on September 30th due to a demonstration and had to vacate the above premises which my father and later myself have owned for 73 years.

Yours sincerely,

(Name)'

Another letter, this time from the local MP, again suggested that we had much to do:

'HOUSE OF COMMONS

London, SW1A 0AA

23rd March 1978

Dear Superintendent Webb,

Firstly, may I say how pleased I am with the way that your officers are involved with the communities in your area and particularly with the splendid work that is done by the various ethnic groups. Further, I understand that with your additional 20 officers, most of whom I gather are on foot patrol, the crime rate has been reduced dramatically and the detection rate increased significantly. This really is very encouraging and I know that local people are commending your actions.

I write only to emphasise again I am afraid the difficulties in the Linwood Road area with vandalism and squatters, all night parties and general disturbance. Enclosed is a letter from a gentleman with whom I have made contact on one or two occasions which is self explanatory. Do you think it would be possible for an officer to call round and have a chat with Mr *** who is a well-established member of the neighbourhood and who is anxious to do whatever he can with his neighbours to improve conditions in the road. Obviously I am aware of the tremendous demands on your personnel, but I do think this would be a useful exercise.

Kind regards,
Yours sincerely,
John Sever MP.'

Yet another revealed a different view and some misgivings.

'To the Officer in Charge,
C Division Police Station.
11th March 1978
Dear Sir,

One needs considerable courage to contact the 'August Majesty of the Police', however, my conscience will give me no rest until I have put on record my appreciation of the great kindness and support I have had from the local men and women of this beat in occasionally knocking on my door 'to see if I am alright', since the break-in last year. At 75 one has very few friends or relatives left to bother or enquire if one is alright, and after it is worth so much to know someone is concerned and near to help. It proved how much hard work was expended by the men on the case that they were able to convict the intruder with so little evidence.

The few English people left in Handsworth depend for their very lives on the Police, and all the best of the black immigrants also, I am sure, but it is, unhappily impossible for us to stand up and be counted against so much evil terror. The courage of the Police cannot be too highly praised, but believe me, it is known and appreciated.

Yours sincerely,
(Name)'

I expected my officers to turn their hand to just about anything that would help to break down cultural barriers. At times the shock could be radical to both sides of the divide:

'20th February 1978

Dear Superintendent Webb,

On behalf of all of us at 61 Soho Road and all the young people from our 'Young People's Meeting' we would like to wholeheartedly express our thanks and great appreciation for making it possible for Police Officer Peter Conway to take part as 'the Friendly Policeman' in our play last night.

Police Officer Conway should be awarded an 'Oscar' for the masterful way that he handled his 'part'. It nearly brought the house down and he had to go back for an encore as the children were all on their feet cheering, he was really great.

So, our special thanks to him, but our gratefulness also to yourself and all the Police officers at Thornhill Road for making our 'Young People's Meeting' such a success.

So very gratefully yours,

(Name)

The Congregation of Yahweh.'

We faced pure hostility from some officers. They saw the traditional status of the Police turned upside down. There were rumblings against our latest heresy; a suggestion that the pay structure within the Force nationally might be altered, so as to reward the man on the beat more than the detective in the office, or the driver in the panda car. We also suggested an improvement in the system of allowances for beat officers. The Police Federation, a powerful trade union for rank and file officers, began to take an interest in what I was doing. The resentment also showed itself in my own more senior ranks. I could sense that they were asking themselves: *'Does this man Webb know more than me? Has he had more experience than me? Has he worked in all the departments? How can we test him?'*

Fortunately there were few things I had not done or seen or experienced or solved in my career, and in time I was able to gain enough trust to continue onward. In that downward spiral of despair in key sections of the community, it was important that my force felt confident that the commander could handle whatever came along. I was fortunate to have around me men and women looking for leadership, and I felt privileged and lucky to be where I was. As news of my new philosophy for policing by consent gained fame and some notoriety, many young aspiring officers asked to move to Handsworth, anxious to gain experience and learn. Of these, several went on to senior rank.

One such was David Ibbs a Bramshill[1] scholarship officer, who asked if he could move to Handsworth as my deputy soon after my arrival. I was happy to take him on and he stayed for about eight months. He got the experience he was looking for and went on to promotion, eventually becoming Assistant Chief Constable, and would retire with an MBE. Our careers followed a roughly similar path and we

---

[1] The national Police training college for Command officers.

competed fiercely. When I was an Inspector and on the Inspector's Course at the Police College, David was a young PC from Wolverhampton. He asked if he could join me on our journeys to and from the college where he was on the 'Special' course. We would argue at length about policing and society and became good friends. He was fast track, quickly gaining rank of Inspector and then the Chief Constable's personal assistant. He used to say to me, *'Look where I am now - ahead of you'*. He got to chief inspector before me so he outranked me. Then I got to chief inspector, then superintendent, and I outranked him. He then requested a move to Handsworth so that he would have a chance of getting ahead of me again, proving himself to be an excellent deputy and a superb cricketer. He helped me to start the Handsworth Park cricket project, and proved to be a real asset and the first captain of Handsworth Police team to play against the local multi-ethnic *Continental Rangers.*

Meanwhile, the already damaged sections of society were expressing themselves in other ways. In April, a man was beaten up by a gang of young West Indian children. A chilling account in the Birmingham Evening Mail confirmed much of the report that came across my desk:

'MAN BEATEN UP IN CHILD GANG ATTACK: A college lecturer was knocked to the ground by a shrieking mob of schoolchildren and kicked and punched several times in a savage attack in Handsworth Park, Birmingham. Shocked and stunned he wept yesterday as he told how his eight year old daughter ran around screaming and trying to stop the frenzied crowd... 'My daughter was running round screaming 'stop it. You are killing my Daddy' and my son came along and saw it all too... When I got up there was an older Rastafarian type standing over me. He punched me twice in the face. He was probably the one who broke my nose.'

Then the mob hounded him for two hundred yards as, clutching his children, he staggered to his car to drive home. A neighbour took him to hospital. He was later quoted: 'I have always been a liberal and tried to set a good example in this neighbourhood. But these people are their own worst enemies. I feel sick and physically and emotionally hurt...''

That same month two of my constables were attacked after a quarter of a mile chase of a suspected stolen car. The drama started when a panda patrol tried to stop a vehicle for a routine check in Island Road. The vehicle drove on and the police car gave chase, forcing it to stop. The two constables were attacked when they went to speak to the occupants. One constable, who had face and groin injuries, was taken to the General Hospital for an emergency operation for internal bleeding. Two men and a woman were arrested.

It was at this time, at national level, that the subject of arming the Police came up, along with the possibility of the use of offensive water cannon and rubber bullets for crowd and riot control. The Daily Telegraph sent along a reporter, Amit Roy, to interview Deputy Chief Constable Maurice Buck and myself. Buck was worried about the momentum building up for an increase in police technology:

'If we are forced to carry guns and use water cannon then it would be a tragedy for the country and the Police. We are a Police Force of the community and I hope we can maintain the traditional system of policing. But recent events have shown how difficult that is.

It is the government's job to tackle bad housing and unemployment in the inner city areas. These are political decisions. If you want to get it right you just look at the underlying causes of discontent.'

My own concerns were, that if only a small section of the Police became an anonymous helmeted army, then the rest of the Force, however human we might try to be, would be regarded in the same light. True community policing, based on trust and mutual respect, would be lost and difficult to retrieve. A severe injury, perhaps death, of some misplaced youngster in a street disturbance would create a national backlash. Death through shooting by a patrolling policeman would be worse. However tight the procedures, something would eventually go wrong. The bobby on the beat is then no longer a servant of the people. He has truly become an arm of repression.

FIFTEEN: A TEACHER GOES TO SCHOOL

You have to learn fast when in command. In Handsworth, with the press always looking for a story, and sometimes the eyes of the world on us, my learning curve had to be exceptional. Everything that my experiences had taught me, from my instincts about the human condition and its complexity, everything that I knew about myself, all had to be brought together into a logical structure. Only by that means might I make sense of the situation that faced us, looking out from the windows of that old Victorian building in Thornhill Road.

Around twenty officers from the United Kingdom were chosen each year for the Bramshill Command Course, designed to prepare senior officers for the role of Chief Constable. I felt privileged to be selected, and that summer was invited to the College to present a paper that would draw on my experiences from my very first days in the army. Those present, including the College Commandant, must have been impressed with my understanding of racial issues, as, suddenly, I found myself regarded as the accepted expert on community policing. From then on the College authorities offered me a standing invitation to return each month to lecture to career officers, and to potential senior force commanders. Very soon, more invitations followed, from every inspectors training course and special constables course all over the United Kingdom, and then from overseas police colleges and commanders. It had suddenly become my duty to teach others from my own experience, tell young policemen and older commanders anxious to improve their understanding, of all that I had learned from my time in Handsworth. Meanwhile, back in Handsworth, I was required to continue my day to day work. It was hard, unremitting toil.

Suddenly I was popular. I did not like current Government policies on society and policing, having seen first hand their deleterious effects on the people of Handsworth. Every day of my life at Handsworth I had tried to tell the world of the effects of deprivation, and at the same time, to assure the world that here was a basically good and industrious people, generation after generation with potential for good. I felt it was my job and that of every politician and social agency to help realise that potential. Meanwhile the Prime Minister would stand each week at the Despatch Box telling us that all was the fault of the people of Handsworth, individuals were responsible for their own success or failure, and that nothing could be done about unemployment and its effects except wait for the market to deliver.

I was later to be ridiculed in many ways, some obvious, some more subtle and corrosive. How naive I was to trust in the sincerity of politicians and some commanders with an eye to their careers and future honours! The reasons for this criticism were not entirely clear to me then; it was only much later that I would understand. They feared that what we were doing was impossible to do in other policing areas. To achieve the kind of contact and understanding required in a typical Handsworth, a superintendent would have a twenty four hour job, and would have to make himself or herself available at times that suited the community leaders and not the Police.

In the eyes of some, my views were too *'touchie-feely'*, but for others community policing became the fashion. Up-and-coming career policeman would join in the enthusiasm, applaud me, ask me questions, engage and re-engage me in discussion. I was getting national, even world wide publicity. People were proud to have been on courses where I gave my lectures. I was the expert, the authority, regularly introduced on stage as *'The man who knows all about community policing'.* I presented my philosophy to officers of even chief inspector rank, superintendents and above, continuing right to retirement.[1]   Later, in 1981, I would be furious at being ridiculed by some senior officers as a *bloody crank*, dismissed as a man carried away with the momentum of what he was doing. This was the dichotomy that I faced, and it is an eternal question as to how you achieve great things without formidable criticism.

Britain's racial and social problems were and still are paralleled across the world, in Kashmir, in America, Northern Ireland, Central Europe, Africa, the Far East. Furthermore, I feel to this day that the same human processes governing day to day relations, crime levels and outbreaks of violence within an area, can be improved by the concepts that we pioneered in Handsworth.

No one ever publicly opposed my views. Young officers were encouraged to see them as the accepted policy. If such officers were seen to be knowledgeable in community policing, career rewards would follow. Everybody fell in line, watching and imitating. Local and national media interest grew and my press files and speaking engagement diary grew apace. Those who did visit Handsworth would go back to their force commander and say what a good situation they had seen. As my understanding of the way things were being viewed at government level grew, I could see that they would not be allowed to do what we were doing, because the necessary support was absent. To be fair, no one solution will fit every situation, and our *Handsworth Experiment* would fit only Handsworth and places like it. Still, there were and are many Handsworths in Britain and around the world, and it remains a source of inner pain to me that no attempt was ever really made to solve their problems in the way that would have been most effective, that is, the Handsworth way.

Outside the Bramshill Command Course, when talking to individual police groups, rotary clubs, Conservative, Labour and Liberal gatherings, it disturbed me to find stereotype reactions from many present. Some suggested that I really should admit, in spite of my praise for the Asians, that they were dirty, smelly and corrupt.

---

[1] After retirement I was never again invited to the College, nor to any Police station.

Others believed that West Indian people were, especially the young men, of their very racial nature lazy, involved in drugs and violence, not interested in getting or keeping a job. Whenever the subject arose, racism would rear its ugly head, the deep uninformed prejudice of the white nation feeling itself threatened. When I spoke in richer, white dominated areas, while, on the surface, people expressed admiration, the implied reaction was *'Great. Handsworth problems are fine as long as they stay in Handsworth.'*

Those with more open minds would listen to my story with amazement. Some would take up my invitation and visit, then discover for the first time in their lives the truth. That black and brown people did wash their hands before cooking a meal; lived clean, god-fearing and respectable lives; wanted their children to succeed just as much as any ambitious white middle-class family; that the fourteen or so races and religions, Sikhs, Hindus, Muslims, Christians, Rastafarians, Catholics, Jews, Anglicans and sub-cultures in our community, were generally living in harmony; that they and their children could mix happily at school and at play. My audiences would sometimes discover to their shame that their own misgivings and prejudices had been reinforced, if not created, by daily stories of crimes in the media. Handsworth would be noticed only if some mugging had been done by a black person, or some Muslim cleric had stepped out of line and criticised the Government for some aspect of policy.

For the record, and so that history will judge our concept of Community Policing fairly, here is the lecture that I prepared in that summer of 1978. I was tempted to add this as an appendix, but if you will be patient, you will see that what I said to the commanders and officers at Bramshill remains as relevant today as it was then. My views have never changed, and all is, word for word, as I read it on that first occasion. It still astonishes me that a detailed *modus operandi,* given enthusiastic applause for four years by policemen of all ranks, became an anathema after my retirement. Sadly it would seem that what I tried to demonstrate then is, in parts of the country, again beginning to find favour. The wheel has indeed turned full circle.

There are a number of technical references included in bracketed phrases to show the modern context. And, since it was spoken with an overhead projector and other aids, I have provided appropriate headings to clarify the structure. Finally, there may remain certain poorly expressed phrases and grammatical errors not apparent to me at the time, for which I apologise.

BRAMSHILL COMMAND COURSE 1978
POLICING A MULTI RACIAL SOCIETY
Ladies and Gentlemen,
The effectiveness of a Police Service depends on the nature and quality of its compact with society, the understanding and relationships, formal and informal, explicit and implicit which connect the Police to the society they serve. Societies

which are reasonably homogenous in their values, purposes and ways of life, and whose groups and institutions act from a reasonable measure of consensus, offer the best material for such a compact and in Britain, its strength has long derived from the strength of a closely woven social fabric. It could be said with some justification that our society and the way it was policed was the envy of the world and something to be copied with confidence.

That fabric is now subject to growing stress in many areas of the country and is probably most intense in the decaying inner city areas where the loss of community identity and alienation are everyday faces and where the population, more often than not, of immigrant stock, coexist having no more in common than the stresses and deprivation of their environment.

This phenomenon in the conurbations coincided with the fall in police manpower and a subsequent shift in policing strategies aimed out of necessity at disguising the deficiencies, whilst at the same time attempting to give the residents adequate police coverage.

Very often the only police/public contact has occurred in response to an incident call and this, coupled with the exodus of resident policemen actually living in the areas that they served and the consequent community involvement that this brought has noticeably altered the traditional relationship and image enjoyed between the Police and their public. The relationship has become distant and sometimes strained, allowing the slightest incident to spark off conflict and recriminations with an absence of mutual knowledge and understanding of respective cultures and problems.

There are many areas in Britain today where the majority of the population now consists of people of diverse race and colour and being possessed of differing cultural backgrounds and expectations, poses a very difficult problem to all social agencies, including the Police.

POLICE ATTITUDES:

I firmly believe that a police officer whose view is that such people should be treated in the same way as anyone else, is not being sufficiently understanding in his attitude. It is one thing to be impartial and possess and practice all the traditional Police skills, but something more is now required. A more subtle approach is called for, based on a deeper appreciation of the complexities of maintaining the peace in a multi racial society.

Many police officers and members of the public alike make the point with some justification that our laws and customs were here before the immigrants and that everyone must obey them with equal intensity whatever their origins. Hopefully in time to come this will happen and the ethnic background of our population will fade into obscurity.

The stark reality however, is that old habits and customs die hard and are being deliberately retained by their users, whilst at the same time gradually varying them to suit the new environment. Racial hostility coupled with economic and social deprivation has added a new dimension to the process of eventual integration and has in many ways hardened the resolve of those determined to keep our Society divided.

The tackling of this problem is therefore a challenge to society as a whole and to the Police in particular. Many sceptics sneer at the ever increasing race relations industry and the prominence given to matters of immigration, creed and colour.

Elections may be won or lost on the way that this subject is dealt with and the way that the Police react and develop their skills in policing a multi racial community could affect their future place in society for generations to come. More important than this is that the peace and stability of our sountry depends upon consensus coupled with a genuine respect for the rights and privileges of all its citizens.

SETTING THE SCENE

The Textbooks, articles and mass media whilst expounding racial co existence in Britain today, are generally full of gloom and foreboding. The tales of police brutality, harassment and malpractice are legion and are rapidly forming part of a coloured folk lore, which if not checked and challenged in an enlightened and determined manner could result in catastrophic repercussions for both the Police and public at large.

The vast majority of recent literature and press coverage examining the problems of coloured people in Britain usually find something to say about Handsworth, the 'Troubled Suburb:' Banton, Brown, Humphry and a host of other academic authors have in turn visited and written about life in the area, and it is true to say that because of the almost unique composition of its multi racial population it has become an ideal location for research and experimentation. What is said about Handsworth is becoming equally valid for many other areas of the British Isles.

Another reason for the consistent publicity is that most of the local community leaders are also national officers of their organisations, and consequently every local matter has a tendency to gain national coverage, and every national matter given local connotations. Fringe and extremist political groups have rapidly jumped at the chance to gain a platform for their respective views and this has resulted in the setting up of district and national offices in Handsworth with an ever present membership eager and ready to make an issue of anything likely to further their aims or cause embarrassment to opponents in the establishment, whether real or imagined.

The problems of Handsworth today could be the problems of a large part of Britain tomorrow. John Brown in his recent publication 'Shades of Grey' describes the problem of Handsworth as of crucial concern to both Police and Society: a key test area where problems of immigrant settlement, youth and age, deprivation, unemployment and housing stress meet and compound each other in an exacting context or urban decay.

Many officers outside the Metropolis and connurbated areas are somewhat sceptical about the problems of both living and policing in an immigrant community and the present preoccupation with the topic.

Many will however, find a parallel with the Northern Ireland tragedy, particularly when they examine the aspirations and difficulties encountered by Ulster Catholics and our own Black West Indian population. The friction between these people and their police forces is not just a coincidence and must surely give food for thought. There are no excuses therefore for being parochial, for perhaps there is something to be learned from Handsworth that is of some moment. There is no possible way that all the problems and suggested remedies can be described in a paper of this length, but I would like to tell of some of them and the efforts that have been made to identify the causes and subsequently effect some sort of remedy: The recent unrest in many parts of the United Kingdom and the subsequent investigations as to the causes has brought home to both Police and public alike the urgent need to find solutions to one of the most pressing dilemmas of modern times.

Can the Police maintain law and order without enlisting the active support of the general public?

Should we allow the Police Service to develop into a reactive style agency similar to those in many parts of the world or should we strive to reverse the present trend and attempt to maintain our rapport with the community and the accountability this of necessity requires?

A brief glimpse into what is a reality might help you to make up your mind.

THE LOCATION

Handsworth itself originated in Saxon times and was later mentioned in the Doomsday Book. The area prospered, and in Victorian times developed into the most luxurious suburb in Birmingham. The large multi-roomed houses built during those years, and still standing today, have been one of the main reasons why immigrants found it so worthwhile settling in the area. It allowed them initially to live in multi occupation whilst they accumulated their capital and sent for their families.

This, coupled with the close proximity to the City Transport Depots, Hospitals, Railway Stations and Black Country foundries, meant that employment was readily available. The response therefore from the West Indies and the Indian sub continent to the British Government's plea for immigrant labour was instantaneous, and almost overwhelming.

The pattern since the end of the War has been one of steady replacement of the indigenous white population, by successive influxes of coloured workers and their families. The process continues, and it is estimated that within the next ten years the population of Handsworth could be totally coloured. This is presently evidenced by the fact that the majority of the central area schools already have 100% of coloured pupils in the classrooms.

The younger generation of white residents have moved out of Handsworth for a number of reasons, not entirely connected with race, and have left mainly older residents to cope with the problems of integration. They, in turn, have sold their property to an immigrant community eager to get accommodation near to their own kind; and this, coupled with the Council's policy of allowing their particular properties to be occupied exclusively by mainly Jamaican tenants, has ensured the creation of an area totally artificial and contrary to all principles of an integrated community.

It must be said, however, that you cannot force people to live where they have no desire to do so, and this situation has meant that, at the moment, the population is almost neatly divided into three roughly equal sections.

An estimated twenty thousand or so West Indians, mainly Jamaicans living alongside approximately forty thousand Indians, and a further forty thousand ageing whites remain scattered on the outer edges of the area. Many of these are of Irish origin.

LIFE STYLE AND ASPIRATIONS - THE ASIAN EXPERIENCE

The Asian community originated mainly from the Punjab and is fairly equally divided between Sikhs and the various Hindu Castes. They have now settled down extremely well in the area, and have managed to find work and remain in employment despite the frequent economic set-backs encountered locally and nationally. An increasing percentage of the town centre shops and businesses are now owned and staffed by Asian businessmen. Because of the strong family associations, much work has been provided and created for wives and children of school leaving age.

The vast majority of the Asian population have either purchased, are in the process of purchasing, or living in, property in the area. This has tended to stabilise their movement and give them a great sense of purpose and belonging.

Three new Sikh Temples have recently been created in Handsworth, two Ravidass (untouchables) Temples, and one High Caste Hindu Temple. Two new Asian cinemas exclusively showing Indian films, Asian Restaurants and Clubs, all add to the growing impression that the Asian community really intends to make a go of things in this country. What is more important, they wish make it a permanency. There is now little inclination to return to India, and their main preoccupation is to bring as many of their family over here to join them as they can, before permanent measures are taken by Government to curtail future immigration.

Their Asian life style and ambition has meant that their relationships with the Police have developed into a cordial and mutually rewarding one.

The initial problems of language barrier, and mistrust of Police and their methods were brought over from India by first generation immigrants. It has been stated that policing in India is very different from that encountered in this country, and it was natural for the immigrant to suppose that he would receive similar treatment from British police officers to that received in his former home. Over the past few years, and in Handsworth particularly, great efforts have been made to dispel the fears that Asians had about the Police Service, and the regular visits to schools, homes, clubs and Temples hasproduced rich dividends.

In their native homeland, Indians from the rural areas tended to settle their differences amongst themselves, either by some form of direct action, or by discussion within the group and with the assistance of the elders. Many of the disorders experienced in the Indian community in the early days, were the results of this 'self help' tradition, and was particularly noticeable amongst the Sikhs. The sight of Indians gathering together on the recreation ground, or on the pub forecourt, possessed of hockey sticks, did not always mean that they were intent on participation in a game of hockey. The eventual call to the casualty department of the local hospital very often resembled something out of World War Two, and it did not take long to establish that another village feud had reached a temporary settlement here in England.

The gradual acceptance of police authority has been very encouraging and is now particularly noticeable in the schools. There, increasing numbers of Asian children participate in projects concerning Law and Order. The Duke of Edinburgh's Award Scheme, with 'Police Work' as one of the major topics, has proved popular. Police officers have been invited to accompany the children on school outings and camping holidays, and an excellent relationship has been established and maintained.

It could be said that this high powered intervention and injection into Asian affairs has increased the work load of our officers. Senior officers now tend to occupy the role traditionally reserved for the village elders, and find themselves advising on, and sitting in judgement on, a host of local matters far removed from our usual experience. Family disputes over marriages, house purchase, temple management, inter-caste problems, all are now an every day occurrence, and this is strengthened by weekly conferences and receptions held with Indian leaders. The whole relationship is built on mutual understanding and trust, with accessibility and availability of senior police officers an essential ingredient.

The most noticeable result of this relationship has been the almost total absence of real criminality in the Asian community. The Indian youth are very occasionally arrested or dealt with for petty theft, and the older Indians still tend to get drunk more often than is good for them.

Inter caste rivalry and loyalty is still strong in the area, and is something that the Police have been actively monitoring. It is now common practice to have joint functions involving Sikhs and the various Indian castes, and they seem to be finding the experience very rewarding. Our initiative in encouraging these meetings was very well received, both locally and by the Indian High Commission. The recent rioting *and inter caste warfare in India during the elections had no repercussions whatsoever in Handsworth, and has not in any way affected the relationship between the various groups. This surely is another very positive reward for the hard work performed by the Police, and good ammunition for those of us who wish to show that Police involvement at an early stage can avoid serious conflict later.*

A recent joint meeting of the Asian leaders with the producers of a BBC television documentary publicly confirmed these assertions. The steady flow of Indians joining the Police Force Special Constabulary, Magistracy and local councils in the area is further proof of the ready acceptance of this minority to accept British concepts and gradual integration. More positive effort is, however, still essential in the need to recruit men and women into the regular Force from ethnic minority backgrounds.

One thing that has caused friction in Handsworth, and which is of continuing concern, is the tendency for young West Indian youths to commit crimes against their Asian neighbours. These crimes range from Burglary to Robbery, with particular emphasis being placed on street muggings and demands made for goods from Indian owned shops. So critical was the situation six months ago that joint meetings had to be arranged by the Police between Asian and West Indian leaders in an attempt to cool tempers. Local MPs and the respective Commissioners also attended, and as a result action was taken, which has subsequently substantially reduced the problem. I will describe these actions in a little more detail when I deal with the West Indian experience.

Undoubtedly in this country prejudice feeds on myth and rumour. It is certainly true that relationships between the Police and the Asian community in Handsworth are now at their highest level, and constant effort made on both sides to keep it that way. Police initiative in organising meetings and functions involving Asians, West Indians and the white population, is now being increased. Several large community projects have commenced, which involve all three communities. This, when completed, will be of mutual benefit. The initial reaction to the construction of a community centre which contains indoor recreation facilities and outdoor sporting areas is encouraging, particularly when it was recognised that these were requested by the Police at recent council meetings as a partial solution to the integration problem, and as a factor in reducing juvenile crime.

Multi-racial cricket teams have been formed this year by the Police with funds and equipment provided by the Cadbury Trust in an effort to bring together the Asian community and their West Indian neighbours. I think it is true to say that the Police effort in relation to the Asian population is a success story, but one which needs continual attention and appraisal if it is to remain so.

THE WEST INDIAN EXPERIENCE
The West Indian experience is a slightly different one, and something which

has strained our flexibility and expertise to its limits. The extremist elements quickly recognised that there was little point in attempting to spread racist and anti-Police propaganda amongst the Asian community. The increasing affluence of Asians and their apparent satisfaction with life in this country meant that the majority of extremist ammunition was of no relevance to them whatsoever. How could you hope to incite a low caste Ravidass follower to get up and agitate forcibly about his plight in Handsworth, when his coming to Britain was the best thing that has ever happened to him. He is now free to earn a living at whatever job he develops the ability to perform, regardless of his caste. He can obtain an education for himself and his family, set up his own property and business, and go anywhere he likes, with no regard to his humble origins. With over twelve thousand followers of the Shri Guru Ravidass living and working in Handsworth, once the essential differences had been identified and remedied, Police-Asian relationships were quickly and closely established.

The Parliamentary Select Committee of 1972 were quick to see, however, that the main dangers and difficulties lay in the fragile, sometimes explosive, relations between the Police and West Indians in the sixteen to twenty five year age range. There have been instances of policemen acting insensitively and officiously against immigrants, and this is particularly true of young West Indians, whose conduct is sometimes calculated to make policemen 'lose their cool'. Past mistakes by the Police are, as I have previously said, apt to grow to legendary proportions. Over and over again it has been said that what matters is not so much what a policeman did or did not do, but the impression created in the minds of immigrants.

It is towards the West Indian community and young British born blacks then that most of the subversive attention has been directed. The poor housing conditions available to the Black community, the high rate of unemployment experienced by their members, and the very low academic attainments of the young school leavers, has created a vicious circle which is difficult to break. There are, for example, not more than a handful of businesses owned or managed by West Indians in the area, and there is apparently little ambition on the part of some West Indian adults to exhort their children to study and work hard to improve their lot.

The greater part of disruption and truancy at school is of West Indian origin, and the majority of the children cannot wait to leave school in order to gain some sort of independence. Academic attainment is rejected, and, consequently, demand for their services on the labour market is drastically reduced. As a consequence, there are hundreds of young West Indian Black youths and girls at large in Handsworth, unemployed and generally disillusioned with their life and prospects. This group are an ideal target for extremist and subversive elements, and have developed a philosophy and sub-culture geared towards an almost total rejection of everything normally acceptable in our Society. I will talk about this a little later.

The vast majority of West Indian population in Handsworth originated from

Jamaica, an island generally recognised for producing the most volatile of all the West Indian peoples. They have a carefree and happy disposition, but trouble and violence can lurk beneath the surface, and martial law in Jamaica is still being imposed quite rigidly.

The first generation Jamaicans initially came to Handsworth to work on public transport and in the hospitals, and this still forms the greater part of their job deployment in the area. Many of those younger West Indians lucky enough to obtain employment on leaving school have found work in local industry, or in a favourite occupation such as garage mechanics.

The older West Indians brought with them a Victorian discipline and genuine desire to gain acceptance in this country. Their Pubs and Clubs contain many adults who are absolutely appalled at the deterioration in their standards and image in the community, and the continual strife that exists between themselves, their own children and with Society in general.

This unfortunate break-up of family association has been the formation of substantial groups of young Blacks leaving home and banding together in the numerous squats and communes, unemployed and completely disillusioned with Society. Most of them have donned the mantle of Rastafarianism, or more precisely the sometimes criminal sub-cult of the dreadlock fraternity.

This group, with its origins in Ethiopia, exhorts young Blacks to study their ethnic and cultural beginnings in Africa, and to work towards black supremacy, and an eventual return to their homeland. Unfortunately, because of the fringe activities of Jamaican Rastafarians, their use of drugs and confrontations with the Police, there has been a break-away of the genuine church goers from those criminally orientated dreadlocks, and a subsequent loss of influence and restraint that was necessary to develop the movement towards acceptance and stability.

As a consequence, we have the spectacle of young West Indians in many parts of Britain, Jamaica and the United States, wearing dreadlock hairstyles, festooned with the Ethiopian national colours either on their tea cosy hats or scarves, trousers at half mast, no socks and open sandals on their feet, the universal uniform of the Rasta man. To some sections of the community, it is a frightening and intimidating sight.

Amongst some Rastas there is a generally accepted belief that any means deemed necessary in order to gain money and sustenance is justifiable. This has seen the emergence of a very violent criminal group with which it is difficult to communicate. The are isolated from Society both coloured and white. In Handsworth, this group of about three hundred or so teenagers gather in groups in the 'squats' and communes, and are largely responsible for the tremendous incidence of robberies, thefts from the person, burglaries and car thefts. Their very existence has signalled the onset of vociferous campaigns from all sides of the local community to have them removed, using whatever force is necessary. Crime statistics revealed that in Handsworth from lst January 1977 to l8th January 1978 there was a total of three hundred and thirty seven reported robberies and thefts from the person. Of these offences, there were positive identifications of five hundred and twelve assailants as of West Indian origin, two Asians, twenty whites and forty two not positively known, but believed to be West Indian. Statistics in recent years have shown a similar trend.

The Asian community became an increasingly frequent target of attack by these youths. Their justification for the plunder and mayhem is that Asians in Africa, together with the white colonialists, have extracted fortunes from the unfortunate Black population. All this ill gotten profit should now be available for distribution amongst its rightful owners, i.e. the descendant Black Rastafarians.

Many elderly whites were also treated in a violent and brutal manner, resulting, very often, in hospitalisation for considerable periods. A broken leg and arm for a seventy nine year old white woman, and severe bruising and shock for a middle aged spastic robbed and pushed out of his wheelchair, are but two examples of the extreme measures that these youths resorted to, in order to gain money for their cause and themselves. The unfortunate label of criminality has, therefore, now been tagged onto the Rastafarian, whether deserved or not.

Such a state of affairs could not be allowed to continue. Going to the squats in an effort to question or detain suspected offenders very often resulted in serious disorders with considerable blood-letting on all sides. The resultant ill feelings between on the one hand the young Police Officers involved in the fracas, the highly emotional young West Indians, and, on the other hand, often adult parents and spectators, has brought relationships to fever pitch. The media, and political activists, both for differing reasons, ensured that the rift received maximum publicity. When these events were followed, in 1977, by the Winson Green riots and the Ladywood By-Election riots, then rumour and speculation really gripped the area by the throat.

The immediate problem was, of course, to reduce the number of robberies and thefts from the person. The most obvious way to do that was the injection of extra officers into the area, and to place them on foot patrol, with instructions to make themselves available to the population. These officers together with those already on patrol made an immediate impact. They were drawn as volunteers from surrounding divisions and were men of some experience and maturity. Use of officers in this category immediately dispelled the West Indian accusation that Handsworth Policemen were all young, inexperienced and prone to spontaneous reaction that is born of immaturity.

The fact that seventy percent of the personnel stationed at Handsworth were Probationers would be obvious to anyone living in the area, and consequently even though the allegations were unfounded, it would not be difficult to add it to the mythology. The publicity given to the injection of these officers into the worst area of

Handsworth was substantial, and was immediately recognised by the general public at large. The subtle assistance given by uniformed Special Patrol Group officers reinforced the general impression that the area was now very adequately patrolled and that it would be unwise for muggers to operate as openly as before.

The local population, MP's and Press welcomed the positive steps taken to visibly improve the situation, with the notable exception of the Socialist Workers Party publication FLAME. The headline in their paper quoted as follows: 'The recent Press attacks on Black youth living in Handsworth has now cooled down. But what still remain is the persistent harassment by Handsworth pigs: 77 was hot, but 78 it go a burn. It as sure as the sun will shine that the pigs are going to make a more ruthless onslaught this year. The Handsworth Pig has received reinforcements. This development can only mean one thing, we must not wait and watch the pigs play 'Supercop' Our position demand that we begin to organise: that every Black youth become a political revolutionary: being organised in order to challenge every Police attack.'

Despite this insidious attempt to inflame local opinion against the patrolling officers, the results were instantaneous. The experiment commenced in January 1978 and from February until the present date, robberies and thefts from the person have decreased by sixty percent, and you may draw your own conclusions as to why this has happened. Overall crime on the sub Division has reduced by almost one third during the same period and this fact has also been widely publicised.

OTHER ISSUES AND POLICE INITIATIVES
It would be wrong to suppose that this is the only thing that is at issue and experiments have been initiated in a much wider field in an attempt to solve the longer term problems of the racial situation.

I have already highlighted the breakdown in West Indian family life and the need for that community to follow the Asian example in encouraging their children to broaden their horizons and improve their academic attainment. Many meetings are now taking place, after Police initiative, with West Indian parents, churches and educationalists in an attempt to demonstrate to the community the advantages of education and aspiration. The need to persuade West Indian parents to recognise and encourage potential in their youngsters, and to relax strict disciplinary codes leading to strife within the family group, and the consequent break up of the homes, is an important factor in creating future stability. Stabilising the home surroundings and drying up the flow of youngsters moving towards the squats and criminal Rastafarianism is of paramount social importance. So too is the removal of the squats and this is being organised in other ways. Attempts to lessen hostility between the Rastas and the rest of the community including the Police must be an urgent priority. They must become acceptable members of the community.

Recognition by the Local Authority that housing and amenities in the area had to be rapidly improved has also greatly helped the task of those pledged to keeping the peace in Handsworth. A large urban renewal scheme is now almost completed, and this will improve the housing requirements of the substantial West Indian population, as well as removing the justifiable criticism that stems from this form of deprivation. The creation of the large sports complex in Handsworth Park, and the proposal from the Multi Racial Mutual Protection Association to build a substantial complex containing libraries, committee rooms, and functions rooms has also taken some of the wind out of the sails of those people interested in causing disaffection within the community.

THE TASK FOR THE POLICE

Senior Police Officers should have few illusions about the nature of the Police task in the multi racial areas throughout Britain. The odds will always be stacked against them by the economic and social context in which they work, and the extent to which that context determines the nature of their functions. There is, therefore, a great responsibility on the part of the Local Authority and Central Government to recognise the needs of an area and to give urgent priority in improving facilities, thereby removing the causes for unrest and disaffection.

In my opinion, the Police of the district who are usually on the receiving end of this disenchantment and frustration have the right and duty to pinpoint the areas where need arises, and to liase with those who can do something towards alleviating the problem. Support and pressure in this direction is, in my view, justified if the long term result is a reduction in crime, violence and improvement in community relations. The knowledge by the community that their Police Force are aware of their problems and are prepared to assist them in improving the situation, has played a considerable part in easing tension and strife in Handsworth.

INTER-AGENCY COLLABORATION

The issue of Police liaison with all the other statutory and voluntary services is essential. All sections of Society confront differing aspects of what are, in essence, common problems. The nature of these problems makes it clear that no service can work in isolation, or with purely reactive policies.

Collaboration with these agencies has, therefore, been firmly established in order to identify the role and needs of the respective groups, and to recognise the areas of operation in which they can all work for the benefit of the community at large. Monthly meetings at the Police Station between the heads of all departments of the Social Services and Probation Service, and their deputies, together with invited community leaders, are now a regular and accepted practice. An exchange scheme between officers of the three agencies has now been established, and allows members of these departments to spend some time out on the ground with their counterparts, so as to gain some knowledge and understanding of the contributions made by each of *them towards the community problem. The acceptance that each agency perhaps sees their role and function in a different context is readily acknowledged, but the improved liaison and accord has undoubtedly enhanced the Police image and demonstrated our willingness to increase our flexibility. It has also been invaluable training to our younger officers in broadening their outlook and understanding of the overall place of Police in Society, and what they as individuals can achieve by adopting an understanding attitude, adapting their methods to suit the need, and thereby improving life for all concerned in the community.*

The fundamental Police priority is, therefore, to bring the reactive and preventive roles of the Police Service into a balance appropriate to long term aims and objectives. It is vital to mobilise community support and preventive resources.

I have tried to show that, in my view, the Police on their own cannot control the destiny of an area. They can, however, bring about a mobilisation of public support more effectively than any other agency because of their unique position within Society.

Officers from areas such as Lewisham and Brixton will no doubt readily agree when I say that much of the distrust of Police was born of sheer malicious rumour and mythology. The mistaken belief that a visit to our Police Stations by any Black was an invitation for his head to go down the toilet was, and is, a difficult image to dispel. The need for a determined Police effort to get out into the local community to educate young West Indians about Police methods and procedures was of paramount importance. School visits, Police open days, advice on arrest schemes and a host of other initiatives, all have gone a long way towards softening the overall West Indian attitude and resentment. Identification of the problems, and publicity to Police efforts to improve matters is also, in my view, an essential ingredient in the was against conflict, and the best means of dispelling public disquiet. Acceptance by the Police of a role as 'the silent service' can lead to grave complications and public reaction. We have, the power to divulge information, and thereby stifle malicious rumour.

To tell a Local Residents' Association about their particular problems and discuss with them what everyone can do to alleviate such problems has, in my experience, proved a very beneficial exercise. Information from the horse's mouth, instead of from an inaccurate and un-authoritative source, has been an ideal way of allaying the fears and misgivings of local populations. This kind of action by Police must not be seen as just a 'one off' exercise. The continued follow-up and monitoring of problems with these organisations is essential if we wish to maintain credibility. The fact that the local permanent beat officer (PBO) attends every meeting, and that the sub-Divisional Commander or his deputy visits and speaks at the Annual General Meeting (of a local community group or local Community Relations Committee), has developed a tremendous rapport between all concerned. Willingness on the part of all sections of the local community to meet and talk with the Police in an atmosphere of cordiality and trust is a target we must all aim for .

THE PERSONAL RESPONSIBILITY OF THE FORCE COMMANDER

To make oneself available at all times in order to meet this criteria is, therefore, an essential and exacting necessity. So too is the need to encourage all your personnel to develop an understanding of their role in Society and to act at all times with dignity and restraint. The challenge of policing an immigrant and multi racial community is an exciting, frustrating and demanding one. The policeman is exposed to everything that is good and bad in the human makeup. He is now confronted with considerable problems in the application of traditional Police procedures to the changing needs of Society.

How do we measure the success of the Police effort at the end of the day? I humbly venture to suggest that if you can satisfactorily show a significant improvement in the following areas of Police endeavour and maintain that progress, then you, as a Commander, could be well pleased with the outcome. The list is by no means exhaustive:

1. Reduction or containment of crime, vandalism and disorder within the area.

2. Reduction in number of complaints against Police.

3. Improvement in community liaison and trust between immigrant groups and Police within the area

4. Collaboration with related social agencies.

5. Informed and accurate press coverage.

6. Job satisfaction, efficiency and high morale experienced by personnel under your command, with an understanding of your strategy and the part that they are required to play in its application.

7. A desire on the part of the local community themselves to understand their problems, and participate in forms of self help and self regulation.

It is my experience that these criteria can and have met, when the Police and public are prepared to work hard in order to achieve success. This genuine effort has demonstrated quite dramatically that there is hope in the heart of hatred.

SIXTEEN: CRICKET WITH A FEW BLACKS

By early 1979 we were in a position to take stock of our *Handsworth Experiment*. It had taken almost the whole of 1977 to persuade people in seminars and discussions that the idea might work, and in January 1978 things had started to move my way. That year saw rapid development of our plans and by 1979 the schools projects were going full swing. Inter-profession exchanges of staff and trainees had grown beyond expectation. That year, fifty five exchanges of staff took place, ten from the Probation Service to Police, twelve from Police to Probation Service, thirteen from Social Services to Police and twenty from Police to Social Services.

When Social Services and Probation officers came to us we made sure they would see the reality of the streets. I would initially meet them to outline how we hoped to make the visit useful. After a brief warning of what they might see, they toured the station with their PBO of the day. They would then accompany the PBO on his beat and later go out with a mobile patrol. At the end of the day I would again meet with them, review what had been learned and myself learn what I could from their experiences. In return, my young constables would sit in on meetings between Social Services and Probation staff and clients, go into the homes of clients, and see first hand the living conditions of disadvantaged people. They would even meet with groups of young offenders, asking their permission beforehand, to discuss their crimes, their problems and their futures. I knew of nowhere in Europe where such techniques were employed and know of none since my retirement.

The word soon got around the community that these interchanges were taking place. I am certain that they helped to develop greater trust between the professions and attitudes by and towards the Police. Many folks began to understand that the Police were not there to just crack down on the young. We were there to assist them avoid a life of crime, or if they had already been in trouble, help them to get straight again. Carole Whitby, local Social Services Area Manager, and several senior probation officers wrote to congratulate us on the success of the experiment. Carole summed things up nicely:

'It is already apparent that the considerable knowledge of local resources held by the beat officers is beginning to be shared with those social workers who have spent days at Thornhill Road. In several cases an early warning from the beat policeman has brought a problem to our attention which prior to the exchanges may well have gone unreported until the situation had further deteriorated.'

In addition, Derek Leigh of Birmingham Social Services was welcomed to Thornhill Road Station each Thursday to liaise with the CID. We achieved a series of well attended forums when all three services exchanged views and information about policies and individuals. Several senior staff from Social and Probation services would come along. We worked through what we called simply *the common agenda.* We jointly analysed problems of homeless young unmarried mothers, squatting Dreads and Rastas, local trends in drug use, how to help young folks avoid a life of drug abuse and consequent crime. We examined problems caused by divorces and family break-ups, and how these would play themselves out in producing potential young minor criminals. We devised ways to help and support the victims of crime, researched what we as professionals and individual practitioners needed to do to equip ourselves better to do the job, in short, everything that affected our Handsworth society.

We set up a sub-committee where social workers, and CID and constables, could discuss individual juvenile cases. This gave an opportunity for the policeman in charge of a case to obtain skilled advice before deciding whether to caution or prosecute. Sir Phillip Knights insisted that we follow clear standing orders in this kind of exercise in that the prerogative in the decision must always remain with the prosecuting policeman. I was happy to follow his instructions to the letter, since by the time the decision had been taken, everything that I had hoped for from *The Experiment* had by then proved a success.

Members of the Police Training Department also attended and the meetings were sometimes described as *Joint Seminars*, an indicator to me that they were regarded primarily as a joint training exercise. I remember that at the very first one on 25th January 1978 we invited James Hunte of the Community Growth and Support Association and also a member of the Community Relations Council, together with Norma Spence, also on the Council, to speak on problems affecting their communities. I tried to break down the barriers even more by encouraging social functions at the station where Police, Social Services and Probation officers could mingle informally, develop personal loyalties, and explore each other's feelings and intentions. An indicator of the changing attitude to an exercise that had begun early in 1978 under a cloud of apprehension was a statement in a memo from Superintendent Bob Snee to my chief Joe Matthews: *'Police initiatives have been maintained in efforts to forge firm links with the departments concerned with a view to increased benefit of the community we serve.'* (My emphasis)

Another aspect we tackled was the much discussed, but often neglected, subject of Victim Support. In Handsworth we had victims and suffering enough to fill a war novel. I arranged for my Chief Inspector Martin Burton to meet with Senior Social Worker Wendy Dale, with the task of developing an effective programme. The Cadbury Trust was the main source of finance for the scheme. We did not have a lot of money, and were not able to offer grants or other financial support, but the scheme allowed us, from May 1979, to train up some thirty helpers in the skills of victim support. The helpers would meet with victims, offer advice, comfort, assist with benefit claims and applications for Criminal Injury compensation. They would also accompany the victims at identity parades and court hearings, both highly stressful, especially for young women and the elderly. It was not perfect. Wendy complained to me several times that she got excellent co-operation from most of my staff, but that the CID were still a problem.

Our cricket games between a police team and the locals were now a regular feature. On 28th July, a so-called friendly game was held against a *Continental XI* which unfortunately for us comprised, this time around, mostly young, tall, very athletic West Indians. An enthusiastic crowd of more West Indians watched as we got hammered. As the day progressed, the audience were to take pity on us and even cheered when we scored. Our men had all worked first watch and were knackered before they walked onto the field. All out for fifty one, we could only get two of the youngsters out for the same score and lost by eight wickets. In true sporting style they agreed to carry on until six o'clock, that is, until our bowlers were exhausted or the pubs opened, or both. I still have the report by PC 7323 Elliott. I suspect that he typed it straight after the match on a typewriter in the back of the pub. The page starts quite neatly, by line twelve the typing is starting to wobble, and by the time he gets to sign his report, both spelling and alignment leave much to be desired.

At the time of the cricket game, we were working at a fun project that would take community policing onto uncharted seas. All around us were fun-loving people, natural dancers, singers, musicians, and costume making traditions brought from the Caribbean. Why not organise a Festival? So, on a hot evening on 26th August 1979 we all, that is, Police, Asians, West Indians, white English and Irish, all sat down in the Crick Lane Community Centre to plan a first for Birmingham, a multi-cultural festival to be held in Handsworth Park in the following year of 1980.

Our Little League football programme was proving more enjoyable for tired constables. For the second year running we had a great turnout, with eleven schools competing and constables, parents and teachers refereeing. William Cowper School won the trophy for the second time, defeating Prince Albert School in a ferocious final. West Bromwich FC captain John Wile was happy to present the trophy in front of a super crowd.

Meanwhile, the pattern of crime in Handsworth created an uncomfortable background to our efforts. January 1978 had seen what was perhaps the height of robbery and kindred offences within our sub-division. These activities had unfortunately taken on an overtone of racial resentment and the white community, and to some extent the Asian immigrants, were looking on all black youths as potential bandits. This type of prejudice was the one I feared most, since it would alienate every section of society. To counteract the spate of robberies and reassure the white and Asian peoples we drafted in one hundred and fifty plain clothes officers, and deployed them to all the likely trouble spots. This gigantic operation was expensive in time and money. More robberies by black youths meant more stops and searches, in turn the excuse for anti-Police propaganda by extremist groups in the demonstrations in Wolverhampton and Digbeth. It was all the more important to me and my officers that our *Experiment* had a positive effect. We began to regain control of the streets, and, as Sergeant Ted Schuck put it in a confidential analysis which accompanied our annual report of January 1979 to the Chief Constable:

'In the light of this development, which in the view of many people warranted even more stringent police actions, we must appreciate the foresight of the senior officers who were responsible for the Handsworth Experiment.

The dramatic reduction in crime can of course be attributed to many factors. One is the hard work put in by the CID and the uniform patrol units who have, up to November 1978 effected 59 arrests for robberies and theft from the person. Another is the increased police activity with leaders of the black community. These men have succeeded in most instances in isolating the black youth who persistently commits crime from the rest of decent West Indian society. Two years ago many West Indians looked upon these youths as a type of 'Robin Hood' character, but today that same black community looks upon each as a force of evil who brings discredit on the decent members of his racial group.

A third factor must also be considered. This is the increased activity in schools. Because of this there has also been a marked reduction in petty crime often committed by school children. Whatever the reason, there can be little doubt that we are moving in the right direction.'

Occasionally, aftershocks from the old days would surface. In November 1979 we had a suspect in custody, and rumours of police brutality were circulating. Around one hundred and fifty Rastafarians mounted a picket outside Thornhill Road Station, and capped the day with a protest march to present a petition. I could understand their concerns. If someone inside passed the message out that he or she had been brutalised, how were we to prove otherwise, other than by a police doctor's report, none of which would be believed by those who did not wish to believe? So I went to meet with them. My comments were caught on tape by a reporter accompanying the march:

'We are trying to improve things for our local community. That includes you. And we in the Police want to hear from you and people living here, how we should go about achieving that.'

The spokesman for the march replied, reasonably I thought,

'One of the problems is the lack of an independent authority to investigate complaints. It is the Police themselves (who investigate and) naturally that causes suspicion. I am sure that many of us taking part appreciated the chance to talk informally with senior officers who (have) noted what we said.' (My brackets).

Were things getting better? They certainly were at times confused. *The Observer* sent a reporter to Thornhill Road to interview me, and then to witness my meeting with some local 'Dreads'. He reported on how the atmosphere had crackled, and then changed to understanding, and then mutual agreement on a solution to a particular housing problem. He then went on to meet with David Jennings, a white clergyman at *All Faiths for One Race*, a church based research organisation.

'It's becoming a joke,' Jennings told the reporter. *'Teach them how to play cricket? It's colonialisation all over again.'* (His spelling) The funny thing was, this was at a time when the West Indian cricket team, with a bowling attack led by the mighty Wes Hall and Joel Garner, was decimating the English batting!

Another local clergyman, who arranged meetings with the Police and young black people to explore ways of agreement on social issues, was accused in a pamphlet signed by several local organisations of: *'Brainwashing the community into believing there can be a rapprochement between the two sides.'*

Sheila Wright, later to become a Labour MP, commented: *'What I'm really worried about is massive unemployment.''* On that we agreed. She then aimed a firm kick to the shins: *'Police running youth clubs and getting pally with a few young blacks isn't going to solve that.'* Yes, it was a confusing time. I hope, though, that you are still with me.

Another press visit took up the theme of our *Angry Suburb Starting to Smile.*[1] I was sometimes surprised how what I thought to be at the time a quite profound comment, could appear, when read in the cold light of day. Did I really say, *'If it moves in Handsworth, we contact it.'?* And, *'I'd rather spend five extra hours over a pint and a curry than spend an extra four hours trying to defend my Police Station.'?* Even so, that summed it all up nicely, at least so I thought at the time.

By now my constables were feeling proud of their achievements. Every school in our area had been helped with a full week of 'Law in the Community' studies, attended by PBOs, school heads and teachers and pupils. We structured the courses to suit the ages and abilities of the children. For those between five and seven we focussed on the Green Cross Code, dangers of playing near water, the dangers of going into empty and dilapidated buildings, and, with the showing of the film *'Never Go With Strangers'*, the dangers lurking in the minds of would-be abductors.

For those between eight and nine, we spoke about the job of the policeman in the community, why we needed policemen, the difficulties of the job, the destructive effect of crime on people and families. In some schools we added meetings with parents and teachers, and they in return laid on multi-national dish and culture displays. We added displays by horses, dogs and gave then a chance to ride in a traffic car, on a motorcycle and in a Range Rover. The pupils from ten to twelve received an explanation of the history of law and order, the make up of the modern Police Force and the kind of jobs that policemen do in the community, and we showed a series of films to reinforce the message. Finally, every school submitted a project and held a prize giving either with the whole school assembled, or at an

---

[1] Birmingham Evening Mail 29th August 1979

evening with the Parents and Teachers Association and all the parents present. Senior police officers gave out the prizes.

For the senior schools we adopted a different strategy, using as our central effort the Duke of Edinburgh Bronze awards. All children attended on a voluntary basis, and surprisingly large numbers did attend, in spite of six long hours lecturing by police officers. We talked about our work in the community, the structure of the modern force, the task of the CID, the various specialist departments, the role of the dog handler, the mounted officer and the police communications network, safety in the home and on the road. In that one year one hundred and three children between the ages of fourteen and fifteen successfully completed their Duke of Edinburgh awards, and we had, in January 1979, enquiries from a further fifty pupils for the upcoming year with more coming in day by day. For the academically serious pupils, PBOs attended fifth and sixth form debating groups to explain how they policed their beats and the day to day problems they faced. At a number of schools officers gave short explanatory lectures to second and third year senior boys, the hardest group of all, about the Police and the importance of their role in the community and society.

Analysed by beat, the record was a proud one. On beat five, Handsworth Wood Girls School had thirty three Duke of Edinburgh Bronze awards with forty more in progress. Eight girls were going forward for the Silver Award. The Handsworth Wood [1] Boys School, under the dedicated and expert guidance of Headmaster John Goss, achieved thirty three Bronze Awards. On beat seven, the King Edwards Grammar School for Girls had fifteen Bronze awards in progress. Beat eleven's Hamstead Hall Senior School had fifteen awards in progress. Finally, on beat fifteen, ten Bronze Awards were due for completion by 2nd April at the Holyhead Road Comprehensive School. A total of twenty eight schools from junior and infant to senior had been part of our programme. Notably, the heads of all the schools we visited would later report to us that all the usual petty crimes within schools, for example, purse and personal possession stealing, fights, vandalism and bad behaviour, were reduced significantly.

I also reviewed progress with the local Residents' Associations. These were self starting and managing organisations, sometimes changing rapidly under the influence of incoming and outgoing personalities. Nine associations had operated successfully. There was, however, in spite of all the changes, a degree of consistency in the day to day problems they faced. I was particularly comforted at the way that the West Indian Friendship Club on Soho Hill had developed. Their relationship with the local PBO had never waned. Our contacts with the managers of the local *Harambee*

---

[1] This school takes most of its pupils from severely deprived families. Since the year 2000, under the divisive School League Tables, it remains condemned among the 200 'Worst' schools in Britain. I often wonder how the 'Best' school in the country would fare with a similar pupil intake and the same financial resources. John later became Headmaster of Broadway School, and was subsequently awarded the OBE for his achievements.

Association had also improved. My beat constable, PC Byrne, regularly visited for discussions, and had the hard task of dealing with a somewhat mixed reception. Some of the Harambee committee were doing a genuine job for black youth in the area, assisting with housing and social advice to young unmarried girls in particular. Other members of the committee were sadly so full of anti-white feeling that relationships were difficult.

The Afro-Caribbean Club at 104 Heathfield Road was the toughest assignment. The place was run by a well-known, somewhat notorious West Indian 'Bini' Brown. Not well attended as a club, it was nevertheless important to local relationships to have good liaison with 'Bini' and his friends, all of whom disliked the whites, the local schools, and above all the Police. My PBO did sterling work in salvaging what he could from a hostile situation.

Ted Schuck and I, plus two PCs, were regular attenders at the Lozells Residents' Association. I made a particular point of attending this one, since Muslims, West Indians and white English were present in large numbers, and it helped me to understand how relationships were changing between the racial groups.

Just down the road from the Association was the Lozells Road Social Development Club. Here things were slightly more complex. The members were a mixture of races, ranging from local Sein Fein sympathisers openly advocating the bombing of civilian targets in Northern Ireland and the mainland, to enthusiastic members of Socialist International. A group also involved was a society known as 'All Faiths for one Race', but preaching distrust of whites, particularly white policemen. No group present had any sympathy for racial harmony. The Police were out-and-out enemies of the people. Contacts at that time were not only impossible, they were inadvisable. I do not think we ever made progress with the club and it would, I sensed, take a generation and changes on a national scale to ease their militancy. The 'All Faiths' group were incidentally invited to and took part in one of the school debating sessions we held. I have no record of the debate, but it was a somewhat stimulating evening.

Our efforts had been noticed by the Scout Movement. District Commissioner Michael Cadbury approached me and asked if we could assist them in some way. With the help of a small contribution from a Birmingham Inner City Partnership grant we looked at a number of options. Three PBOs were interested in becoming Scout Leaders, and we formed a project group to liaise with local immigrant leaders and organisations to recruit scout leaders from the community. We also looked at the possibility of a pilot scheme for a 'Police Badge' for senior scouts similar to the one already awarded by the Fire Service. I was touched to read a slightly affronted comment made by my reporting officer, somewhat envious that the Fire Brigade had got to the scouts ahead of us: *'Rather surprisingly, no contacts have been made with the Police Force to assist in a similar scheme.'* Attitudes in the old station were changing.

One report I received contained a plaintiff note (his capitals): *'It is important to emphasise that the listed commitments are in ADDITION to any commitment which is normal to a Resident Beat Officer's work on his beat, i.e. weekly visit to schools to discuss any problems with headmasters and the bringing to any headmaster's notice problems with his pupils in any given area. Such commitments are carried out automatically by any PBOs on this sub-division.'* It was exhausting work for all of us. Things would get even harder as time progressed, but in many ways even more rewarding.

In May 79 we were approached by the Anti-Nazi League who wanted to march against an imminent National Front gathering in West Bromwich, just to the north of Handsworth. I called a meeting with all the ethnic group leaders, the Asians, West Indians and all the other agencies who might get involved. We sat down in a local pub, ordered non alcoholic drinks for some of the Asians and pints for me and the West Indian representatives, and talked it through till closing time. Recently there had been trouble at a similar event in Southall in London, things had got nasty and people had attacked the Police. So I asked them all: *'Is that what you want to happen here after all the good work you've put in over the last two years and all we've achieved?'*

To a man they agreed that we needed to ensure a peaceful day. There might be over a thousand on the march out of Handsworth heading towards West Bromwich, while we could muster just a couple of hundred constables. So, they volunteered to police the event themselves. *'We'll come on the march ourselves, be in the front row, keep it moving. We'll take it straight through Handsworth and pull out when we get to West Bromwich.'*

So they did. We put out a token presence, while the ones I had met in the pub proudly marched ahead of the waving banners just like it was their march, and their friends walked alongside as stewards. Groups of uninvited agitators joined in at stages along the way, hoping to stimulate some aggression and conflict. Sadly they found themselves, as the local newspaper[1] put it, *'Punching at cotton wool... The 'bomb' was effectively defused before the march ever began, thanks to the often unglamorous work they call community liaison. The agitators found themselves up against local community leaders who had given Police an undertaking that there would be no violence. Apart from the actions of the inevitable sprinkling of hotheads, this was a mutual trust which could not be broken. It was born of what appears to be a new understanding between Police and the racial minorities.'*

That day in Handsworth we did not have a single arrest connected to the march. There was violence within the West Bromwich hall where the National Front were meeting, and some stone throwing outside, with three demonstrators arrested, all pretty quiet compared to what had happened in Digbeth and elsewhere just a couple

---

[1] Sunday Mercury May 6 1979

*1954 Egypt
Full Sergeants' Mess
Bedfordshire and Hertfordshire
Battalion*

*1957 Wilbury Wanderers
Standing Second Left*

*Christmas 1954, Letchworth. We Had Just Returned From Egypt.
(Fifth From Left Front Row)*

Aiding The Fight Against Leukaemia
With Dr John Stewart and Dr John Browne

New aid in leukaemia fight

With 'C' Police Division
Squash Team

Walsall Police Division Football Team

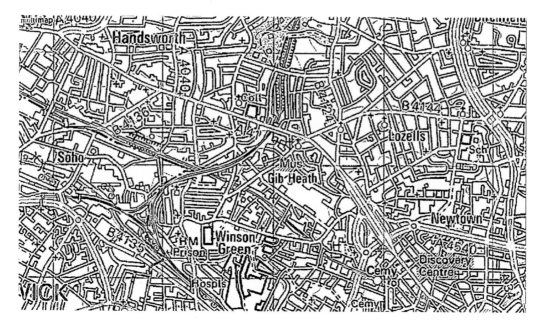

Map of Handsworth
Sub Division

Thornhill Police Station
(Birmingham Post and Mail)

Presentation Ceremony For a Retiring Inspector
with Supt Gerry Finch (2nd Left) and Chief Superintendent Joe Matthews (5th Left)

Winson Green
Asian Protesters
(Birmingham Post and Mail)

Winson Green. The Battle Begins
(Birmingham Post and Mail)

Boulton Road School, Anti-National Front Demonstration
(Birmingham Post and Mail)

*James Hunte and wife Sharon
(Birmingham Post and Mail)*

*The Moment of Truth
I Step Forward and Listen
to the Complaints of an
Angry Resident*

*With Delegation of Senior Officers
on the Overseas Command Course
From Bramshill Police College.
Also James Hunte, Local Magistrate
Darsham Bhogal, David Ibbs and
Joe Matthews*

Constables Doug Shuter and John Bennett Repair
a Wheelchair for a Local Resident
(Birmingham Post and Mail)

Addressing Asian Leaders
in the Local Ravidass Temple.
Standing is Gurmeet Summan

April 1979
In Uniform with a Young Anti-National Front Protester
on an Anti-National Front March
(Birmingham Post and Mail)

Crackdown
We Raided Serval Illegal
Gambling and Drugs Dens

Sharing a Curry
Gurmeet Summan,
Chief Inspector Martin Burton,
Bet's Dentists Dick Harrison,
James Hunte,
Tulsi Das,
Leader of the Guru
Ravidass Association

Digbeth, Birmingham, 1978
Police Lines Protect a
National Front
Rally Held in the
Digbeth Civic Hall
(Birmingham Post and Mail)

Digbeth, Birmingham
Anti-Nazi Taunting Begins
(Birmingham Post and Mail)

Ted Schuck
The Real Laughing Policeman
(Birmingham Post and Mail)

PC Tony O'Loughlan Receives the
BBC Nationwide Golden Helmet Award
Nominated by the Children of
St Mary's Church of England School
Handsworth

*Escorting the Procession
in Celebration of the Birthday
of the Shri Guru Ravidass*

In My Office

*Duke of Edinburgh Award Class
WPC Louise Bamber, a PBO Assists
(Birmingham Post and Mail)*

John Wile
Captain of West Bromwich Albion
Presents Winners Trophy to
William Cowper School in
Little League Tournament
(Birmingham Post and Mail)

Around 1980 the
West Indian Cricket Team
Visited us to Support our Efforts

From Left to Right:
Fast Bowler Joel Garner
Martin Burton
Me
Captain Clive Lloyd
Alvine Kallicharran
Saoud Bacchus

Visit to India

From Left to Right
a Local Punjabi Policeman
Norman Taylor (Handsworth Rotary)
Punjab Member of Parliament Mr Chitty
and to My Left
Chief of Police for the Punjab

*Mrs Ghandi's Visit
to Handsworth
(Birmingham Post and Mail)*

*Bet and I at the First
Handsworth Festival
Held in Handsworth Park*

*A Hearty Punjab
Home Welcome*

*More Hearty Meals
in the Punjab*

*Sergeant Ted Schucker
Receives the Cobra Cup
from Councillor Ron Wootton
Chairman of the Police Committee
for his Outstanding Contribution
to Police/Community Relations.
Ted also Receives the
British Empire Medal
on Retirement*

*Rudy Narayan
Barrister in Law
(Birmingham Post and Mail)*

*With Special Constables
I Recruited and Trained for
Handsworth Patrols
and Community Work
(Birmingham Post and Mail)*

*July 1981
Shopkeepers Clean Up after
the First Handsworth Riot
(Birmingham Post and Mail)*

*July 1981
Police Check a Car Spares Shop
After the Looting
(Birmingham Post and Mail)*

Lord Scarman
(Birmingham Post and Mail)

Receiving One of Many
Retirement Gifts from
Chief Supt. Don Wilson MBE
at the New Inns Pub
on the Soho Road
A Sad Day

Christening the New Pool Table
at All Saints Hospital
With Bassant Singh,
George Harrison
Basil Clarke, Sidney Caro
(Birmingham Post and Mail)

June 1987
General Election
Perry Barr Candidates
Jeff Hunte
John Taylor
David Webb
(Birmingham Post and Mail)

Mohammed Ali
and That Famous
Left Hand
With James Hunte at the
Opening of the
Mohammed Ali Centre
(Birmingham Post and Mail)

Mohammed Ali in the Crowd
(Birmingham Post and Mail)

1985
The Lozells Road
Riots Begin
(Birmingham Post and Mail)

1985
Lozells Road Riots
by Night
(Birmingham Post and Mail)

1985 Lozels Road Riots Press Coverage
(Birmingham Post and Mail)

*1985 Lozells Road
The Morning After
the Riots
(Birmingham Post and Mail)*

*1985
Funeral of Lozells Road
Shop Keepers
the Brothers Kassamali
and Amirali Moledina
(Birmingham Post and Mail)*

*1985
Chief Constable Geoffrey Dear
Consults with James Hunte
(Birmingham Post and Mail)*

1985
Home Secretary Douglas Hurd
Meets Local Residents
After the Riots
(Birmingham Post and Mail)

1985. Restoring the Trust
Permanent Beat Officer
Steven Homer with a
Handsworth Youngster.
Steven was one of my First
PBO Trainees
(Birmingham Post and Mail)

1985
Julius Silverman
Announces his Inquiry
(Birmingham Post and Mail)

The Silverman Inquiry
Boycotted by
the Community Leaders
(Birmingham Post and Mail)

September 1989
Famous Chicago Bears
Running Back Walter Payton
in Birmingham with Some
Birmingham Bulls.
Bulls Manager Leigh Ensor
is Front Left
(Photo by Peter Biddulph)

Bulls Head Coach
Sam Timer Coached
US Heisman Quarterback
Doug Flutie at Boston
College before coming
to Birmingham
(Photo by Gary Mayell)

August 1991
Alexander Stadium Birmingham
British Championship

1992, Wally English. Miami Dolphins Offensive Co-ordinator
and Personal Coach of Dolphins Quarter Back Dan Marino is Centre Second Row
Wally Coached the Bulls for Most of the 1992 Season
I am in the Back Row. Peter Biddulph is Front Right

Granting of the Shawl is a
Traditional Greeting for an Honoured
Guest. With the Ravidass Sant (4th from Left)
and his deputy (Far Right). I was in Jalandar
on Behalf of the Ravidass to Assist in the
Resolution of an International Problem

*Provincial State Governor
Harana Presents the Doctor
Ambedkar Award at Talkatora
Stadium, Delhi, Before an Audience
of 8,000 Dalit Writers*

*Bet and I
Most Formally Dressed*

**With Business Colleague
and Friend John Eyre (Centre)
at a Masonic Lodge in India**

The Foundation Meeting of the Lodge of Universal Brotherhood, West Bromwich

Socialising at Rockey Road Junior School

Soho Road Shop Keepers (Birmingham Post and Mail)

February 2003
Punjabi University Conference
on Human Culture and Values.
Behind me is a Portrait of Guru
and Sant Valmick, Founder of the
Movement and Author of the
Maharamayana

The Valmicki Sabha
(Organising Committee)
Raised £100,000 to Build
Three Schools in the Punjab

July 2001
With Lachman Singh
Arjum Dass and Pakhar Singh
All of Whom were Affected
by the 1981 Riots
(Birmingham Post and Mail)

2002
On the Soho Road
(Birmingham Post and Mail)

2003
Just Me
(Birmingham Post and Mail)

of years before. I was fascinated to see the press reports, a vindication of all I was trying to achieve.

Photographs have a wonderfully innocent way of catching the moment. In one shot the marchers file past, many sporting university scarves and the long hair typical of the late seventies, accompanied by a lone grim faced constable thinking of home and an overdue dinner. Behind them is a huge political poster foreshadowing the imminent 1979 election *'BRITAIN ISN'T GETTING ANY BETTER.'* Just below is a photo of me in uniform[1] marching along a Handsworth street. Beside me strides a proud, cute, ten year old boy, chin determinedly jutting, placard held high, *'BLAIR PEACH FOUGHT THE NAZIS - THE POLICE MURDERED HIM - DISBAND THE SPG.'* We two walked together, chatting, for a couple of miles to the Handsworth boundary to where our colleagues from West Bromwich would take over. He was tough, old head on young shoulders. I am sure he went on to great things in life and wish him well wherever he may be.

This was not a matter of hard versus soft policing. Everybody knows, even the criminal, the difference between right and wrong, between the benefits of a peaceful community, and what you can lose when the peace breaks down. It is that human instinct for bad behaviour or survival that steers a relatively small number of people off track. So, the only real issue for me was effective versus ineffective policing. You take the little things and build on them so that when the big problems come, maybe two or three times a year, you have contact, you have trust, you have willing helpers, because your problems are their problems.

A reporter[2] of the Handsworth to West Bromwich march later came to visit me at Thornhill Road: *'I arrived there to the accompaniment of excited children's chatter as another party made the now regular tour. On the walls were essays and paintings from previous young visitors, including one that says, pertinently, that Policeman Do Not Bite. The style of the men inside is affable. Superintendent Dave Webb, emerging from under a pile of paperwork, is able to point to the unsolicited testimonials piled high beside him. He can talk about a growing understanding on all sides and of the local community 'policing itself' when it chooses to exercise the democratic right of a protest march... The place which once had such a fearful reputation has turned into a pace-setter for improvement.'*

Earlier that year, street muggings had dropped from sixty per month to just a few a week, and overall were down by sixty percent. Letters of congratulation flooded in from all sections of society and newspapers took up the theme. The Birmingham Post, more a business paper than a popular broad sheet, reported Joe Matthew's comments and the tale of our cricket and football games for the children, our Duke of Edinburgh Award scheme, and the success of our beat patrols in reducing street crime. James Hunte, by now a nation-wide traveller for the Mutual

---

[1] *Shops count the cost as wives stay away,* Birmingham Evening Mail 30th April 1979.
[2] Richard Williamson, Sunday Mercury 6th May 1979.

Protection Association, a West Indian organisation, commented on policing nationally and the progress we had made: *'Handsworth is ahead of them all.'* The Birmingham Evening Mail [1] reported our positive policing and its benefits: *'Beat Bobbies are Taming Tough Suburb.'* In reality, our *tough suburb* was finding a new identity and taming itself. Especially pleasing was the publicity shining on my new Chief Inspector Martin Burton, the ever willing work horse Ted Schuck, and all of us at Thornhill Road. I drove home quietly satisfied that evening and next day read the story under the headline: *'THE ANGRY SUBURB FINDS NEW HOPE.'*

Militant did what it could to stir things up, but the best they managed was a somewhat confused report by a Handsworth People's National Party Youth member, telling of one or two allegations of Gestapo type Police harassment of West Indian and Asian youngsters. In evidence he produced a photograph of five young socialists on a protest march in South London.

[1] 22nd March 1979

SEVENTEEN: GOLDFISH, INDIA, CHILDREN AND A FESTIVAL

We were living in a goldfish bowl. Everything bad or even just questionable was reported, analysed, often criticised. Yet the majority of the readers and watchers really hadn't a clue as to what the problems were really about. I suppose it is like that in most public professions. The West Midlands Police magazine *Beacon* [1] did a special centre-page feature on us:

'Sitting on a powder-keg with a smouldering fuse and the whole world looking on to judge the effects of the explosion - that's the general concept of policing the Thornhill Road Sub-Division. Indeed no other sub-division can have been subjected to greater scrutiny; it has been the subject of six television documentary programmes, featured in many books on race relations and is regularly visited by police officers of all ranks from other forces and by students of all courses at the Police College. Life for officers at Thornhill Road is like living in a goldfish bowl, but they enjoy it.

Five or six years ago, it would have taken 20 or 30 bobbies to arrest one West Indian for a minor offence. Today, policing Handsworth is comparable with any other sub-division in the Force area. This situation did not come about by accident. Thornhill Road has become the hub of a vast wheel of public relations with 22 spokes, in the form of permanent beat officers, extending into every section of the community. Superintendent Webb and his Deputy, Chief Inspector Martin Burton are at the centre of things.'

Our Residents' Association contacts were proving a great success. In only two years my PBOs had attended two hundred and nine meetings, and from the reports by the resident group secretaries, the numbers of people attending had varied between ten and three hundred. Everything I had hoped for had happened. We were in touch with local problems and social needs and could pass on the word to Social Services and local councillors. We could anticipate problems between neighbours. We knew by indirect information from neighbours, sometimes through information supplied in confidence and with good intentions, whether a young person was likely to get into trouble, or was keeping bad company. Occasionally we could ensure that formal meetings with council officers and environmental health staff put the problems on their agendas. Finally, we could keep the local MP in touch with what was going on.

We supplemented all this with mobile police offices which we set up and manned with our PBOs. This allowed the local people to call in on their way to and from work and from the shops, and ensured that children going and coming back from school were aware of a friendly presence. We visited on a regular basis all the British and West Indian churches, the local Sikh, Hindu and Ravidass temples and the West Indian, British and Indian clubs and social organisations. It reached a stage

---

[1] *Living in a Goldfish Bowl,* November 1980

where we were pretty much in touch with everything going on. I was available to anyone in the area at any time and place, in meeting halls, offices, in the homes of people, temples, churches, shops, cafes, pubs and clubs, squats and cellars, in my office, and on the streets and many times in my own home.

John Brown walked the streets with me on most of his visits and commented: *'To walk the streets and frequent the meeting places of Handsworth with Webb, as I have done frequently in recent years, is to be constantly waylaid, often every few yards, by individuals and groups seeking contact, consultation, advice on a host of matters, personal and collective, ranging far beyond the call of police duties. Almost wholly unrecorded and therefore rarely acknowledged within the Service. These contacts are the cornerstone of Webb's effectiveness as a police commander... Now as a moderator in community action. Now as a catalyst for community actions. Now as a mobiliser of community resources for care and order. Now as a mediator in community conflict... Almost, at times, as local ombudsman.'*

***

Mrs Indira Gandhi, re-elected to a second term as Prime Minister of India invited Bet and I to visit her at her home in the Spring of 1980, and after an amazing and somewhat devious journey through customs, speeded by the mention of Mrs Gandhi's name, we emerged into the kaleidoscope that is India. Our tour took in many villages, and we saw first hand abject poverty interwoven with the most opulent of hotels and houses. We experienced the wonderful landscape, walked through the gardens of the Taj Mahal, and visited the famous Golden Temple of Amritsar. How ironic that the great gleaming temple of holiness and peace would, but four years later, prove to be the cause of Mrs Gandhi's death. [1]

We were to be honoured and welcomed on three occasions by the Prime Minister at her residence, and met with members of her Cabinet, all of whom were fascinated by my tales of life as a policeman in Handsworth. I wrote an account of our visit for Police Review.[2] I told it like it was, opulence, ox-carts, poverty, beggars and all, knowing that not a few of the readers were likely to feed their prejudices on stories of foreign lands and poor Asians, with relatives living in Handsworth sending them valuable British currency.

Our 1980 Handsworth Festival, on which we had been working and planning for over a year, proved a great success, and became the second biggest ethnic festival in Europe after the London's Notting Hill Carnival. Things had not initially gone smoothly. I was in the Rotary Club, in a strong position to get things moving. Still, while we in the Police were deeply involved as initiators of the whole idea, we wanted someone other than the Police to organise things. The Rotary at that time

---

[1] November 1984, killed by two bodyguards in revenge for an attack on the temple earlier that year.
[2] *'A Taste of India',* Police Review, August 1980

nominated Barry Langston to chair proceedings. Barry lasted about three weeks, then retired, beaten, he confessed to me, by the size and complexity of the racial mix that faced him. They were too diverse, too lively.

Then we settled on James Hunte. He was a councillor with connections and the ability to get things moving, a well known public figure, Chairman of the Birmingham Community Relations Council. He lasted a few weeks. Then we tried one of the Asian leaders, and he lasted four days. He was a *Ravidassi (Untouchable)* and some of the higher castes did not want him in charge. So the thing fell into disorder, and they asked me to be the Chairman. I was the only one who they all felt did not bring any political baggage. So much for the charge of being a dictator.

I did not want the chair. I wanted the community to run their own show. I wanted to be in the background, but I wanted the Festival to succeed. The objective we all shared though was to prove to the world and the cynics, of which there were multitude, that Handsworth was changing and growing, and that different races could work and live together. As a result of the success of the 1980 festival, they would prevail on me to stay in the chair for the 1981 Festival.

The West Indian and White communities, that is how they were happy to describe themselves at the time, formed two separate organising committees. They were quickly followed by the Asians who arranged a singing and dancing competition for the party afterwards, together with a Kebadi tournament. Attractions for all the family included a cricket knock-out competition, an open tug-of-war, dominoes knock-out competitions, eight-a-side football, parachute exhibition, bhangra music and dancing and a boxing tournament. Our mighty wrestler *Sucha Singh*, did battle against *The Unbeatable Executioner from the USA*, and featured on all the posters in a pose that could but frighten the horses. One distinguished guest enjoyed himself so much that he took the trouble to write to Chief Constable Sir Phillip Knights:

'14th July 1980.

Dear Sir Phillip,

I thought I would drop a line to tell you that I was at the Handsworth Festival on Saturday morning and afternoon and attended the party in the evening. What an astonishing transformation has come over Handsworth! It is quite extraordinary how the personality of Superintendent David Webb has altered the whole tone of the area. I was much struck by the friendliness of people to one another; and a happy gathering both in Handsworth Park and at the party afterwards of multicultural character in an area in which there has been such tension in the past is an extraordinary testimony to what he has done, and to the way that Rotary, through him, has helped.

I am of course chary about writing to you concerning any of your officers who has done so well because I suppose they are in danger of preferment and then they will have gone. In any case I am sure you know all this yourself. But I had to write and congratulate you. I think that the reduction of crime by 60% in the area tells its own tale. I am taking the liberty of sending a copy of this letter to the Sunday Times in the hope that they may be moved to say something good about race relations rather than the usual dismal story.

Yours very sincerely,
Hugh, Birmingham
(Hugh Montifiore, Bishop of Birmingham) '

Our Holte School activities revealed more than we expected. It was a mixed senior school with around thirteen hundred pupils just on the edge of Handsworth. After debating the options, we had chosen three fourth-year forms with the aim of improving relationships between young people and the Police. According the age groupings, classes would participate for various numbers of hours per week in a special session. The intention was to bring policemen and pupils together throughout the entire school year. An outreach worker, Bob Storr, a friend of mine later to join me on the local Rotary Club, was concerned to bring both sides together. It meant that both sides could meet in a non-stress situation, engage in small discussion groups, go on fact finding visits outside Handsworth, and reinforce all this learning with role-playing excercises and films.

Jointly with F1 Sub-division, I allocated a team of six officers; Ted Schuck, three constables from C1 sub-division, and two from F1. We ran the programme with Bob Storr under the guidance of headmaster Steve Allatt and Chief Inspector Martin Burton. The sessions gave us a fascinating insight into the minds of the black pupils, all less than fourteen years of age. Even after three hard years work trying to change the attitude of the young, those children revealed just how far we had still to go:

'The Police tell lies. Like at the station. They say no one beat anyone up there. But they do.'

'Young ones the worst. One call me a black bastard.'

'An uncle of mine. They beat him up in the police station. Put a pillow on his head so the mark wouldn't show. Then they flushed his head in the toilet. And charge him with something he didn't do.'

'They see a black youth in the street, they stop him. Call him a black bastard. Jump on him. Put him in the meat wagon. For no reason at all. Oh God, Oh God, its true.'

'Coppers coming into schools? It's a waste of time.'

At one of the sessions when something was said about beatings up in the station, an officer declared that it never happened in Thornhill Road. John Brown, who was present at the class, later commented: *'The shutters came down. Blank. End of story. One PC muttered to his mate 'The bloody fool. There's only one way to deal with these children. Tell them the truth, explain how violence can sometimes come about, but tell them that we try to guard against it.''*

Back in 1979, Birmingham Social Services had been concerned at the high level of truancy and minor crime among children of all races between the ages of eleven and thirteen. Many were already beyond the control of their parents. A senior social worker, Derek Leigh, approached one of my more experienced staff, Detective Inspector Victor Green, and between them they began to discuss problem cases on a regular basis. We called the project *Citizen 80*.

Derek Leigh came from what might be called a radical background. He later was to confess share of involvement with the Police, describing himself when younger as *'a revolting student'*. He was involved in the infamous Grosvenor Square riots and hit, severely, over the head by police batons, almost trampled by a police horse, and searched by police officers for drugs at student parties. It took him until Handsworth 1978 to discover that all policemen and sub-divisions were not the same.

We were concerned to change the youngsters' views of themselves, to improve their self esteem, to encourage them to understand that life held more for them than they realised, in short, to change their futures. *Citizen 80* sessions were held in the school holidays at Holte School, with classes and discussions, and not a few arguments, on the role of the various agencies in society. The policemen speakers had a hard time at first. At one stage the girls in one class looked blankly out of the windows for the entire sessions for a whole month, until the barriers came down. Then we added a series of five-day camps out in the country, away from the Handsworth streets, involving them in adventure problem solving, teamwork, having fun finding themselves as persons.

By the middle of 1980, our Lozells Project was in full swing. We were not achieving all that we hoped for, but we were achieving a great deal. Crime associated with young immigrants was down substantially, and, equally important, people felt safer in their homes and on the streets. Policemen could talk to the policed, school children had new and better role models, Handsworth was becoming a better place to live. Sadly, our projects and cricket games and festivals would prove but tiny against the forces massing across Britain, as unemployment climbed towards three million, and the hopes of a nation began to fade.

EIGHTEEN: IDLE HANDS

It was comforting to know that I was not alone. Even within London's Metropolitan area there were attempts to develop policing by consent and with public approval. Superintendent John Smith of P Division in Lewisham and New Cross had changed his beat system: *'I'm seeking a contract with people to solve their problems. We are trying to get together with people... It's a question of trust, of people working with the Police in their own self interest.'* [1]

When asked if it was not a bit late for London to rediscover community policing and the value of that public co-operation after much had been destroyed by city-wide policies of saturation stop-and-search, he insisted that what he was doing was still the correct thing: *'We now have the ability to do this kind of policing -because we have more Policemen. We couldn't do it before, because we didn't have the staff. If it (racism) comes to my notice, I will stamp on it.'*(my brackets).

In Skelmersdale, Lancashire, an experimental community policing scheme was set up with structured patrols by four area teams, each comprising a sergeant and eight officers. All operated on foot, each to his or her own separate patch, and all were involved in school and community projects.

Southwards, in Devon and Cornwall, one of the patrol officers operating under John Alderson's regime reported: *'Operating without community consent, direction or control is wasted effort. Policing should therefore remain a negotiated contract between the public and ourselves. We can then identify the law as a co-operative rather than a delegated responsibility...'*

Yet, on a wider front, travelling Detroit Police Commander Daniel McKane discovered a different world. He visited West Yorkshire to study that version of community policing, and found a wide disparity of attitudes to the scheme, with almost seventy percent of policemen against the whole idea. When interviewed in confidence, they would refer to community constables with disdain[2] as *'Hobby bobbies'* or *'Officer Plod'*.

My own Force too, in spite of our successes, harboured conflicting views. A correlation emerged between job and attitude. Constables deployed on face-to-face contacts felt that they had benefited personally, attracting fewer complaints, less aggression, and finding an easier processing of arrests back at the station. I felt that the reason for the improvement was my decision to use older, more experienced

---

[1] Labour Weekly, June 12th 1981

[2] This same concept, with parallel implications for CID and uniformed officer grading and status, surfaced as a government backed initiative in 2001 - *Uniform plan for Detectives,* BBC Internet News 27th August 2001

constables for beat patrols. In mid 1977 younger probationers formed fifty three percent of my force yet, by mid 1981, the proportion had fallen to forty four percent.

Some among the Handsworth Force revealed bitterness against the changes and, as they saw it, the predictable side-effects. A typical example was the issue of fixed penalty parking tickets on the Soho Road, a busy main route in and out of Birmingham. The Asian shopkeepers were all strong supporters of the Police. I knew many by their first names. The most prominent among them were on community representative groups so important to us, and I relied upon them to keep their people calm when elsewhere life became tense and violent. They had helped me greatly during the Handsworth Festival and the Anti-Nazi League march in 1979, and they no doubt would assist in other ways in the future. Yet they suffered from a lack of parking space, and would use our relationship to unfair advantage, parking delivery vans, and sometimes their cars, on the main Soho Road. The biggest problems seemed to occur on Saturdays, which were usually quite busy. A frustrated officer talked about this to John Brown: *'I talk to the shopkeeper and instead of saying 'Yes, I'll move it,' he says, 'Go talk to Mr Webb'. So I say to him, 'Sod Mr Webb, here's a ticket!'"*

From outside our sub-division came other whispers. I knew that however successful I might be, some constables in face-to-face contact and arrest work would still face abuse and occasional violence, sometimes involving distressing crimes. One young constable noted: *'When you see some old lady bleeding in the road, done over by a group of young blacks, you don't have to be racist to want to come down on them. And it's bitter if you nick them on one shift, take them to court the next day, see them bailed, and then arrest some of them next shift for the same kind of offence.'*

One allegation running among the CID in other divisions was that I was *'More involved with people on the outside than the inside'*. A phrase that told me a lot about the thinking of the critics. I wanted my constables and officers to be neither on the inside, nor the outside. We were part of the Handsworth community, there on behalf of the community.

By contrast, others were supportive. One constable was quoted as saying: *'He (Dave Webb) puts a lot more time and effort in than any other superintendent I have ever known.'* Another said: *'Without Dave Webb, make no mistake, this place would have gone pop years ago.'* The most telling comment was: *'It was tense until three or four years ago, until Mr Webb came along. His approach has made a vast difference'.*

The CID in Handsworth offered more serious criticisms. Some felt that my community approach had no real effects. One confessed: *'The PBOs might as well not exist as far as we are concerned.'* They felt frustrated and at times bitter, pushing always for a reactive style, genuinely believing that the answer to crime was always and only to employ saturation tactics, hit criminals hard with the Special Patrol Group. I knew that it would not work. We would merely displace the criminals and their crimes, and become a hostile and feared organisation with disastrous effects on the ethnic community. Some in the CID felt that not to employ such tactics was a 'betrayal'. Yet I knew that down that road were fields sown with dragons' teeth.

This cynicism, this bitterness towards me and like minded commanders was known to me then, but the public saw little of it. Such views were reserved for internal discussions, policy meetings, and bar-room philosophising. I defy anyone to believe that the views revealed in the following extract, published two years later, did not carry through to the man on the beat, did not influence his attitude to the young potential criminal, to the black and disadvantaged, to the homosexual. The writer must have held these views for years, and took the opportunity to speak when it was offered. It typified the attitude of many in the Force throughout the 70's and into the 80's toward our concepts of community policing. The words are written by a practising Superintendent from the Suffolk Constabulary, regarding a person with similar views to my own, John Alderson, Chief Constable of Devon and Cornwall: *'Not only has poor old John Alderson gone careering off the rails, he's fallen off the wagon. Remember him? He is the outspoken former Chief Constable of Devon and Cornwall; the pleasant-looking, grey haired gent with the cultivated accent who preened himself on the telly before treating us to his doctrinairism on this, that, or the next thing.*

John is now shacked up with the Liberal Party (the Who?), the lot who, last year, noised abroad allegations of police corruption, demanded all manner of police reform, without thinking too much of the implications, and advocated the lowering of the age for homosexual activities between consenting parties. When he packed his bags at the College and took himself off to milder climes and a chief constableship to boot, some people reckoned that with a bit of luck, and a following wind, he could aspire to greater things - but they were wrong...

As Barry Pain put it, when he was Chief Constable of Kent: ' I've been engaged in community policing for years. The only difference between me and John Alderson is that I don't go shouting it from the rooftops.'

I, like many, saw him as a re-jigger of past notions and ... a latter day re-inventor of the wheel.. And there have been questions of his loyalty, too. Long before he announced his intentions to bed down with the Libs - although politics was his game - he was to do the Police of these islands the greatest disservice that any serving officer could do...

That brings me to the Libs gag, or Gay Action Group, and the latest brainwave from the prophet. In an interview with Gay News, Mr Alderson said it would help the Police service to a greater understanding of minority groups if homosexuals were recruited. I think the idea stinks. Mr Alderson knows perfectly well that the service had one high ranking homosexual. And he knows too the public reaction when that story broke.' [1]

---

[1] Police Review, February 18th 1983, page 310.

It was appalling to see a senior colleague attack another colleague in this way. Members of the Force should at no time involve themselves in politics, religion, or sexual orientation issues. I wrote a determined rebuttal which fortunately was given fair prominence in Police Review. Sadly the damage was done. I wondered at the time what a member of the public would think to see senior officers engaged in such personal attacks. What would someone who was gay imagine would happen to them if arrested in Suffolk, particularly if they had cause for some kind of complaint over the way their case was handled?

***

Our Holte School and Citizen 80 projects were by now fully fledged. By mid 1981 we had extended the programme to sixth forms over thirteen week sessions, but it was hard going. Our biggest enemy was apathy. We had unfortunately started with an age group with an already established mind-set. To add to this they watched day by day as parents and brothers were made redundant with no hope of alternative jobs.

Crime figures for my sub-division were a worry. Looking back over the previous four years, reported crimes increased from six thousand six hundred a year to seven thousand, one hundred and thirty seven. Burglaries had grown from two thousand, one hundred and fifty three to two thousand eight hundred and seventy nine. The crimes that most concerned the press and the public, street crime and muggings, had, though, dropped significantly, from three hundred and twenty two to two hundred and fifty three. Within these totals the number per month had varied from as high as forty seven to as low as sixteen. And over the four years as a whole, robberies and thefts from the person fell by fourteen percent against an overall rise for the West Midlands of ten percent. The involvement of young West Indian and Asian lads in local crimes still concerned me greatly, and I felt a sense of failure. Out of reported street robberies, eighty nine percent were by West Indian youths. More cars were being stolen or robbed of belongings and radios, and young Asians of around eighteen years of age were getting into crime this way. Surrounded by the culture of Handsworth, losing the family discipline of their Hindu, Sikh or Muslim parents, they were seeking new identity in destructive patterns of behaviour. To boot, there were indications of a higher level of local crime than was revealed by the official figures. Petty theft from shops by young West Indians was sometimes accompanied by abuse and hustling of the ageing whites, and we knew that some Asian women were sometimes reluctant to report minor robberies.

We wondered whether there were new unrecognised forces at play, a new type of criminality for which we had not planned. One theory was that the uniformed enforcement side of my Force had initially forced a drop in street crime and this had transferred attention to other types of crime. We had identified and arrested many of the ringleaders and while they were in jail, robberies reduced. When they came out of jail, the figures went back to the previous level. Another view was, that the reduction in the number of squats had reduced the number of local minor criminals, but had made detection more time-consuming. In 1976 we had twenty six squats containing around two hundred *Dreads*. By 1981 my policies had reduced the number of squats to eleven. This had moved some crimes around, and changed their nature. Now we were unsure where to find the youngsters, and a detective would have to consequently spend more time tracking down suspects for each stolen property crime, thus adding to his frustrations.

Another of my constables reported on a burglary at the home of an eighty two year old lady. She was woken by two intruders at 2.30 in the morning, but did not report it until 8.30 a.m. because she did not have a phone, and was too scared to go out of the house until she thought the coast was clear. The Rastafarian youths, whom she estimated to be fifteen years of age, had headed straight for the pantry, taken all her food, and left her with fifty pence in her purse. The constable was bitter. He put the Social Services in touch with the old lady, but he never forgave the two lads, who we were never to catch.

We suspected, too, that a more corrosive force, unemployment, was stalking the streets. John Brown was free to access all the data sources available. His problem was that his data sources were incomplete and in some ways unreliable, so if politicians wanted not to see the truth, they had several avenues of escape. Between January 1977 and January 1981, in the area covered by the Handsworth Office, unemployment for those under eighteen rose from three hundred and sixty nine to four hundred and five. For those over eighteen the picture was startling, growing from four thousand, six hundred and seventy eight, to seven thousand, two hundred and thirty, an increase of fifty six percent John Brown tracked these changes on a graph, and from January 1980 the rise of some four thousand locally unemployed young adults moved almost parallel to the increase in reported crimes. He also noted that in spite of a known increase in the numbers of young unemployed males in the area, the number registering at local unemployment offices went down. There were other changes within the figures which suggested that of the total registered as unemployed, forty percent were of West Indian origin or descent, and fifty six percent were of Asian and other ethnic groupings.

I was also worried about the disappearance from the unemployment register of many leavers from local schools, both boys and girls. West Indians averaged around thirty percent of all fourteen hundred local school leavers. Yet at the beginning of 1981, several months after the end of the school year, only one hundred and fifty three had registered with the Handsworth Employment Office, and a total of only ninety two placements of West Indian youth had occurred on the Youth Opportunities Programme over the years 1979 and 1980.

Indications were that with qualifications so limited, so few jobs around and discrimination in employment so obvious, the children felt it was not worthwhile. Instead, they drifted to a hopeless day to day existence, living on handouts from friends and parents, odd jobs in the black economy (interesting how we still so easily say that word 'black'), and some on the proceeds of petty crime. For the older citizens too, work was a rarity, as many local foundries closed down across Birmingham and the Black Country. John Brown confessed his frustration and sadness: *'The consequences are a growing number of young people, often on the move, living semi-independent hand-to-mouth ways of life in which, as necessity presses, distinctions between legal and illegal become increasingly blurred... In such ways as these, attitudes are justified, values modified, and new norms established - with what implications for society? And this great energy potential of under-employed young people will be channelled which way..?'*

Government policies offered nothing. The tone for the country was typically set in the House of Commons debate of Wednesday June 24th 1981. Michael Foot's weakness as leader of the Labour Party was compounded by Margaret Thatcher's formidable combative skills and intransigence. She swept Foot to one side, insisting that monetary policies to control inflation, and increase unemployment, would be the priority. *'The figure (of unemployment) is already too high[1] and the danger is that it will rise higher still for several months to come.'* Continuous enforced idleness in the late 80's and 90's would be regarded by a future Chancellor of the Exchequer[2] as, *'A price worth paying'* for controlling inflation. Sadly, the Government had failed to allow for the views of young school leavers and their parents, who, also, could read and understand Commons debates. They recognised themselves as that price; and so idleness, cynicism, hostility to the state, and our thin blue line of defence, would be their watchword.

Still, what did all this prove? Handsworth people still mattered to me, whatever the figures. Those children were our future, criminals and innocent alike. If we could change their behaviour just a little, then we would have used our time well. I would never abandon them, never give up, never despair.

A couple of years earlier, John Brown had visited the Handsworth Wood Girls School and talked to headmistress Clare Hinchliffe. The girls were furious at the BBC's failure in 1977 to include their achievements in an award winning documentary *Shades of Grey*. Clare, later herself to be awarded the MBE, looked back over the four years that my PBOs had been visiting. I will quote her in full, since she said great things about Ted Schuck personally and whatever may be the fate of this book, I want it to go on record that I was proud to be in charge when Ted Schuck BEM was around.

'The local police are a great help in sorting out the problems. First, with the great throughput of West Indian girls in the late 1970s, and now (1981) with the second wave, the Asians who make up the greatest majority - 80% -of the lower forms... If a girl gets into trouble, or runs away from home, the policemen help a

---

[1] 2.6 million and rising.
[2] Norman Lamonte, First Secretary to the Treasury under Mrs Thatcher, from 1989-91

great deal. If we have a disco, Sergeant Schuck may be about unseen, in case of trouble. Recently an Asian girl ran away from home, and Ted Schuck was running round in the back streets until the early hours, to all kinds of addresses we thought she might be.

About 1978 we had trouble in class, a kind of restlessness, an anti-spirit we hadn't had for years. There was trouble from children going to the Summer School and Saturday School for Black Studies. There were... some people who were infecting the youngsters, so they became anti-parent, anti-Police, anti-teacher, anti-school. The feeling was very distinct in the second and third forms, those who hadn't had regular classes with Sergeant Schuck... As a result, Ted has come on a regular basis, and has contributed to a teaching programme throughout the year. This covers not only law and order and young people, but also goes back into the history of the migration of peoples. Ted has a marvellous feeling for history, and that's very important to these immigrant children...'

Clare then spoke bitterly.

'The shame is, we see nothing of this in the newspapers or on television. The girls were appalled when they saw the programme on community policing because all the emphasis was on the Rastas. The media seemed only interested in conflict. The girls are sick of programmes like this. The say they don't want to show the truth about us. It's always the Rastas. I've told the media about Sergeant Schuck, but they've never used it.'

We knew that Handsworth had changed. When John Brown returned that year he carried out one of his renowned *Brown* tests, walking the local streets in the bustle of the day and at night as the pubs turned out the last of the drinkers. He discovered a Handsworth new in many respects: *'The contrasts of Handsworth seem even more vivid. As before, black, brown and white children play in littered, derelict streets not far from where Canada geese strut head in air over green pleasant and very select golf links. But now the contrasts jostle with each other everywhere... Rusty bangers park bumper to bumper with newly registered Mercedes. Elegant ladies in bright saris, hovering over fruit stalls like birds of paradise, almost rubbing shoulders with black boys in woolly hats, rubbed jeans, worn gym shoes... Clothes seem sharper, rhythms more insistent, a place to come to rather than to go from, in no sense a place apart.'*

John interviewed me at length early in 1981 during one of our many walkabouts. He recorded on tape something which, until I saw the published work a year later, I had forgotten. Sadly my prediction would become all too true: *'Some senior officers say it doesn't matter what the public thinks of us. They say 'They get a service from us. They shouldn't be complaining about it. We should be impervious to criticism. That's often been Police thinking... If we don't get the mixture right, there's going to be demonstrating, there's going to be knocking on the front door, there's going to be brutality, violence, tremendous upset, and there's going to be a lot of outside focus on this place. And I suggest things are moving to that critical level in places other than Handsworth. The warning signs are out...'* As I said these words I knew that, day by day, my relations with Headquarters were corroding. Events beyond my control inside and outside Handsworth would soon find a momentum of their own.

NINETEEN: WONDERFUL MISTER WEBB

Brixton, in London, exploded over the weekend of 12th - 14th April 1981. Police were pelted and fire bombed, shops, property and buildings were destroyed. Many were injured, amazingly no-one killed. The immediate press reports were a lurid affair, a recurring theme of black rape, white virtue, darkness and light. *'A WHITE woman was raped by a black youth as she prepared to flee from the Brixton riots, Scotland Yard said last night... In another attack a young nanny was attacked by a youth who tried to rape her in the lift of a tower block near Brixton police station. 'He was in a frenzy, it was terrifying...''* (Their capitals). A balancing story of a white workman talking to a black priest helped, but the damage was done[1].

In the same tabloid, a twelve column inch story of the forces of Revolutionary Communist Tendency involvement almost obscured a four line account of the realities of Brixton. Tucked away in the bottom left hand column of page thirteen Scotland yard's figures of three days of violence were: *one hundred and ninety nine people arrested, one hundred and forty three Policemen taken to hospital including nine still detained, more than thirty civilians treated in hospital, and seventy shops and homes seriously damaged.*

It was pleasing to see our Handsworth story taken up by the national press as part of the reflective journalism that tends to follow big news stories a few days after the event. In one national, the typical black versus white theme was accompanied by an account of Handsworth's importance in the development of community policing. We were described variously as a *'model race relations experiment... a new approach'*. The Metropolitan Police were said to be studying Handsworth, *'... a rundown area, where half the population are coloured.'* I was named and praised for my partnership with local immigrants. The Times included Handsworth in a full page feature[2] on the theme of rioting and its causes in Brixton. We were praised for our sense of purpose and ambitious programme: *'Superintendent Webb has made himself a reference point for community thinking and action through the range and quality of his personal contacts with community leaders. He has helped to reduce local hostility and greater compliance and co-operation. The CID has had some notable success in the detection and arrest of local key offenders. And his permanent beat or neighbourhood police officers have developed closer operational contact with schools, temple, shops, clubs and neighbourhood associations and on the streets.'*

Handsworth was on the visiting rota of senior officers on the advanced courses of the National Police College. Officers from all over the world were coming to visit us to watch our experiment in operation. James Hunt, described by one

---

[1] *A night of terror,* Daily Mail 14th April 1981.
[2] *Are there lessons in the way that Handsworth became quieter?,* The Times, 13th April 1981.

national paper as *'... a militant West Indian leader, who admitted that in 1973 he had advocated that blacks should shoot local policemen'* was quoted:

'Handsworth's social problems are worse than those of Brixton or Bristol. Here we are living on a volcano. It has been the good relations between the police and the local black communities which has saved things from exploding. Superintendent Webb and his men have created the good relations themselves by coming out and meeting the people. They treat us fairly and we respond.'

Our outward-bound camps were by now a great success. We started in 1979 with twenty five youngsters. By 1981 the word had got around and we had seventy five. These may not seem to be high figures, but remember the famous *Terror Gang of 200* headlines from 1977. If we could change the lives and attitudes of even half of those seventy five youngsters, future youth crime figures would start to fall.

Most of this, like so many of the positive things we did in Handsworth, went either un-noticed or un-reported by the media. Where bits of information did emerge, they were highly misrepresented. A typical comment, which one still hears on the radio from time to time was: *'Fancy Social Services sending young thugs on holiday at the taxpayer's expense. What a waste.'* [1] Those who hold this view forget that it was we, the well disciplined children of yesteryear, who produced the sad, dysfunctional children of today.

As the Citizen 80 project grew I decided to allocate a greater share of our time, and put two of my best men into the formation of a new project group at Centre 3 Social Services, in Dawson Road. The idea had been forming in my mind from the late sixties, when I had seen a similar project attempted in Walsall. That had not succeeded because it was run by the local police and comprised only policemen and youngsters. My scheme would involve other key agencies responsible for those young minor criminals we had formally cautioned at Thornhill Road Station. By this means we could monitor their behaviour and progress as they moved from the age band eleven to fourteen, up to fifteen to nineteen.

We trained them with lessons in social skills, literacy, films, youth club activities, sporting outings and residential weekend camps. Rodney Reed, the *'Centre 3'* Intermediate Treatment Officer was joined by a social worker, a probation officer, a volunteer group worker and one of my best achievers, Tony O'Loughlan of Golden Helmet fame. There were still rumbles below the surface. The social worker and probation officers were at times reluctant to lay all their cards on the table, particularly if a court case was pending. In spite of their reservations, overall it was a success, of which all those involved should be proud.

Meanwhile, from those who saw our Lozells and other projects as money wasted on young black work shy criminals, we had carping and criticisms. Was it *'...*

---

[1] BBC Radio WM, Summer 2000. Spoken by a friend, who I will not name, about Walsall Social Services outward bound activities for juvenile first offenders.

right or appropriate to use untrained policemen in professional youth work?' Was money being spent at the Wallace Lawler Centre *'... to the detriment of other local youth activities?'* Was the Lozells area being *'... favoured at the expense of equally needy parts of Handsworth?'* Finally, the big one: *'To what extent was this a genuine multi-disciplinary initiative, rather than simply a police project?'* [1]

This last one worried me greatly. It challenged the basic assumption on which my entire Handsworth philosophy rested: *That the Police, in the absence of any effective political or administrative alternative, must lead in the development of social cohesion, and be accountable to the people they serve.* If in the future things improved, then all could be safely handed to whatever organisations, or whichever people, would be willing to take up the reins. If we failed, all would have to accept street violence and crime, wasted generation after generation, social decay on a biblical scale.

I did not concede. I challenged the critics head on. I fought to have the work of the Wallace Lawler Centre extended even more to cover a wider range of activities and population groups. We bought furniture for a Rastafarian self-help group, and set up and ran another youth club at Westminster Road School.

I had, through hard work and commitment, created a momentum that some were beginning to doubt I could maintain. I did all kinds of things not normally expected of a policeman, including advice to starving Rastafarian youths on how they could draw unemployment benefits. It was no good to say *'Go get a job young man'*, or *'get on your bike.'* There were no jobs, none at all. Or we would liaise with the Housing Department to get a squat regularised. Or we would negotiate with local charitable trusts to obtain grants for Rastafarians. Or we would seek ways to make up for the failings of parents and the education system. In other words, our aim was to help society to find a way of producing good citizens.

James Hunte, my colleague from the days of the 1977 *Free Africa* march, had matured greatly. He was by then a member of the West Midlands Police Authority. As the 1981 summer came on, the Brixton troubles were followed by other outbreaks, including Toxteth in Liverpool. The Toxteth riots were quelled by what was euphemistically described by Mrs Thatcher as *'vigorous action'* which included the use of CS gas.[2]

A month later, Hunte, unknown to me, recorded an uncanny prediction. *'Webb has done more than anyone deserves to ask of him. He's worked hard. He knows the area. He knows its various problems. But how much further can he go without greater recognition or support from his superiors? If I were him, I would have*

---

[1] Anonymous quotes by local Policemen and politicians confidentially noted by John Brown in his research and passed to me for my elucidation.

[2] *The Downing Street Years* - An autobiography, 1993.

resigned long ago. But who can follow him? The problem that really concerns me is that of continuity.' [1]

Rudy Narayan, a local barrister, wrote under the nom-de-plume of *Troubleshooter* in the *Caribbean Times*. In May 1981 he wrote:

'Most of the immigrant leadership figure in Webb's network of projects and committees, and he is no stranger to Indian weddings and meetings all over his 'patch'. Doing a drink-about with Webb calls for the ability to walk fast and drink hard... All in all, while Handsworth's MPs have been absent from the constituency's streets, it is Superintendent David Webb who has effectively been Handsworth's Police Chief, friend and MP.'

I had a feeling as I read this, that it might not win me many friends back in the Council House nor among local MPs. I must have seemed to the Chief Constable, his deputies and assistants, to be the star of the show, a cuckoo in the nest. People were coming from all over the country, and the world, to see me and not them. Once in Handsworth, they would make a bee-line for my office, and off we would go to walk the streets, meet the people, visit the shops and clubs, see life in our suburb, warts and all.

By that time our ethnic recruitment into the Sub-Division had improved significantly. By mid 1981 twenty out of forty of our special constables were Asian or West Indian. With community workers increasingly coming into Thornhill Road Station as part of their liaison duties, the old place was at times a multi-racial bustle of constables, temple and church representatives and members of the public. Some said the place more resembled a town hall than a police station.

My Chief Inspector Martin Burton persuaded the Rastafarian movement to supply speakers who would attend training seminars for our newly appointed constables. These two hour sessions allowed free exchanges between the newly appointed constables, local community leaders and spokesmen from other local organisations. My heart raced as I read Martin's report. He truly recognised the value of what he was doing: *'The meeting with the Rastas was the most successful we've ever had. They were due to come for an hour, and they stayed for three. Both sides had a good go at each other. It was a very healthy atmosphere. Police began to understand what it means to be an unemployed black around here. The Rastas began to understand the problems of the young coppers. And now of course they know each other as individuals: this by-passes the stereotyping on both sides.'*

I felt at times that some outsiders were intent on mischief. Others were feeding in agendas of top-down, didactic policing. Telling, rather than listening; talking down to the children that *being a good citizen was the accepted duty of a school pupil*. True, it was, but how does one foster this instinct in the heart of the child raised in decaying streets and a workless family? By lectures in an atmosphere

---

[1] Said in a recorded interview with John Brown.

of discipline, or by face to face discussion and personal exchanges, in an atmosphere of mutual trust and self learning?

We in the Handsworth Force were now part of a complex structure combining Education Services and head teachers, Social Services and the City Council. Large committee meeting followed large committee meeting, agenda followed agenda, minutes and reports and phone calls and visitors unlimited. I was dealing with powerful organisations beyond my sphere of influence. Uninformed critics among the staff and politicians on the City Council and national bodies had ways of getting their sniping into meetings of the Council. My critics were not calmed by one embarrassing local headline: *'WONDER WEBB'S THE NEW MASTER OF THE MIDLANDS.'*

TWENTY: RIOTOUS FUN

Handsworth's 1980 Festival had been a great success. I was determined that 1981 would be even bigger and better. This time we persuaded groups of all kinds, even from well outside Handsworth, to join in. The central focus was the Handsworth Rotary, the Round Table, and the West Indian Faith and Confidence Fellowship Club. Then along came the Rialto Club, Lloyd Blake's West Indian Federation Association, the Guru Ravidass Temple and its Association, the Birmingham Community Relations Council, James Hunte's Midlands Community Growth Association, the local Rangers and Continentals Cricket Club, The Lozells Project, Lucas Industries Tug of War team, the Sikh Temple, the Federation of Indian Organisations, the Brotherhood of Justice Youth Council, and finally the West Midlands Police, in the form of myself, Chief Inspector Martin Burton, Sergeant Ted Schuck and two constables, Charlie O'Donnell and Tim Green.

As we prepared for the Festival, from the south came news of clashes between skinhead youths and Asians in Southall in London. The highly destructive Brixton riots in April some two months earlier had resulted in the Scarman Inquiry, and conflicting evidence between the Police and the Brixton organisations was raising the temperature. There was conflict between Police and Policed, and the papers were full of it. My heart was full of hope, and yet doubt. Was our tiny ship strong enough to survive whatever might come?

In the weeks and days leading to our Festival, groups from all over Britain with a cause to fight littered the walls with anti-Police propaganda. We were portrayed as using black and Asian Uncle Tom assistants to control society. Every kind of allegation flowed across handbills given out on street corners. The Socialist Workers Party joined forces with the Pan-African Congress Movement, although what support they might have from Nelson Mandela from in his cell on Robben Island I much doubted.

I had travelled to Warwick University a couple of times at the invitation of Professor John Rex, and lectured to the students on my theme of Community Policing. Someone in one of the organisations intent on trouble, had got to hear of it, and one leaflet proclaimed that I was a perpetrator of a plot, using university facilities to access information on the black community, so that I and my force could dominate the black races. *'Policemen posing as social workers take black kids swimming and play football with them. They then go into schools in Handsworth and give lectures on how nice the Police really are...they organise discos so that people can dance away their frustrations. But the people of Handsworth know that things are far from calm and cool. The police in Handsworth have not stopped framing and beating up black people, the police haven't stopped ignoring racist attacks. BOYCOTT THE POLICE CARNIVAL!'*

I was angry and puzzled at the vehemence, yet was comforted by the knowledge that all our people involved in our carnival would speak for more folk than any militant carpetbagger. Mischief crossed my mind, and in an irresistible fit of connivance I issued the following pamphlet, with the help of a few friends among the West Indian community: *'The Police and Friends Handsworth Festival on 4ᵗʰ July must not be supported by Black People even though it is being run by black friends and the Asians joined together with the whites. Let us go backward and not forward.. Don't go to the Police and Friends Festival. Don't enjoy yourselves to make them happy. Stay away and come to Bini Brown's place at 104 Heathfield Road instead of the Festival on Saturday, and to the school on Sunday to hear from Robin Hood[1] himself. Free refreshments and entertainment will be provided by courtesy of the Socialists Worker's Party. FORWARD NEVER. BACKWARD EVER!!'*

On the day of the Festival, Bini Brown's place would remain deserted for the entire evening. Meanwhile, ten thousand people, including a thousand Rastafarians, gave their answer, wending through sunlit streets to the throb of drums and music from three continents. Dreadlocked West Indians rubbed shoulders with white bearded Asian priests and followers in flowing robes, Bhangra groups twirled and twisted, beautiful young ladies in amazing costumes danced around and with my constables, black, brown, white and blue in a rainbow parade. In the park were stalls and side shows of every kind; from Victim Support to Gee's take-away, with Mrs Edward's Jamaican pastries and jerk pork, and ice cream stalls. A cricket knockout competition put the lives of a few spectators at risk, and a tug-of-war competition included the national and European champions, plus the Punjabi Farmers Association, who put our obviously less fit West Midlands Police team to shame. The Far East laid on a Karate display, and the giant Sucha Singh destroyed all white ambitions in the wrestling ring. We had eight-a-side football, a police mounted display and dog handling show, a West Indian Gospel girls choir from Handsworth Wood School, a multi-racial *Its a Knock-out* run by West Midlands Fire Service, Reggae bands, and cultural events by all the Rastafarian groups. Elderly West Indians, fresh from thirty years of practice in their Faith and Confidence Club, destroyed all comers in a knock-out competition of dominoes.

The policing for the day? Myself and four other policemen from the organising committee, all in casual clothes, plus two uniformed PCs in an information vehicle. We patrolled the procession and perimeter of the park with three PBOs and four specials, including a proud Sikh in his specially designed blue-grey turban. We felt no collars the entire day, made no arrests. Everyone learned a little more about their fellow citizens, and themselves.

That evening all the community leaders and organisers met in the big assembly room at The New Inns pub to celebrate the success of the day. We shared a

---

[1] DB, A local criminal with many convictions for robbery with violence, revered by some agitators.

146

well spiced local curry and drinks, speeches were made, and prizes presented. Bishop Hugh Montifiore came along to restore some dignity to our somewhat relaxed proceedings. The only spoiler was the presence of some six Socialist Worker activists who heckled and demanded to be heard. So we let them spout the stuff we had seen on those handbills and posters, to a chorus of total disapproval. As they rose to leave, a group of Rastafarians challenged them at the door and threw them out.

Next day, smarting from their rejection, the group published another series of handbills. Our old Thornhill Road Station was now *The Torture Centre, the focus of a world-wide model of community policing designed to beat down black resistance to oppression.* One claim looked ominous: *'If we get rid of Webb, we can have this place.'* In the same week, each evening, Thornhill Road was picketed by a group of West Indians and Socialist Worker activists, representing a DB who had been arrested for carrying offensive weapons.

Meanwhile, around Britain, talk and debate on the recent riots were filling TV screens. Commentators speculated from the safety of studios, newspapers wondered. The Guardian expressed its fears on Tuesday 7th July: *'WHICH MULTIRACIAL city in Britain is next in line now that Liverpool, London and Bristol have erupted? Will it be Birmingham? Or will the community policing experiment in that midlands city save it from the riots that have exploded elsewhere?...'* Next day, Manchester's Moss Side would explode into forty eight hours of disorder.

On the morning of Friday 10th July, several of my beat officers told of rumours on the streets, that the National Front intended a march along the Soho Road. I put as many men as I could spare on patrol and contacted headquarters to ensure that we had units on standby at Walsall Road, Tally Ho Centre, Bournville, Bradford Street, Tipton and Ladywood. Telephones and fax lines buzzed, messengers helter-skeltered the ring roads, defensive helmets and shields were hurriedly unstacked, husbands telephoned frightened wives to reschedule their coming days. I walked our patch in my civvies, talking to groups of men, young and old, who were standing apprehensively on the corners. We had noticed that several white, Asian and West Indian youths had been seen hanging around with members of the Socialist Workers Party. I tried hard to reassure everyone. *The rumours are false. There will be no march, we will not allow it. It is a ploy, an attempt to create mayhem.*

It was getting dark, towards ten o'clock. I strolled down Thornhill Road to the corner with Soho Road, down by the *Frighted Horse Pub* and the Handsworth Library. All around me were people, black, white and brown. That picket crowd was still there, grouped menacingly opposite the station, along where an old brick wall protected the fronts of some terrace houses. Some shopkeepers were thinking ahead and hammering home the last few nails, boarding up the big plate glass windows. They did not say a word, just looked at me. In their eyes I saw stone cold fear.

I thought to myself, *If you want trouble, get your kicks in Handsworth. Just march up the main street for immediate worldwide coverage.* Every organisation seeking publicity had its office in or came to Handsworth. The Socialist Workers Party, the National Front, the reports all read like Special Branch files. No good going to Solihull or some posh area. Go to the place where the tools of revolution; poverty, unemployment, frustrated young men, all are readily to hand.

Was a moment of truth approaching, a turning point? I knew that if Brixton had happened, and we survived, then my way would have been vindicated. We *were* the news and I, David Webb, in my fifth year of senior command, the man who had challenged the accepted policing mantra, was responsible for all that would follow.

I was talking to the crowd, telling them that nothing was going to happen, there would be no trouble by the National Front, no battle, nothing. If anyone tried to march through our neighbourhood I would stop them. I told them to relax, go home, not to worry. Then just before ten, the citizen's band radio crackled: *'There's a National Front March in the main street Handsworth! There's a riot going on! Quick, get to Handsworth and defend our people!'*

We guessed that if true, then something was about to happen, and if not true, it was a ruse to stir up a riot. So I walked up and down the road, telling the people; *'Look, this is the main street. There's no riot. Look for yourselves, you can see. It's just a rumour, don't believe it.'*

I reached the corner of Soho Road and Thornhill Road and turned to look back. The night exploded with a thud and I saw stars. Blood trickled down my face. Another thud and something hit me on the forehead. A third brick hit me but I did not feel it. As my head cleared, people were trying to kick and punch me. I heard shouts of *'GET WEBB!... GET WEBB!'* I cannot remember how I got back to the station, but my constables afterwards told me that a group of Asians, West Indians and whites had gathered round to protect me and bundled me back inside. Meanwhile, a hail of bricks and bottles from across the road flew over the crowd aimed mainly at me.

As I was in the Station trying to clear my head and being patched up by a constable, the windows along the Soho Road were being smashed and shops looted. Eye witness statements the next day claimed that a crowd of youths, some white, some black, all armed with bricks and sticks and clubs, had started to throw whatever they could grab, and then had immediately turned their attention to the shops. They went up along the Soho Road and within minutes twenty five shops had been smashed up and looted, with six or seven torched.

Sergeant Ted Schuck wrote later:

'We had the first news of the violence, and of activists at the centre of things, when Mr Webb came back injured. We went down in the van, and were being badly stoned. I think the police officers were shook up quite a bit. We were very few in number, but had no alternative but to charge the rioters. We numbered about fifteen, and two sergeants, and of course at my age, I'm not a great deal of use anyhow. But they were very brave when they went to break up a crowd of about one hundred and fifty. It made me immensely proud of the our people, of a spirit that must never be

chipped away. Then reinforcements arrived. The looting was gradually quelled. The great thing was that within two hours of us gaining control of the situation, we were able to establish our traditional rapport with the people, the police officers were openly talking to groups of black and brown and white youths on the streets.'

An eye witness, a Mr Taylor of Great Barr, who had been passing through at the time, told the Birmingham Evening Mail: *'A group of Rastafarians vehemently pointed out to an excited group of young people that they were being agitated by white political extremists who had no interest in the well-being of Handsworth. The Rastafarians told the crowd that the agitators had lied about there being an imminent attack by skinheads. The group respected the feelings of the Rastafarians and the gathering broke up. I saw a West Indian peacefully disarm an excited young man of a brick. I heard a European pleading with Handsworth people to end the violence.'*

Our casualty list was enormous. Four pages listing bruises, cuts, gashes, torn muscles, including one page of thirty from our station. I was first on the list: *'Superintendent Webb - 3 blows on the head.'* Out of all the police eye-witness reports one of the most telling was by Chief Inspector David Blick of the Bournville Station. He and his men had been on standby for the entire day and were called to Handsworth at around ten that evening. *'As the convoy of police vehicles travelled along Soho Road towards West Bromwich, near to the junction with Villa Road, we were attacked with bricks and bottles thrown by West Indians from both sides... Approximately 100 persons were involved in this incident. The vehicle I was travelling in lost its windscreen and side windows and Sergeant Adamson, who was in the front passenger seat was hit on the side of the face by a lump of concrete which caused a serious gash to his lower jaw, rendering him semi-conscious...'*

Most of the force were allowed off duty around 4.00 am day as the streets quietened. Many local children would that morning walk to school in new jeans and new trainers, boasting of new TV's, new refrigerators. I remember one story of a man who looted a refrigerator, pushed it away from a shop in a wheelbarrow commandeered from a builders yard. As he went down the road someone hit him over the head and pinched the wheelbarrow and fridge. And the same happened to the second man. That fridge was looted and re-looted five times.

The sun rose next morning on a peaceful scene, with smoke still rising from smashed and burned out cars and shops. Fortunately no people had been burned. By 7.00 am some senior members of the Police Committee and a number of community leaders of all races were at my house, crowded into my tiny living room. All were insistent that there had been no fault in the way that the police had handled things. Our good community relationships had restored order and harmony quickly. To a man, they offered full support for any actions I might take. I had room for just two armchairs and a couch that seats two people. They sat on the chairs and the floor, my wife Bet made breakfast for us all and we debated what to do. I knew that on our decisions might hinge the whole future of community policing, a concept into which

I had poured every waking moment, and the whole of my learning and career as a policeman.

An outbreak of looting occurred next evening, Saturday 11th July, and then Sunday 12th, but from then on it all went quiet again. Our arrest list was fascinating. We pulled in forty two young men that first night, fifty seven the second night, and nineteen on the Sunday. Only fifty one out of the total 118 came from Handsworth and the immediate areas. All the rest had come to our suburb for an evening of fun and looting. Some had come from as far away as Wolverhampton. One had travelled from Hollymoor Hospital Nurses home some fifteen miles to the South. His ensuing discussion with Matron must have been interesting.

Sergeant Ted Schuck would sum things up in his own way as, later, we reviewed what had happened: *'I think the last three and a half years has given me a chance to look back at the Police Service and perhaps reassess its place in society. If I had any doubts about the new ideas I'd gained during that time, they were dispersed by the Friday evening riots. I saw then that those ideas were right. Without the backing of the general public in Handsworth we would not have had the flexibility to put down the riots firmly and decisively and then immediately revert back to friendly relations with the community. Some policemen think you cannot do both. We were able to do both. That's what 'policing by consent' means.'* Good old Ted. He got a British Empire Medal and the Midlands Police Cobra Cup for services to the community when he retired later that same year. Along with the cup came an award of twelve pounds in cash.

We had proved that our concepts worked, but that thirty minute street battle, and the 'copy cat' troubles over the next two nights were the opportunity some were looking for. Those who were safely far enough away from the facts could now claim that Handsworth was no different than any other place. *'All that wasted money.'* they would say, and *'Handsworth is really just the same black violent ghetto it always was.'* Community policing Handsworth style was *'... a myth, a waste of Police manpower, a diversion from the real job of the Police, to fight crime.'* [1] Whatever we may have proved within Handsworth, I knew that now, beyond our tiny community, few would be listening.

---

[1] Quotations passed to me by friends. I never discovered who said them.

TWENTY ONE: FAME AND THE GOOD LORD

Tuesday morning, 14th July, 10.19 a.m.. Ted Schuck calls me across the office. *'Sir - its for you, BBC Radio, Jimmy Young Show, Gloria Hunniford'*

Gloria explained that the Government's response was beginning to emerge, after what Mrs Thatcher had called the most worrying ten days of her premiership. A proposal had emerged from Home Secretary William Whitelaw for the use of army camps as overflow prisons. For the Police there would be water cannons and armoured vehicles. New tactics would include snatch squads and national co-ordination for riot control. Across the country there would be a significant change in how Police chiefs did their job. And according to Jim Jardine, chairman of the Police Federation, the old Dixon of Dock Green image would simply have to go. So, how did all that look to me in the cold light of day? Did I accept that the events would knock my projects back?

Not a bit of it. I told Gloria that when I got home early that Saturday morning and finally got to bed, there were thirty five calls in the first hour from members of the community all reassuring me of their support in keeping our projects going. They saw the role of the Police as crucial to success. I knew that those of my men who had been injured might feel that the whole thing was not succeeding and would lose enthusiasm. Our projects relied on their good will. There was, too, a risk that such a traumatic event might drive a wedge between the Police and the People. That would be exactly what the instigators of the trouble wanted the Police to do. Throughout, the morale and spirit of my men had been tremendous. They were not at all deterred. All the shopkeepers whose shops had been looted had said to me, that they were pleased that Friday's troubles had not developed into something more serious, and they were urging me and my force to continue with our projects. Next year's Handsworth Festival would involve everyone as it had before. No rioter would overcome what we had achieved, and were trying to achieve. If the rioters came back a thousand times, we would not give in or fail.

Gloria asked, *Was the nation moving towards a para-military police force?* I told her, not at all. Recent riots had revealed that some police equipment was antiquated. When a policeman faced fire bombs you had to give him the means of defending himself, that was all.

Gloria pressed the point, asking for my views on water cannon, rubber bullets, armoured vehicles and personnel carriers. I told her that as long as I was in charge of my sub-division, we would not use them. Those suggestions were predictable when society felt pressured. Hopefully we could show in Handsworth that by living and working together on our joint projects we could avoid the need for such things. Sometimes when large crowds gather it had to be an available tactic. The trick was to create a situation where large crowds would not gather, keep people moving on as happily as could be achieved. There were other things too that I did not want to discuss publicly. I was not convinced that we had to go down the heavy equipment road, even though certain of my colleagues in the Federation might disagree with me. I feared that such things would drive a wedge between Police and Public.

I added that, I was not a chief constable. I could not refuse such things if ordered, by superior officers, to use them. But I would be very sad to see that kind of thing happen. The problem for society was that once the equipment was available, police forces would be bound to want to practice on it to know how to use it. Once you practice on it, there is always the possibility that an individual commander will want to use it. Then, once you start to use it, then it becomes just another standard piece of hardware and an everyday feature of policing. When you get to that point, there is no way back. Should policy move nationally and locally to such methods, then it would be a sign that my policy had failed.

***

Confusion reigned nationally throughout that year. For Brixton, Southall, Toxteth, Moss Side, Handsworth, every commentator, every politician, knew the cause and the solution. Prime Minister Margaret Thatcher had, in May 1981, accepted Home Secretary William Whitelaw's suggestion that Lord Scarman, regarded as *'That distinguished Law Lord'*, should undertake an enquiry into the causes of the Brixton riots and make recommendations. Michael Heseltine was nominated as an inner city supremo, and was despatched, with a team of civil servants, up the M1 to Liverpool, for a two week pilot study. The move was immediately condemned as cosmetic by a number of his conservative colleagues, among them John Stokes. *'This looks like appeasement. What about the rest of the country who abide by the law? Do they have to riot and loot to gain special attention?'*

Enoch Powell thundered on the dangers of new large Commonwealth populations in British Cities. The Commons shouted him down as he claimed that Britain was in danger of Civil War. Conflict echoed back and forth from Westminster's panelled walls. Mrs Thatcher countered the argument that riots had been caused by unemployment. She was correct; unemployment was not the sole cause. Explosions of the kind we were witnessing had many components, assembled, one by one, in the mind of the child, from the age of five up to the young man of twenty. It then required but one or two external factors to form a critical mass ready to explode on the streets.

Some of Mrs Thatcher's own Government members complained that the social fabric of the nation had been *'... torn apart by the doctrinaire monetarism the Government had espoused.'* She retorted that this overlooked the fact that riots, football hooliganism and crime generally had been on the increase since the 1960's, most of that time under the very economic policies that government critics were urging her to adopt.[1] The merits of water cannon, rubber or plastic bullets, CS gas and armoured vehicles ricocheted around the hallowed lobbies. Ulster's policing methods were said to be an example which most British people would wish to copy.[2]

She visited Brixton's main police station and talked to the West Indian tea ladies. She claimed that her point was proved, by their determination to continue to supply tea and refreshments to their constables while the street riots were running. Everyone, she claimed, was as disgusted as she was with those who were causing the trouble.

Mrs Thatcher also went to Toxteth to see for herself the results of the troubles, and recorded the day out in her memoirs. She found housing by no means the worst in the city. She had been told that some of the young people involved got into trouble through boredom and not having enough to do. She added that people only had to look at the grounds around those houses with the grass untended, some of it waist high, and the litter, to see that this was a false analysis. They had plenty of constructive things to do if they wanted. Instead, she asked herself, how could people live in such circumstances without trying to clear up the mess and improve their surroundings? What was, to her, clearly lacking in the inner cities, was a sense of pride and personal responsibility, *something that the state can easily remove but almost never give back.*[3]

To be fair, she did accept that the causes of such troubles might go deeper, but her analysis and remedies sadly missed the mark. She controlled her Cabinet with a firm hand, and it was her philosophy that set the tone and agenda against which we in Handsworth and elsewhere had to battle. Her ministers were expected, as it later emerged after a number of Cabinet resignations, to produce analyses and conclusions that fitted with her own understanding of life, otherwise they were regarded as *'wets'*. *'What had become',* she asked, *'of the constraints? A sense of community, including the watchful disapproval of neighbours, is the strongest such barrier. But this sense had been lost in the inner cities for a variety of reasons...'* These she perceived to be the uprooting of natural communities to artificial ones in new estates, the creation of large *'ethnically mixed'* neighbourhoods, a welfare system that encouraged dependency and discouraged a sense of responsibility. Finally she accused the great demon, television, of undermining those common moral values that once united working-class communities. The results, she claimed were a steadily increasing rise in crime among young men, and illegitimacy among young women. All that was needed for these to flower into full-scale rioting was a decline of authority, and that was what had really been at the heart of it all.

---

[1] *The Downing Street Years, p 143 - 147.*
[2] The Times, July 16th and 17th 1981.
[3] *The Downing Street Years, p 143 - 147.*

Two days later my phone at the station rang. It was the Chief Constable's office. *'Lord Scarman is due to visit Birmingham on Thursday, and he has asked to come to Thornhill Road as part of his programme. He's seeking information that will help him put the Brixton situation into context. He has meetings all day and a press conference and some TV interviews, but he would like to start his day at Thornhill Road. We'd be grateful if you would show him around and answer any questions he might have.'*

That is how, on the morning of July 16th 1981, but a few days after our Handsworth riot, a sparrow of a man in the slightly crumpled suit and with a shy charming smile, came to be facing me in my office. Helping himself to a couple of chocolate digestive biscuits he began a quest for information that might change the face of policing in Great Britain, and in major cities around the world.

We hit it off right away. A press conference at the Council House would end his day. There, he would publicly say all the things the public wanted to hear. He had met Sir Phillip and examined the issues of water cannon, CS gas and other technology and techniques. He would meet Gordon Morgan, leader of the West Midlands County Council, then the Police Committee, then Birmingham City Council and many others. Most of all, he wanted to know about Thornhill Road and our policies, and by then I had the advantage of knowing about street riots from every angle. He said he would like to return to Handsworth to undertake more research.

On 10th August he was there in my office again. I knew what he wanted to see and why. He knew that in the backstreets and shops and cafes of Handsworth he would find some of the truths about Brixton. Until then his information had been based mainly on unreliable national and local TV and newspaper coverage, the confusion of parliamentary questioning and debate, and whatever he had been able to glean from his briefings in London. Evidence was were flooding in to him, volume after volume, from Councils and Policemen and committee after committee, group after group. Much of it was voluminous, strident and confusing. The opportunity to look at things in Handsworth in his own time, explore relevant issues, was invaluable.

I set up a pie and pints lunch for him at Bernard Whyte's club, and he walked the busy streets, and strolled down Soho Road. He visited local clubs and talked at length to the owners about crime and drugs, and the problems of running a business in a deprived area. He surveyed the damaged shops and burnt out buildings, talked to old and young, the shoppers and the shop-keepers. He met the Rasta men and their spokesmen. He talked with Bernard Whyte and James Hunte. He met excited Asian gentlemen and their brightly dressed ladies, and community leaders of every colour. His mind was sharp as a razor, questioning everything, challenging and then re-questioning. Occasionally he would pause to make notes in a small leather-bound book.

Back at Thornhill Road he met some of my staff. Then he questioned me on my policing policy, the weakening bond of the family, deprivation and unemployment and their effect on young and old. We examined the role of education, probation stage counselling, how to divert criminal tendencies from the minds of school children. We considered the successes and failures of our Lozells Project. He was most interested in my views on how policemen should behave towards citizens, especially ethnic populations. Finally we talked about the importance of Police Consultative Committees, representation on them of ethnic minority groups, and the role of community leaders in helping the Police to do their job with the consent of the people.

I later discovered Lord Scarman to be deeply disappointed at the resistance shown to his report on the 1981 disturbances.[1] He and many others on the right and left of politics had warned repeatedly of the consequences of inaction. That failure to act would bear bitter fruit in the nation-wide rioting of 1985. His 1981 terms of reference had been consciously defined so as to effectively exclude any investigation of social factors. William Whitelaw made clear that he should focus on policing and only on policing. Scarman threw down the challenge and refused to conduct any enquiry unless the terms of reference were widened. So, under an inevitable compromise he was allowed to include 'suggestions' on social policy.

Basing his conclusions on evidence gathered in Brixton, Handsworth and elsewhere, he made thirty eight recommendations on policing, and two formal recommendations and twenty 'suggestions' on employment, housing, education and race relations. He was later to be disappointed to discover that all but two of his conclusions on the influence of social factors proved of passing interest to the Cabinet and virtually none would be implemented. Indeed the Birmingham Post, not renowned for its left wing views, would, four years later, conclude that the Government's attitude to Lord Scarman's conclusions *'was not altogether surprising, considering Mrs Thatcher's known views about the purpose of his original report'.*[2] Scarman himself would later reveal that what he considered to be the central conclusion on Brixton: *'... the rule of law would only be achieved if it reflected social justice for everyone, including deprived and frustrated young blacks.'* had not only been ignored, it had been, in effect, scorned.

In the years leading up to 1981, and for some twelve months afterwards, Mrs Thatcher's colleagues seemed determined to take as much notice of Lord Scarman as they did of me. From the beginning of our conversations in Handsworth I sensed that he would be viewed, as Mrs Thatcher would say, as *'Not one of us...'* The nation would, in time, in the light of more disastrous riots in 1985, look backwards at his 1981 conclusions. Commentators would, all too late, attempt to draw some lessons from his 1981 report. Everyone would know that Scarman, as a Law Lord, could never publicly say that the Government had done nothing between 1981 and 1985 to

---

[1] Published 25th November 1981
[2] Birmingham Post, Nov 27th 1985 *'Years on, and still no further.'*

change things for the better. But as history would move on and interview follow interview, every Fleet Street journalist, indeed anyone who understood the realities of Britain in 1985, would know exactly what he meant.

***

I was under scrutiny. The Chief Constable's office were even more convinced than before that I was neglecting my duties, spending too much time running around the country talking about community policing, meeting too many visitors. A polite but sinister memo dated 23rd September 1981 from my Chief Superintendent Joe Matthews requested me to report on my visitors and visits over the last twelve months. When I listed my diary between January and August 1981 I did not feel it was too bad:

January: 4th - Indian Assistant High Commissioner; 5th - Staff of Link House Project; 6th - Undergraduates from Aston University; 8th - Interview on BRMB Radio; 9th - ABC Weekly interview; 12th - Interview on Beacon Radio; 16th - Staff from Aston and Handsworth Institute;, 21st - Visit from Leicester Constabulary; 28th - Meeting with Deputy Chief Constable.

February: 5th - County Councillor Binney.

March: 2nd - Visit from Student Nurses of All Saints Hospital; 10th - Professor Eterhuyse of The University of Stellenbosch South Africa; 12th - visiting social workers of Bournville College.

April: 3rd - Central Office of Information visit by Father Panton Director of SERVOL; 13th - Commander Patterson and six officers from Senior Command Course Bramshill; 21st - Interview by Independent TV.

May: 2nd - Interview by Daily Star; 8th - Interview with BBC TV; 19th - Commonwealth Trust, ten visiting national broadcasting directors.

June: 12th - Visiting party from Oxford University with Sue Smith; 24th - Visit by Rev B. Thurley.

July: 3rd - Interview with The Times; 13th - ATV interview and panel discussion; 22nd - Interview with Hannan Peschar, distinguished Dutch Journalist; 22nd - Interview by The Washington Post and other American Newspapers; 23rd - Visit by Government Inspector; 28th - Interview with Daily Telegraph.

August: 10th - Visit by Lord Scarman; 11th - BBC Panel programme; 14th - Visit by the Executive of the NCCL; 17th - Visit by Representative of the Home Office; 20th - Three officers from Cambridgeshire Constabulary; 21st - Visit from the Department of Education of Nigeria.

Over 1981 the tempo had grown, adding to my hectic schedule of the previous year, and new invitations were flooding in. Chief Constable John Alderson insisted that I should speak at the Devon and Cornwall Regional Inspectors' Development Course, scheduled for October. Rotary International welcomed me to their annual conference in Torquay between October 23rd to 25th. The University College of Wales offered an opportunity to expound my views to a joint audience of staff and students. Bramshill requested of the Chief Constable that I should present a paper on *'The Handsworth Experience'* on 24th September, and again on 23rd October. The requests bounced around the Chief Constable's office like errant golf balls gathering questions, comments and initials until I finally obtained permission. Then it all started to unravel.

TWENTY TWO: A HARD DAY AT THE OFFICE

'Dave Webb looked a little fragile. He had been to two weddings the day before and in Handsworth they do like to treat their policemen properly. Next week he expects to attend two more weddings. He goes because he obviously enjoys them, but also to maintain good community relations. For that's how he runs his patch. Part politician, part peacemaker and part policeman, his methods of community policing were shown to pay off during the recent riots that swept England...' [1]

You may ask, objective reader that you are, how it came to be that everyone - the Home Office, the Chief Constable Sir Phillip Knights, little me, all appeared to sing from the same hymn book, all saw the light. Yet, when matters were tested a different picture would emerge. A collision became day by day inevitable.

When, in 1975, I arrived in troubled Handsworth, Sir Phillip was highly impressed, promoting me to Superintendent within twelve months. Impressed he might have been, but he never gave me a single instruction in six years. No guidance, no comments, no re-direction, no questioning, from the first day to the last. I like to think that in some way my policies became his policies, Handsworth's fame became his fame. He got a deserved knighthood in office and even more deserved life peerage on retirement.

From around me came rumours of disapproval among the top echelons of the Force. The reason and source were impossible to trace. It reached my ears that I had been described by one senior commander as *'That bloody crank'*. Inevitability was in the air, but what to do? I seemed to switch into auto-pilot, doing the same routines, all the same things that I had done for the previous five hectic years. It just would not go away. I detected no rumours around the office. Whatever Sir Phillip was up to, he was not letting on to anyone outside Lloyd House. [2]

The first move was not long in coming. The phone rang at home. It was Assistant Chief Constable Les Sharpe. He would later be promoted and rewarded to Sir Lesley Sharpe, Chief Constable of Strathclyde. We went through the usual exchanges, then he said: *'We think you need to reassess your career. We feel you would benefit from a change. We'd like you to move to Stechford, and there you could take charge of football security at Birmingham City FC.'* Les Sharpe had said *'We...'* It was one of those moments. I felt a cold flush of adrenaline.

Should I fight them? I was at the climax of my career. Our policies were having an amazing effect on community relations, yet there was still so much more to be done.

---

[1] The Catholic newspaper *THE UNIVERSE*, 4th September 1981

[2] Lloyd House is the headquarters of West Midlands Constabulary in Birmingham.

I replied, *'Sir, if you think that you're wrong. Career move? I did football policing for eight years at Walsall. Do you take me for a fool? I'm doing the right things for Handsworth and you know it. I don't know what they've told you to say, but I'm not moving voluntarily.'* I can still hear my words, icy smooth, unnatural, confused. *'... But you're in charge. If you post me I've got to go. But I've so much to do here. I'm not going, not yet.'*

There was a short silence, then he said. *'... I understand. We can talk about it some other time. Goodbye David.'* He knew when to retreat. There would be another message.

Les was new to Birmingham, had been in the Force for only three months. Maybe that is why he was the messenger. There had been no mention of Sir Phillip, yet how could a Superintendent be so pressured by an Assistant without the Chief Constable himself controlling events? All I could conclude was, that they wanted to wind down what we were doing in Handsworth. Those outside Handsworth wanted a sanitised, easily managed version of community policing. Put bobbies on the beat, put on a few talks in the schools, call it *Community Policing.* I knew it would not work, especially in Handsworth. Within three or four years we would be back to where we were, state versus citizen, harassment, violence, another lost generation, more riots, all my good work undone.

My philosophy was too difficult, too expensive in time and effort, too radical, too ethnic for some. Black and brown would be seen as politically more important than white. The Police Force nationally could not do it. It meant that the superintendent and his superior officers would have to commit to twenty four hours a day availability, at the beck and call of disparate and not too well organised groups of non-British people.

Sir Phillip was, deservedly, greatly respected at the Home Office. He played by the rules, but one of his local commanders was making waves, challenging official policy. Perhaps he felt that now was the time to move me to pastures new. Or maybe he believed that I was losing sight of the role that my colleagues and the Home Office thought senior officers should play. Many of those who had praised me back in 1978 during my lecturing at Bramshill would depart quickly and quietly from the ranks of the believers, when the Home Office reacted to Scarman's initial 1981 findings. Then it was that senior and middle rank members of the Force converted to the Thatcher mantra on street disorder.

Critics, including some notable academics[1], were saying that my system was not true community policing, that I was getting involved in things that policemen should not do, that I should keep out of things that were the responsibility of others.

---

[1] A prominent local critic was Professor John Rex, Research Professor of Ethnic Relations at the University of Warwick. He undertook research In Handsworth in the mid 1970's, but we never met in Handsworth.

The cruncher was, that under my philosophy, policemen would have to be involved in virtually everything that went on in society, and that was seen as dangerous. In the eyes of some, it then becomes a police state, albeit a benevolent one. They said that what I had in Handsworth was a dictatorship. That I did exactly what I wanted to do, and all my cultivated friends, as leaders of the community, did what I told them. They said I had total control, that nothing happened unless I said so.

Some referred to the policy followed by John Alderson in Devon and Cornwall. His style, they said, was true community policing. After twenty years, however, it baffles me still how they could really believe that a policy right for the rural white communities of our South West peninsular, could, to any significant degree, be right for Handsworth and similar inner city areas.

Admittedly, some acknowledged the success of my policy, but felt it could not be copied within available resources. A London Metropolitan Police senior commander was quoted as saying that London could not do what is done in Handsworth. Handsworth was a one man band, imposed from above by sheer force of personality of the chief, and when the chief leaves, the policy will fail.

Furthermore, I knew that whatever happened, there would be no more promotion. I did not want to stay at Handsworth for the rest of my service life. I had ambitions like anyone else. I still wanted to get to the top, be in the running for a chief constable, use the opportunity to implement my style of policing from a position of senior command. I had been on the command course, and had the qualifications and experience.

Sometimes a man is forced by circumstance to stand for what he believes. Back in 1956, at the start of our life together, I made a statement to my wife Bet that the day I did not enjoy going to work, then I would be out. By now I was 46. I had worked seven days a week, twenty four hours a day, giving my time and health to my love of Handsworth. I had immersed my life in the place, in the people. Yet I did not feel burned out. I just felt powerless to achieve against the pressures around me that resisted change. I felt at times like Galileo. I and the leaders of the Force were looking at the same facts, but we each saw a different world. I had others to consider; a wife, son and daughter both starting a Police career. If I played things wrong, would their careers be affected? Women always want their men to be strong, the dominant dog. I had let Bet down and all those who trusted me to protect them. I cried many times, but never in front of Bet. I could not show it. Toughness was all. The hard men would soon get me out, take charge in Handsworth. It would take another twenty years of changes in society for people to understand that what I had fought for was right for its time.

I waited and waited for the next message. Then on the evening of Thursday 8th October it came, unusually, to my home, from his home. *'Hello David, Les Sharpe. We've been thinking about things. Maybe that Stechford job wouldn't suit you after all. We were wondering if you would prefer a senior job in administration at Lloyd House. It would certainly benefit your career at this time of life.'*

This time I was ready. Did he think I would change my mind? What would happen to all that I had built, everything that I had devoted my life to for five years? All they wanted was a simple *'Yes'*. Then they would claim I had volunteered to go. I replied firmly: *'Sir, you know my reply. These people need community policing and that's what I'm giving them. Please tell Sir Phillip that I'll consider what he says, and be in touch.'*

There was a polite *'Goodbye David....'* and he put down the phone.

It was then I decided. I wouldn't let them have the satisfaction of getting me out. I would do it my way or not at all. I would retire and tell the world why.

Next day I went to work as usual and late in the afternoon sat down with pen and paper. A typewriter would be too public. The following wording is approximate. I cannot recall exactly what I said. Maybe it buried itself into my sub-conscious. I just remember it as a hard, hard day.

'Friday 9th October 1981

Dear Sir Phillip,

I feel sad that my policies are not being appreciated elsewhere. There is resistance across the country to what I want to do, and my policies are no longer welcome. I have twenty six years of service and feel that now is the time to retire, with effect from 31st December 1981.

Yours sincerely,

Superintendent David Webb'

It was like signing my death warrant. I did not keep a copy. Today, the first in six years, I would leave the office on time. It would be a long journey homeward to my softly weeping Bet. I carefully sealed the envelope, endorsed it *Private and Confidential*, put it in the post tray and strolled through the old Victorian doors into bright autumn sunshine.

TWENTY THREE: GOODBYE SIR PHILLIP

Next day, Saturday 10th October 1981, I phoned the Birmingham press and the story was out. I was determined to tell the world first. I did not want a press officer dressing it up as some mutually cosy agreement. At the same time, I did not want to reveal the unacceptable job offers from headquarters. Reactions within the Force might affect my children's careers. So, I would co-operate with the smoke screen, aim my criticisms at some vague national target. If anyone then chose to criticise my work, then let the cap fit where it may.

The BBC were quickly on the trail. Monday morning Jimmy Young's producer phoned and within five minutes I was national news. Young explained that Handsworth had become widely recognised as one of the most successful community policing projects in Britain. I had brought my men in closer contact with the people by putting them back on the beat. I had encouraged the younger of them to play football with residents and to join in with other community programmes. My work had been praised by race relations workers in Britain and abroad. However, within the Police Force itself, the reaction had not been quite so generous. The phrase 'Bloody crank' was now in the public domain, and I was taking early retirement. Why after twenty six years had I done it?

I could but explain that after twenty-six years such a decision was deeply regretted. I was sadly disappointed by the reaction of many across Britain, to our achievements in Handsworth. Now I would have the opportunity of voicing my views on community policing across the country, at colleges and universities.

Would the black and Asian organisations be disappointed at my decision? Of course they would, and I was most conscious of their feelings. But what alternative had been open to me? I could only hope that they would understand that I could probably do more good by making this protest than I could if I was in Handsworth, where, for the last six years it felt at times as if I had been bashing my head against a brick wall. Across the nation people were aware what had been happening in their own areas and cities. Whatever the police forces in all these places said about their own role and, what they had been doing, unfortunately, their public in many cases did not agree with them. It seemed to me that a terrible breakdown of communication had occurred.

In Handsworth we had good relations with our people because we had insisted on involving them in all sorts of projects where we could inter-relate with each other. Going out to youth clubs and away on adventure trips, visiting the schools, organising Duke of Edinburgh projects. Still, to many senior police commanders, all this was unproductive, a waste of Police time. They were so wrong. I felt I had a duty to pay tribute to those few colleagues in other forces who supported what we believed, for their own positive work going on outside of Handsworth. As for those who followed what I considered to be a negative road, I honestly did not care. I had visited places across the country, and I knew for sure, in my heart, that what we were doing was right for the people of Handsworth.

The rank and file policemen of Handsworth were behind me one hundred percent. If that had not been the case, we could not have got off the ground with the hundreds of projects that we pioneered. It was a sad time for all, but I would still live and work in and around Handsworth. I would stay with those projects and committees that retirement allowed. I would still be there, keeping an eye on the situation and chasing up whoever took over from me.

Within a day[1] I was on the radio again, this time in the first floor studio of Pebble Mill, interviewer Ed Doolan. Sitting next to me, sharing the microphone arm, almost breath to breath, was Ronald Broome, Deputy Chief Constable of the West Midlands. Ronald had known, and been part of, the unacceptable job offers to me over the previous four weeks. He and the people at headquarters knew that, had I chose, I could have made it hot for them. There had been no gentleman's agreement, but we all joined in a kind of game, hiding the real truth.

I will not re-run all the conversation with Ed, as I repeated much of what I told Jimmy Young. I would just say that Ed was puzzled at my reasons for retirement, repeating the question *'Why?'* several times. He was an experienced journalist with a nose for a story. Perhaps he guessed there was something more behind our friendly words. Ronald Broome's answer to his final question summed up the Headquarter's stance.

Doolan: *'Can I ask you one question that is important to all of us. We've heard Superintendent Webb tell us of some of the reasons that he is leaving the force, because of an unhappiness of attitudes elsewhere in the country, to perhaps a different form of policing to that which we know in the West Midlands. Is the West Midlands likely to follow other areas of the country and does what is happening elsewhere give you concern?'*

Broome told him *'No'*. As long as he was associated with the West Midlands, and as long as the Chief Constable's Policies were carried through, the nature of policing in the West Midlands would stay as it was. That is, consensus policing, with a community thread running all the way through everything that the Police did. This would extend from the youngest recruit, right through the Force. He stressed in particular that community policing of the kind that I had pioneered would carry on. There were people within the Police Service who saw the Police as having nothing to do with helping to run youth clubs. Such people, he claimed, believed that the job of the Police was simply the enforcement of Law and Order. The Chief Constable and

---

[1] Probably Tuesday 13th October. My tape is undated. I am unable to directly quote Ronald Broome. I would require his permission and feel a request would prove futile.

Ronald Broome did not share that view, and community policing would, in future, be seen at its best in Handsworth.

By this time, Lord Scarman had published his Report on the Brixton Riots of 1981. The day after the publication of his Report, Westminster's Supply Day included a debate on Law and Order[1] with a motion proposed by David Steel, that called for the introduction of community policing methods, and an independent procedure for the investigation of complaints against the Police.

David Steel noted that in 1980 there had been seven thousand four hundred and sixty complaints against the Police, but only on hundred and seventy six charges had been brought. Among the figures were many complaints of racial discrimination, yet, he continued, *'it is astonishing that, as far as one knows, not one police officer has been dismissed for racial prejudice.'*

He referred to the need to introduce the recommendations on social issues by Lord Scarman, and hinted that he suspected that the Government, represented in the debate by Patrick Mayhew, Minister of State at the Home Office, would implement few of them. *'In my experience of speaking about police matters... I have found that if one attempts to criticise them, one is accused of being anti-Police.'*

Moving on to the role of the special constabulary, he commented: *'A few weeks ago I raised the subject of the resignation of Chief Superintendent David Webb in Birmingham, on the grounds that he felt obliged to abandon his community work, because he was not getting sufficient support for it from senior officers. It is interesting to note that, among other things, he had been recruiting more and more people, particularly from the ethnic minorities, to the special constabulary.*

Time and again, the approach that has come to be known as community policing has proved to be correct. Again, therefore, we look to the Home Secretary for a lead and an assurance that that approach will be given higher priority, and will be accepted as Government policy for the future. Community policing should not become merely a minor cosmetic for any police force that wishes to be considered progressive. It will be no more than a token if it is suffocated beneath general policing methods which amount to a direct contradiction of it.'

Sadly his words would fall on deaf ears, as a friend of mine in the Lords would discover in the following year.

***

Seeing your name on the front page of *The Times* is an experience. It was a good obituary, a top left corner trailer plus a full spread on page two, continued on the back page.[2] All the nationals had something or other on the story. I even made

---

[1] Hansard, 26th November 1981, 1009 - 1016.

[2] *Community Police Chief retires early,* The Times, 13th October 1981.

BBC News at One. More radio and TV interview requests flooded in, including *Newsnight*, and *Left Right & Centre*. David Steel, leader of the Liberal Party raised the matter with the Home Office and around the Westminster lobbies. The Birmingham Mail grabbed home advantage with *'Why I quit - Police Pioneer'*. They even honoured me with an editorial.

An immediate reaction came from Jim Jardine, Chairman of the Police Federation, the body representing many of those groups who had most criticised me behind the scenes: *'I am in favour of community policing. It has long been practised in the Force. But it can only be brought in gradually and it requires the education of both police officers and the public. Positive policing methods are needed to control riots and maintain law and order.'*

The spokesman for the Birmingham branch of the Federation was equally enthusiastic: *'Some police officers feel that community policing involves too much latitude... Some feel that it should have gone further and some that it has gone too far...'*

Next day, 13th October, the headline in the Birmingham post, *'Community Police chief tells of lack of support'*, was supplemented by a Sunday Mercury editorial, *'We must act on race alert'*.

Responses within the Force generally ranged from *'sad'* and *'dismaying'*, to *'understandable'* and *'inevitable'*. Some were more strident, ranging from *'regrettable'* (that good old code word!), to *'good riddance'*. Martin Burton was promoted and appointed to follow me, and Sir Phillip issued a statement that community policing in Handsworth would continue, both in policy and practice. How effective all this would prove we were to find out four years later. Many of those fourteen year olds we tried so hard to help in 1980 and 1981 would then be blooded among their peers in the 1985 Handsworth riots.

Letters flooded in from around Britain and the world. Many of the writers caused me to wonder if, perhaps, I'd made a mistake, pleading with me to think again, continue the good work in Handsworth. Robert Kilroy Silk, Chairman of the Home Affairs Committee, wanted to know why I was retiring.

One letter especially troubled me, from the mother of a young policeman in the London Metropolitan Force. She had married an Indian naval officer, by then sadly dead, and her son wanted to prove himself, make a success in what he saw as a worthwhile career. *'... Please understand that I am asking you for advice. He would probably be extremely angry with me if he knew of this letter. The point is that he suffers considerably from the somewhat contemptuous treatment he undergoes at the hands not only of the general public, but more specifically from the Police themselves. He joined the Police Force determined to be a good Policeman and that has not changed. But how long does he have to suffer and if the answer is for ever, do you honestly think it will be worth it in the long run?'*

I replied as best I could and asked her to encourage her son to stick at it, but I was not hopeful. The history of the Metropolitan Force since then has not been a good indicator for the future of that young man.[1]

I received just four letters which we might describe as, *not in favour.* Phrases such as *'Good riddance'* peppered a letter from a middle aged lady. I wrote a long apologia in return, and she followed up with a milder rebuke, but I was still her least favourite policeman. A Mr G. R. told me that he was glad that I and others like me were leaving the force: *'Things were never so bad since the immigrants came...'* An anonymous missive arrived on 29th December, a kind of New Year greeting, *'Sucking up to wogs - TRAITOR!'* Another gentleman sent a copy of an open letter addressed both to William Whitelaw and me, claiming that, *'You are responsible for the trouble. You and the immigrants...'*

One letter I did not receive was published in the November edition of the local Police Newspaper, *Beacon.* It was written by a Birmingham Detective Superintendent based at Lloyd House, exactly at the time of my retirement, and revealed a little more than the writer intended.

'The term Community Policing has mystified me for some time now. In the past I thought it merely meant a policeman doing his job in the community of which he was a part. It has been obvious for some time that I was wrong because the media have for some two or three years now credited the Chief Constable of Devon and Cornwall with its creation. However, the media have now admitted their mistake and inform us that the answer is much nearer at hand and community policing was really invented on the very sub-division on which I worked for several years.

If only it had been invented earlier and I could have joined in the fun of such things as having community leaders come along to sort out the problems when the station was besieged by an angry crowd because somebody had been arrested. We were so ignorant in those days that we thought community leaders were elected by the people. There must be many like me who feel they toiled in vain before the great revelation. Why, only two weeks ago I and my wife were able to be part of that community for much longer than we would have been in the past as we sat behind the bus completely blocked by illegally parked cars. To think, in the 'bad old days' we used to move them and let people pass straight through.

Ah well, when I joined they told me I would learn something new every day.'

***

Just a few short weeks to go in a lifetime's career, yet still the pace increased. I cannot here list everything. The list of invitations seemed endless. The Inner

---

[1] See chapter Thirty Two, *Race Memories,* for the proof that things were more corrosive and dangerous than neither I, the Government nor Chief Constables around Britain could ever know.

London Education Authority had visited our Lozells Project and were most appreciative of our hospitality in Handsworth. The University of Technology in Loughborough, after reading my story in the Guardian, offered the possibility of a departmental job on community research and teaching. Chief Constable John Alderson invited regular lecturing at the Devon and Cornwall constabulary training college. Rotary International welcomed me to their annual conference in Torquay. Aberystwyth University invited me to speak to a joint audience of staff and students some time in November. John Moores, later Sir John Moores and founder of the world famous university in Liverpool, invited my contribution to a major study on community policing. As he beguilingly put it, *'A page or so will do...'* Malcolm Feuerstein, documentaries producer at ATV asked for my views on his latest achievement, *'An arranged marriage'.* The BBC invited me to partake in a Newsnight Special on the night of the publication[1] of Lord Scarman's long awaited report on the Brixton affair, sitting alongside a spokesman from Scotland Yard, Roy Hattersley, Paul Boeteng, and a spokesman from the Conservative Party.

In late November Ronald Broome and I sat side by side in the Ravidass temple in Handsworth, and we put forward our views on community policing. No surprise, we appeared to agree. I managed to drop a hint with, as the Evening Mail put it, *'Superintendent Webb warned the leaders of the community and the Police that there would be serious trouble if community policing did not continue.'*

I spent a short time visiting friends in India at the end of November, and sadly missed a letter of invitation to Aston University's open lecture series planned for Spring 1982. The subject of *Police in a multi-cultural society* was one of an on-going series. Speakers included Roy Hattersley MP, Dr Alec Dickson, Founder of Voluntary Service Overseas and Community Service Volunteers. Also present would be Wally Herbert, famous for his three thousand eight hundred mile journey from Alaska via the North Pole to Norway, Phillip Strick the film critic, and Dr Peter Jarman of the *Centre Europeen pour la Recherche Nucleaire* (CERN), famous for his work on quarks, leptons and black holes. A touching pot-pourri.

I returned from India on 2nd December and three days later lectured for the last time at Bramshill to command officers on *'The Handsworth Experience'.* I knew by then that there would be no more invitations to lecture there, and my heart was heavy on the train back to Birmingham New Street. Meanwhile, the British Association of Moslems invited me to their annual dinner. Baroness Seear, Chairman of the House of Lords select committee on unemployment and former President of the Institute of Personnel Management wrote: *'We are sorry to hear that you have resigned. Would you like to speak at a special conference we are holding in the new year to focus on inner cities and the problems these zones face? It will be held at the BBC's Pebble Mill Studios on a Saturday in late February or March 1982.'*

---

[1] Wednesday 25th November 1981.

A host of job offers came in, mainly from security and insurance companies. None of them were of interest. Call it intuition; I wanted to be free, to look around, see the world the way that I saw it, say what I wanted to say, not to be afraid of what I knew to be true, simply because I owed someone a favour. Even at university I could research and teach, but still I would have to conform, be a different kind of pc.

***

They held my retirement presentation at the New Inns Pub on the Soho Road. Chief Superintendents Don Wilson and my successor Martin Burton were there, plus all my PBOs and many from Thornhill Road, and a crowd of my friends from the community. We put on a splendid buffet and something to drink. I was presented with the usual retirement rewards, watches, whisky decanters, brief cases and other things. All tried hard to make it a special event, with happy speech after happy speech, but my heart was heavy. I did not invite anyone from Headquarters. I knew they would not want to be there. The publicity might not fit their agenda. As for me, well, I was just happy to see all my friends, some of whom, fearful for their career, would never speak to me again in private or public.

I asked to see Sir Phillip to say goodbye. Only once before, in 1977, was I in his office, for my promotion to Superintendent. My retirement and public statements had raised questions. Enquiries had circulated in Westminster in the privacy of the Home Secretary's office, and more widely on the floor of the House. Some folks guessed I was exiting under pressure. The Home Office may well have been on the phone to Sir Phillip, *'What the hell is this Webb up to etc.'* No doubt some chief constable colleagues had asked him what was going on. He had been effectively challenged by the West Midlands Police Committee[1] behind closed doors and questioned about my departure. I was later informed that Chairman Edwin Shore had asked, *'What is going to happen to Handsworth? We've tried to persuade Webb to stay but he won't stay.'* As a result the Deputy Chief Constable had been forced to make statements reassuring the public that community policing would continue.

Sir Phillip was not the confrontational type. He would sometimes phone me and ask:- *'Mr Webb, will you do the BRMB phone-in on Handsworth?'*, or *'Mr Webb, will you do the BBC phone in?'* and I would do them. On one occasion Mrs Knight, his wife, phoned to ask me to do a radio programme and thanked me afterwards when I did it. Yet he had given no directives on policy. Over six long years, there were no standing orders, not even a memorandum saying, *'This is what I want you to do.'* So, our second meeting was somewhat frosty. I waited outside for an hour and a half, and was finally ushered in.

'Well Mr Webb,' (He always called me *'Mr Webb'*). *'They tell me you are going.'*

---

[1] *'Pledge given on Police Methods',* Birmingham Post, November 1981. I do not have the exact date.

'Yes Sir.'

'I agree with your recommendation of Chief Inspector Martin Burton as your successor.'

'Yes Sir'.

'After all that has happened, I hope you will not be engaging in a battle of wills with us over Handsworth.'

'No Sir.'

We talked of other matters which will remain confidential, but none suggested I was flavour of the month. There was no *'Thank you for 26 year's service,'* no *'Well done on community policing.'* It was clear that whatever might be said publicly, my community policing Handsworth style would slowly wind down. There was no handshake, no sadness, no friendship. I was going, and that was that. Our conversation drifted to an uneasy conclusion, I stood up, said a crisp *'Thankyou Sir Phillip'*, turned and walked out into the rest of my life.

TWENTY FOUR: A VERY INTERESTING RETIREMENT

It is amazing how quickly things can change. I had signed that letter to Sir Phillip on the 9th October 1981, and was on national radio on the 12th. Within two weeks I was courted by three political parties, each with an eye on the 1983 general election. Then I was scheduled to speak at six British university groups, invited by Robert Kilroy Silk to submit a paper to the Parliamentary All Party Penal Affairs Group, and to explain to his members the reasons for my early retirement. Finally, as the end of 1981 approached, two television programmes were pencilled in for the following January with more programmes on the horizon.

My official last day in the Force was due shortly, but had not yet arrived. Graham Thornton, a local founder member of the Social Democratic Party, had written a mysterious letter saying that he would call round to collect me on the steps of Thornhill Road Station on 4th November. From there he would take me to meet *'a prominent person...'* at the Regional Directorate of the Department of Industry. There must have been some curious glances from those upstairs windows as I walked the few short steps to the waiting car.

Shirley Williams then wrote in her unique style to ask me to speak at a meeting in her Crosby constituency on the subject of community policing. On the local front, Handsworth Labour MP Sheila Wright was to retire at the next general election and there was press speculation that I might succeed her. David Steel invited me to visit him at Westminster to meet with his colleagues.

As a conservative for many years, I had even won the Conservative Bowls Championship. My experiences at Handsworth, however, had proved most educational. As a local police commander, for several years, I had witnessed first hand the effects of Conservative economic policies, and I knew that there were no easy answers to our problems. Moreover, it was the Government's appearance of *not caring* that I found difficult to handle. So, my instincts were somewhere between Labour, Liberal and Social Democrat, and it took me two months to decide. By January 1982, David Steel had seen enough to be confident that I would make a good candidate. My nomination forms for initial membership were despatched and seconded by February 1982, and in April a personal letter from Simon Hughes arrived at my home inviting me to become a member of the Liberal Home Affairs Panel, with special reference to policing issues. It would take until August before David Evans of the Liberal Candidates Committee would write to confirm that my name had been added to the list of Approved Parliamentary Candidates.

After the difficulties of 1981, my heart was once again full of hope. I believed that perhaps in a new role I could fight for the kind of policing that was right for Britain. I would then be in a position to influence matters on a national scale, not just for Handsworth. I revealed my hopes to David Steel:

'It is of course part of my strategy to convert Handsworth and the numerous constituencies over which the community leaders exert influence away from the Labour Party to the Liberal Party...' As events unfolded, it proved harder than I ever imagined.

Elsewhere in the land my friend John Alderson was finding resistance to his policing methods as firm as I had found it, and he, too, decided to seek pastures new. On Tuesday January 5th 1982 he retired five years early, and would soon follow me into the Liberal Party, standing in the June 1983 general election as the candidate for Teignmouth. A perceptive half page feature by Times Home Affairs Correspondent Peter Evans conveyed John's disillusionment. Alderson explained:

'A myth is being perpetuated that the anonymous motorised cop of the 1960s and 1970s can somehow be plucked from his car and transformed overnight into a composite community worker, youth leader, friend, confident and law enforcement officer all rolled up in the catch-all definition - community policing. Cosmetic community policing of this kind devalues a genuine attempt to motivate neighbourhoods against the threat of crime and disorder through the organic evolution of a partnership between Police and public... Under true community policing, Police and community are a controlling influence on crime and disorder.' [1]

Evans concluded his interview by expressing a fear that would be seen by many, within four short years, as a prophecy: *'The departure of Mr Alderson and Superintendent Webb is a warning that, unless Police and government are prepared to act on Lord Scarman's proposals for community policing and greater accountability by the Police, black people's suspicions, already strong, will turn once more into dangerous discontent.'*

The pace on the invitation front increased day by day. 1st January 1982 had seen the annual Ravidass community celebration of the birthday of their guru, and Bet and I spent a wonderful day renewing friendships. The University of Leicester organised an Easter conference on *Scarman and After*, and invited me to partake. The audience included Kenneth Oxford, Chief Constable of Merseyside, and Patricia Hewitt of the National Council for Civil Liberties. The Police and Society Research Centre asked if I could submit a paper of four thousand words on *The Handsworth Community Policing Experiment*. The Royal Forest of Dean Grammar School asked if I could address their sixth form, and the Cranfield Institute welcomed me to Denmark to a conference on *Crime Control Policy*. The University College of Wales at Aberystwyth offered dates in March for an informal talk to a gathering of students and staff. The University of Exeter brought together an intimidating audience of over two hundred post-graduate students to listen, learn, and doggedly question. The hallowed precincts of Cambridge's St Catherine's College housed the 1982 Konigswinter Conference and members of the Social Democratic Party led by Roger

---

[1] *The Times*, Wednesday 6th January 1982.

171

Morgan and Shirley Williams, plus myself, at a large international gathering. The Law School at the University of Warwick asked if I could speak at their Socio-Legal Society Dinner. The Birmingham Association of University Women won my heart with a conference at the charming Winterbourne House in Edgbaston. Birmingham's Swanshurst School sixth form gave me a good grilling. The young men of Handsworth Grammar School joined in my toast to, *'The Bridge Trust Old Boy's Society'*, and sat politely through my entire, over-long, after-dinner speech.

Central TV invited my presence on *Here and Now*, with the final cut shown on 10th January. In the meantime, three more TV appearances loomed ahead. Finally the Apex Trust's conference at Pebble Mill went ahead as planned on 13th March. I managed to meet many of the speakers ahead of the conference, including Paul Boeteng, who examined initiatives for disadvantaged minorities and employment issues. A notable member of the audience was former Deputy Chief Constable of the West Midlands Maurice Buck, by then promoted to Chief Constable of Northamptonshire.

While all this was going on I decided that I might have time to spare, so I contacted Guy Cumberpatch at the University of Aston. Guy, who had worked with me on the Lozells project, found room for me in his programme, and the post of part-time research assistant for three months enabled me to complete my thesis for the Cranfield Institute on the predictable subject of Community Policing. The salary of some £7,000 a year pro-rata was not a fortune, but it helped.

Meanwhile, the world that I had tried so much to change continued on its way. There were rumours of imminent trouble in Toxteth, and inter-racial and Police-versus-community tensions exploded, in St Paul's in Bristol.[1] After what was described as a full scale gang war, lone policeman PC Ian Bennett, returning home from a pub, was set on by a group described as *The St Paul's Gang*, receiving serious injuries in a ferocious attack. One witness recalled: *'We were all very excited. I walked across the road and told the others to forget it. But one boy hit Bennett on the back of the head with a half-brick. Fifty hit him with bricks and glass. Another boy hit him on the head with a baseball bat.'*

Next day, a squad of policemen were accused of a serious attack on a West Indian housewife, a Mrs Royal, as they *'... rampaged through her house looking for the ring leaders of the gang... Neighbours, both white and black, who watched the police raid, are helping Mrs Royal draw up a letter of protest to the Home Secretary... A neighbour of the Royals said 'It was a sight to see. They belted her a right one.' Another neighbour, Mrs Sarah Pearson said: 'I saw her being hit. I was shocked.' ... A Mr Henry said 'We know there are some policemen who don't like us. There's one who came to search my house. I asked him for his warrant. He said 'I don't need a warrant where you coons are concerned..."*

---

[1] *The Observer*, Sunday 7th February 1982

Further invitations flooded in. The National Union of Teachers asked me to lead a workshop on Police, Probation and Community Relations on 20th May 1982. Peter Newsam, Chairman of the Inner London Education Authority, Roy Hattersley and Sir George Young were in attendance. St Martin's College Lancaster was my next venue, followed, in June, by the Convention of Sikhism in Handsworth. The Rotary Club of Tamworth welcomed me to a lunchtime meeting to talk about *Living in a multi-racial society*. The Fabian Society, meeting at Winterbourne, at the University of Birmingham, asked me to talk on *After Scarman - The Police and the Community*. My contacts with local radio bore fruit in an invitation from the BBC, to become a member of the Radio WM local Radio Advisory Council.

My diary took a sinister turn in summer 1982, with an invitation to travel, as a member of the Liberal Home Affairs Panel, to the Friedrich Naumann Foundation seminar, to be held at the frequently bombed Belfast Europa Hotel. It was marching time for the Orangemen of Ulster, and the height of the troubles. I brought a memento back with me, a tiny sky-blue handbook for use by Policemen in Northern Ireland, *General Guidance on Personal Security Measures*. A section entitled *Your Children* contained chilling advice: *'DO NOT:*

1. Allow children to answer the door especially during the hours of darkness.

2. Allow younger members of your family to open your mail.

3. Encourage young children to answer the telephone as they may unintentionally give out information which may be detrimental to you.'

As we sat there in the summer heat discussing possible solutions to that seemingly eternal crisis, I reflected on the stress that my own constables had undergone in the streets of Handsworth. Their unease seemed small compared to the brave men of the Ulster Constabulary. I could not but wonder whether my work in Handsworth might have, after all, some relevance to the people of that troubled province.

I was fortunate to have a repeat opportunity to spread the gospel in Northern Ireland with an invitation to be principal speaker at a conference on policing organised by the Committee on the Administration of Justice, held in Belfast on May 14th. Other speakers included Terry Shields, a member of the Northern Ireland Police Authority, Chief Constable Bill Wilson of the RUC, and the day was chaired by Lord Blease of Cromac.

On 18th November 1982 John Brown's long awaited book, *The Handsworth Experience*, was launched by the National Council for Voluntary Organisations in Bedford Square, London. I had the pleasure of speaking at the launch, alongside Margaret Simey of Liverpool, and John Brown himself. In previous chapters I spoke of the theme and content of John Brown's study, with a host of illustrative quotes, so I will not repeat them here. I will, though, give due attention to the lengthy foreword by Lord Scarman.

The distinguished Lord was to be misquoted and misunderstood by many who had not read his Brixton Report, and sadly, by many that had. The latter included a number of prominent policemen, using selective quotation to justify their own positions, ranging from soft, to hard reactive policing. One that caught my eye was Basil Griffiths, who retired from the Chairmanship of the Police Federation in 1982. His views fairly reflected, I believe, those that I fought so hard against and failed to change while in the Force.

Basil contributed to a conference on *Scarman and After* at Leicester University between 16th and 18th April 1982. I was scheduled to speak but could not attend due to business in India. Basil was then invited to submit an essay to a compilation book of the same name published in 1984.[1] He first examined Scarman's views on the accountability of the Police to society, and the need for chief constables to consult local representatives within the community. Then he moved on to comment that Scarman had made much of the need for senior police officers, when determining action for such offences as misuse of drugs, sexual offences, pornography and public order, to consult local representatives within the community. Yet, Basil believed, such judgements, whether made by a constable exercising his discretion or by a chief officer making a major policy decision, must inevitably be influenced by public expectations.

So far so good. Sadly he then twisted the value of positive local consultation, by quoting a case that he knew of, where a group of locally elected politicians had expressed a wish to assume operational control of the local police. From there he concluded that words spoken by Lord Russell of Liverpool, the British Neuremburg judge, when speaking of the Hitler regime, were relevant to this issue. *'Those who advance the notion of Police accountability might consider that there are those in British politics who show a taste for totalitarianism.*[2]   Thus, within the space of a mere seven sentences, he had taken the argument from a police chief rightly consulting the elected members of his Police Committee, to guilt by association with Hitler's Nazi regime. Sometimes we defend ourselves with steely hoops so strong that belief makes us the prisoner.

Back to Lord Scarman. His Brixton Report was long and detailed, covering every aspect of the Brixton riots and associated matters, providing a rich harvest for those who would cherry pick his thoughts to justify seemingly every social and policing activity imaginable. Lord Scarman's foreword to John Brown's book contains, I believe, the crux of Scarman's entire philosophy, what in his heart he knew to be the reality of Brixton, Handsworth, and every similar community throughout the

---

[1] *Scarman and After - Essays reflecting on Lord Scarman's Report, the riots and their aftermath.* Edited by John Benyon, Pergamon Press, 1984.
[2] This same argument was used by some to describe the activities of the Anti-Nazi League during the National Front meeting in Digbeth in 1978. See Chapter thirteen, *Stormy Weather.*

world. His views on the reluctance of the Police generally to accept the central role of good community relations still strike home.

'My experience has taught me two fundamental truths, The first is that successful policing depends upon us tackling and eliminating basic flaws in our society. Currently the basic flaw is a compound of racial disadvantage and racial prejudice. This truth has to be learnt, and the appropriate cutting-out operation devised and carried out, by society as a whole: by all of us.

The second truth does relate primarily to policing methods. I would simply repeat what I said in paragraph 9.2 of the Brixton Report [1]: 'The Police are not responsible for the disadvantages of the ethnic minorities. Yet their role is critical. If their policing is such that it can be seen to be the application to our new society of the traditional principles of British policing, the risk of unrest will diminish and the prospect of approval by all responsible elements in our ethnically diverse society will be the greater.'

Unfortunately the Police cannot wait for us to get society right. They are on duty now: and in the inner city as well as in the country. They must act swiftly and effectively to suppress public disorder, protect life and property, and enforce the law. The Handsworth Experience, faithfully and vividly told by John Brown in this book, reveals the devastating awkwardness of the Police dilemma. Have they a way through? Are they to stand inevitably condemned - by some as ineffective or by others as oppressive?

Handsworth points to a conclusion, which I suspect many policemen are reluctant to accept. Success will come, only if the Police take the initiative. They have to go out into the community and talk. [They must] talk about their operations and their problems as well as about anodyne (but valuable) things like football, social events, club activities, and winning the interest and confidence of the children. This is not easy, as the uncertain history of the Lozells project shows. If people feel they are the object of imposed Police benevolence, they will turn away. But if the people see the Police as co-operating in their ventures, mutual trust can develop.

I confess that the most disturbing feature, which John Brown wisely does not conceal from us, is that many policemen do not accept the central importance of 'community relations', as sadly the basic British principle of policing by consent has come to be called. They are, I believe, the victims of the technological myth. They appear to think that technological advance is the true professionalism of the Police. They mistake the part for the whole.'

John Alderson too had such issues in mind. He had addressed the Liberal Party Assembly two months previously, on 23rd September 1982. In his view community policing meant local committees controlling operational strategy, but not day-to-day control: *'It is critically important because we need to retain the best*

---

[1] Cmnd 8472; Penguin Books 1982

policing traditions and offer an alternative to the Police becoming the repressive arm of the state.... a repressive police force becomes attractive to some people when economic difficulties arise.'

On the Scarman recommendations, he felt the Government had accepted most of the hard line measures, such as the deployment of plastic and rubber bullets and CS gas, but they had not shown the same fervour on humanising the Police, such as moves to combat racism among police officers.[1]

***

Once I had a friend who was an Earl. He rubbed shoulders with Lords and Princes in the House of Peers, but was not really rich. He would visit Bet and me in our tiny house, and sometimes sleep on the couch. As well as speaking in the Lords on behalf of the Police Superintendents Association, he would drive around England in a bottle green taxi donated by the cabbies of London, whose patron he had become over the years. When not earling in the Lords or taxiing in London, he would go to Algeria to give his time, strength and as much as he could spare to a quarter of a million refugees displaced during the Franco-Algerian wars and now forgotten by the world. Rejected by their own Government, they lived in tents, dilapidated homes and in squalor on the edge of the Sahara Desert. It was there, among that tired persecuted nation, he learned the realities of life on earth. Singer Cliff Richard and actor Bob Hoskins were active with him during the 80's. His wife Shirley was born in Handsworth and they loved the place, following every move I made with great interest. They loved to walk the streets with me and talk to the people on the sidewalks. Sadly, he died many years ago and I miss him greatly. His name was Christopher Winchelsea, Earl of Nottingham.

One day in July 1982 a wonderful letter arrived from Christopher and Shirley, enclosing an invitation to visit the House of Lords. Christopher was hoping to test the Government's record on implementation of the community policing measures advocated by Lord Scarman. He had scheduled several questions of the Minister.

Although I had seen it from the outside on visits both as tourist and student on Police courses, it was my first visit to Westminster's Parliament building. I knew many of the people responsible for policing the building and its surroundings, so all was not too strange. As Christopher and I were treading the wide stairway up to the public gallery, a sparrow-like man in a dark, slightly crumpled suit was coming down. It was Lord Scarman. The dark suit reached out to shake my hand and that mischievous face wrinkled into a shy, charming smile. We exchanged a word or two.

---

[1] *Warning on dangers of Police State,* Conference report in The Birmingham Post, 4th September 1982.

Nothing special, just a *'Nice to see you again David'*. Still, we knew each other's thoughts.

Christopher's questions did not make it through the order paper and he had to be content with written answers. Usually such answers might take up to twenty three days, yet the reply arrived within a week. Christopher was convinced that the speedy response meant that the Home Office did not want the same question to be repeatedly published as it made its way up the order paper. Furthermore the minister's reply seemed, Christopher later confessed, somewhat suspicious: *'The Police Service generally has responded well to the Scarman Report and many police forces have introduced community policing schemes tailored to local conditions. Statistical information about these schemes is not collated centrally and can only be provided at a disproportionate cost.'*

In other words the Home Office did not know, few police forces could provide evidence of any kind of community policing strategy or action, and it seemed to the Government to be rather unimportant. The Home Office knew why the question had been put and my role in it all. Yet it would have taken only forty two phone calls to discover the truth, a good and worthwhile day's work on behalf of the people of Britain.

I once asked Christopher what he thought about my enforced departure from Handsworth. He thought for a moment and smiled. *'It always seemed to me that Sir Phillip and his colleagues were confused. They couldn't understand the message so they decided to shoot the messenger.'*

TWENTY FIVE: INTO POLITICS

Westminster's hurly-burly came at me faster than I had ever imagined. From those first probing letters from the main parties, I had eventually settled on the Liberals. Yet which constituency should I represent? In August David Steel had offered an October 1982 by-election chance at Birmingham Northfield. After thinking about it for a couple of weeks and after many attempts by my friends at persuasion, mainly by my close colleague Sidney Caro, Secretary of the Handsworth Liberal Association, I reluctantly turned it down. I just did not feel ready to take on a strange suburb, one in which I would be a virtual stranger. In the event, Labour's John Spellar fought a good campaign, easing home just three hundred votes ahead of Conservative Roger Gale.

The General Election of June 1983 offered more hope. There were several options, but I was not the one who would decide. Many things had to be weighed in the balance by the two Davids, Owen and Steel. I dearly wanted to stand in Handsworth, confident that if I did, my contacts and experience would almost guarantee success. Others did not see it that way, and the SDP/Liberal negotiations failed. David Owen refused to concede Handsworth and my only remaining option proved again to be Northfield, containing what is now the great Rover/MG complex, and still far outside my experience. David Steel was really apologetic about it all, but there was nothing he could do. To make a special case for me would create a precedent in the remaining negotiations.

Eyebrows in police circles must have furrowed curiously when I laid out the SDP/Liberal Alliance policing manifesto in the June 1983 edition of *Police Review*. I restated everything I'd tried to do at Handsworth, hoping that most of the officers who had experienced the 1981 riots would now agree that the only hope would be one of joint collaboration between Police and People. With more policemen on foot patrol we could increase the potential for personal communication and rapport with individual members of the public. I feared that respect for the Police would rapidly fade if rubber bullets and water cannon became a natural part of Police armoury. We supported the creation of an independent authority for the investigation of complaints against the Police, all highly unpopular in police circles. Even less popular, we proposed the setting up of a new controlling body in London, with an all-party Select Committee composed of London MPs, to which the Home Secretary would be answerable.

Even though it was but six days before the Election, I felt it was important to make these statements. Michael Meacher, at that time MP for Oldham, on an opposite page, also supported our proposals for community policing and was against the insensitive use of SPG type units. He felt it was too easy for five year's hard work by community officers in one area to be ruined overnight by the deployment of an SPG unit with a fire brigade approach. I could not have expressed it better.

Campaigning was a thankless task. Bet and I did all our own publicity, printing leaflets, cards and reminders, *'Sorry you were not in...'* letters. Then we walked the patch, all of it. Occasionally, against much competition from established Liberal candidates around the Midlands, we managed to get the services of the tannoy van, charging up and down the Bristol Road, frightening shoppers and dogs alike. Since we were far from my contacts in Handsworth, it was impossible to obtain local help. It felt like me and Bet versus the world.

Spellar had the advantage of being in office for some two hundred days following his 1982 victory. Conservative candidate Roger King had been a former Austin-Morris apprentice before setting up his own business, and the Rover/MG works and the surrounding suburbs held a rich vein of willing assistants. Luckily my contacts with the Birmingham Post and Mail, and links with newspapers around the suburbs, helped somewhat, and I got my views well into the public arena. It was hard going. You learn quickly how to accept rejection, even contempt, right in your face. Still, I felt I could give them all a run for their money. In the event, King swept in, translating many of his Rover contacts into votes and beating Spellar by two thousand, seven hundred and sixty votes. I got more than ten thousand, pretty good for a first timer and an outsider. Headlines in the local papers included *Bitter-sweet night for City's Hopefuls*, and above was a photo of Roger King celebrating with hands held high, and Spellar and myself standing glumly behind him. I determined then that next time things would be different. No more Northfields for me.

From shortly after my retirement I searched for a new career which would pay the bills. My pension was half pay and I had a mortgage on the house. Fees for visiting speakerships, and sometimes not too generous expenses, added little to the weekly income. So, what to do? I knew that my contacts in India and the Asian continent might prove useful, as well as those in and around Handsworth, extending across the entire city. In the event I chose a combination of activities that would hopefully use all of these factors in a productive way.

In 1982 I had rented an office in Soho House lying on the boundary between Handsworth and West Bromwich. I developed three activities, and by the end of 1983 deserved, I believed, a pat on the back. My legal and policing experience was useful to a local solicitor and an association was formed under which I advised him and his clients on court and other cases. Many clients initially sought my advice maintaining that they were innocent when I knew they were not. Their faces were a picture when the advice bounced back across the desk to the effect that they had better plead guilty or find another adviser.

Frequent visits to India enabled the creation of some good business relationships. The concept of an import-export company based in Handsworth was realised with the purchase of a small factory warehouse in Booth Street, and the formation of a sports supply company, *Aries International*. I hoped to develop it as a family enterprise. Bet was our company secretary. Even today not many folk understand that many of the high quality sports goods they buy in the shops are made in India, and much of the software used and sold by major suppliers is written in India and shipped by satellite to the West.

The third strand to my bow was my knowledge of Asian businessmen around Birmingham. Many I knew to be victims of bad legal advice and poor insurance policies. Indeed the location of their premises and frequent troubles in the city meant high insurance premiums. In some cases cover was refused by all the main companies. A close friend of mine, who ran an insurance brokerage in Nottingham, came to see me, and together we worked out a method that would give Asian businesses a better and faster service than ever before. To boot, I would supply quality advice on legal matters, social problems and import-export complications. I put the whole thing together under the name *Federation of Asian Businesses*. I made sure that my West Indian friends were not excluded, and within months I had two hundred members with more added each day. Thus I survived.

Mohammed Ali came to town in August of that year and James Hunte was like a dog with two tails. His work among the West Indian peoples had reached the ears of the great man himself, and James was honoured by an invitation to visit Mohammed's home in Los Angeles. From there came a promise that there would be a visit to Handsworth to officially open the Mohammed Ali Centre, a social and sports club in Lozells that James and his colleagues had set up with support from the City Council. On 6th August the long, gleaming convoy arrived, driving through streets littered with crumbling houses and shops. Just about every politician, journalist and sports fan in the Midlands tried to get in camera shot. There was shouting, singing, confusion, almost a riot, until the man himself could squeeze into the place and cut the ribbon.

In 1987 I was to try again for election for the Liberal Democrats. After that 1983 failure in Northfield, this time around I would try closer to home. David Steel wrote on 30th October to say that the news was not good. The Ladywood constituency, which I preferred, could not be agreed. There was even a suggestion that I might fight as an independent Liberal, but David advised against it as *'both politically and personally damaging'*. Perry Barr, which included the Handsworth ward, was inviting an approach. Nevertheless it was unfamiliar territory and Jeff Rooker seemed unshakeable. The Tories shipped in barrister John Taylor from the comfortable suburbs of Solihull. John came from a black West Indian family. He was a councillor and the son of a Test cricketer. So, for me, against these two heavyweights, standing even this close to home would be an uphill struggle.

As the Alliance candidate, I told the potential voters: *The electorate in Perry Barr are a unique set of people. They are multi-racial and live in an area which outwardly reflects the extremes of wealth and opulence, as well as the most abject poverty, deprivation and despair.*

How can even well-intentioned Conservative supporters relate Tory policy on the national scale to what has happened to their fellow constituents in this area? Massive unemployment, poor housing, unacceptable levels of crime and disorder are now the everyday face of living in the constituency. The present Tory policy will do nothing to alleviate our plight.

Labour supporters will also be only too well aware that the spectre of the Loony Left lurks menacingly over this City, and that internal strife will burst out into the open as soon as this General Election is over.

There is no longer any need to choose between the two extremes previously available to the people of this constituency. Alliance policies combine moderation with practical common sense, and will benefit the people of Perry Barr, whatever their previous political allegiance, creed or ethnic origins.

My friend Said Abdhi was a Labour man, working for Jeff Rooker. Said had the job of standing outside the polling station to persuade all his Asian friends to vote for Rooker and not me. He was most apologetic. *'I cannot help it, David, you are my best friend, almost a brother, but Jeff Rooker is the Labour Party candidate and this is what I have to do, I have to help him...'* All the Indian ladies, due to the tradition of following their husband's advice, would also be persuaded.

Knocking on every door would not win, in spite of an ever present TV camera at my shoulder. Most windows had a big poster - *Vote Labour.* The door would open and I would explain who I was. *'Yes, hello Mr Webb. It's nice to see you. I supported all that you did in Handsworth. You did a great job.'*

I would say, *'Do you know what the Labour Party policy is on this, that and the other..?'*

'No.'

'Well what if I explained my policy to you on this and that and the other..?'

'I would agree with you one hundred percent'

'Then why are you voting Labour?'

'Because I've voted Labour all my life.'

Party experts calculated that a candidate could expect around four thousand votes from floating voters and members of the opposite sex. The rest was traditional. In some constituencies, a monkey could stand and, provided his photo did not appear in the papers, he would get elected. I came third, losing by around three thousand votes. Taylor lost by two thousand. The Tories of Cheltenham had turned him down as a potential candidate, probably because of his colour, and he was later to be given a peerage, probably by way of compensation for his sterling work as a councillor.

TWENTY SIX: MORE RIOTS, TWO DEAD

The Policemen are helmeted in traditional high helmets, badges gleaming, pristine uniforms, soft leather gloves. Behind them some wise shopkeepers have boarded their windows, amid a row of shops already empty and secure with corrugated sheeting.

The sergeant in charge points to something in the distance. A large stone flies past, skipping along the tarmac. The squad retreats in chaos to the shelter of a big red fire engine.

Along this terraced street, a crazy cocktail of dustbins and milk crates forms a barrier, and behind that, like beached whales, are overturned cars, one already spitting smoke and fumes from its filler tube. Further behind is an always moving, running flock of young men and teenagers, some hurling missiles high over the barriers towards the police.

Now the ranks have regrouped. Still in those old helmets, but now with body length perspex shields, arms locked in a human python that stretches from wall to wall, undulating towards the distant rioters. A dark cascade of bricks, sticks and smoking fire bombs arcs over the burning cars towards the snaking line, and it shudders and rejoins as a young constable falls bleeding to the pavement, to be claimed and dragged away by colleagues.

By their side, in simple terraced doorways, seeming cocooned from all danger, stand curious residents, some black, some Asian, some white. An old couple lean across their doorstep, the husband manoeuvres his false teeth around his mouth into a grotesque smile, glances at his tiny grey wife and then back at the distant baying crowd. He seems far away, dazed, perhaps recalling halcyon days when neighbour doorstepped with neighbour as a warm sun whiled away a tradesman's weekend and all had a job. He draws his grey pullover tight around his shoulders, licks his lips nervously and moves his upper dentures once more into that most peculiar smile.[1]

***

It was 1985. I was no longer a Policeman. Still, there remained that promise to the people of Handsworth that I would not go away. I was not going to pack my tent

---

[1] This account of the 1985 Handsworth riots is based on some 500 press articles, interviews, TV recordings, magazines, each containing different versions and interpretations. I cannot in this book give each its due and will inevitably be accused of selective bias. I hope in time to find a way of making them available for students, historians and policemen. I would also recommend a wide ranging study by Elaine Thomas, which surveys world literature on the subject and is available on the Internet. Do not be discouraged by the title. *Muting interethnic conflict in post-imperial Britain: the success and limits of a liberal political approach.*

and disappear into retirement as others had done. Within the limits imposed by my December 1981 promise to Sir Phillip of non-interference in policing issues, I was determined to ensure that community policing would stay in the public eye. I have never changed my view on that and never will. It is too important.

Dave Boucher, Bini Brown and all my old contacts were still there on the various panels, committees and action groups. I met them every week or so, together with beat constables and other officers, some of whom had worked for me at Thornhill Road. We all sat on the panels alongside or opposite each other. It was interesting for me, and for them.

My friend Sidney Caro retired as Chairman of the Patient's Social Committee of the All Saint's Psychiatric Hospital[1], and I succeeded him until 2001 when the place, after seemingly decades of impending closure, finally closed. I also stayed on as Chairman of the Handsworth panel of the Community Relations Council for Birmingham. Sadly, personality clashes would develop between members of the main council. Immediately after the riots that summer, the Asians would allege that the West Indians were beginning to dominate. All twenty Indian, Pakistani and Bangladeshi members resigned and reformed into an independent group called the *Birmingham Advisory Liaison Committee*. Eventually the national Commission for Racial Equality and the City Council became so disillusioned that they agreed to disband everything. After that the City Council employed a permanent staff running various advisory groups among the different communities.

Between 1981 and 1985 I had no access to police intelligence or information, and I never asked. I knew though, in spite of assurances to the media that *'Community policing is continuing'*, they were steadily winding down the projects that we had pioneered. Unknown to the Chief Constable, several officers contacted me during the summer of 1985, telling, in confidence, of a general drop in morale, of the dismantling of projects, and the substitution of watered-down ideas that were intended to pass for community policing. The intense methods of community policing that I developed, leading from the front, accessible to anyone, night or day, had disappeared almost immediately after my retirement. All that important leadership and momentum was lost. I had repeatedly warned in the press, and at those meetings I was able to get to, that there would be further flare-ups similar to the 1981 outbreak, due, as I put it, to: *'A potent mixture of massive unemployment, social deprivation, lack of amenities, cultural ignorance, and a jigsaw of racial backgrounds.'*

Martin Burton, by then a superintendent, responded to the same reporter's questions with the comment that *'David Webb's version of community policing went with him in 1981.'* There was now *'... a much more realistic approach'.*[2]

---

[1] A vast Victorian complex, built around 1900, on the Handsworth - Winson Green border.
[2] Express and Star, Monday 16th September 1985

Those Superintendents who succeeded me, even though the job was later up-graded to the level of chief superintendent, were never given the autonomy that I had enjoyed. Those projects that did continue became just a job, no longer a vocation. Over a relatively short span of four years, most of our pioneer schemes had disappeared. Reactive policing was seen to be back and given a free hand. Under the new policy, Handsworth would be policed by the same methods as those used by every other force. Every year, or in one case, six months, a new chief with his own style and priorities was appointed to Handsworth's Thornhill Road Station. None of them were allowed the time nor opportunity to develop the required personal relationships with all levels of the community. Their policies failed to allow for the truth that the eleven-year-old juvenile of today, surrounded each waking hour by unemployment, poverty and criminal role models, is the eighteen-year-old thug of tomorrow. Or, maybe they did understand it, but they did little to prevent it.

In May 1985, seventeen people had been arrested for drugs offences at the Villa Cross pub. In July drugs with a street value of £1,500 were found in a raid on the Acapulco Cafe. In the first week in September angry residents claimed that a *softly softly* approach was proving ineffective against the drug pushers. Even children, it was said, were being used as carriers. Eric Faux, Chairman of the Handsworth Soho Road Residents Association said that people were frightened to leave their homes at night or even in the day for fear of mugging attacks. Local MP Jeff Rooker commented that the Villa Cross pub was a disgrace. A spokesmen for Ansells, the owners, said that there had been a problem with drugs, but it had been cleaned up.[1]

There seemed to be an increasingly reactive Police stance towards youngsters on the streets. The Villa Cross pub should have been closed down long before, together with the Acapulco Cafe. The Police had the power and means, official and unofficial, as I had in 1977 and 1978, to move the pushers to another area. Their hope that drug pushing and purchasing would stop with a few doors smashed in and two dozen arrests was an illusion. The drug trade, after that first addictive purchase, is driven by insidious demand, and addicts will always find a way. Headlines like *'Police chief serves notice on drug barons'* and *'Rubber bullets the answer - Police Chief'* might reassure the public that something was being done but would, predictably, prove ineffective.

There had always been high unemployment, but things seemed to me to be even worse than in 1981. Listening to my friends and colleagues in Handsworth, and some of the young West Indians and Asians who came to me for help with employment and other advice, Handsworth seemed to be a tinderbox waiting for a spark.

A hint of impending troubles occurred on Sunday 14th July 1985 after the sixth Handsworth Festival, opened officially by Chief Constable Geoffrey Dear. A

---

[1] Wolverhampton Express and Star, Tuesday Sept 10th 1985

group of around thirty youths, some black, some Asian, some white, hurled bricks and bottles at policemen called to investigate a disturbance. Reinforcements were called in and three constables suffered minor injuries.

On Monday September 9th the major Handsworth riot began. From the many reports in national and local papers and from statements by eye witnesses, it appeared to start at around 5.00 pm that evening. Geoffrey Dear's account seemed to be the most accurate, but I fear that the total mistrust between community and Police caused potentially important evidence from eyewitnesses among the West Indian and other sections of the population to be studiously ignored.

A patrolling motor-cycle policeman noted that a car parked outside a cafe recently raided by drug squad officers had no tax disk. The driver was recognised as someone disqualified from driving, and an arrest was attempted. West Indian youths, allegedly mostly involved in the sale of drugs, poured out of the cafe to rescue their *brother*, reinforcements were called up and a pitched battle followed. Eleven officers were hurt in hand to hand fighting. If you have read my earlier chapters on 1976 to 1978, and managed to get this far, the sequence may sound familiar.

An eyewitness, a local worker for NACRO[1] saw something different, claiming that all was sparked off when the police motorcyclist gave the driver of the car without a tax disk a ticket for parking on a double yellow line. *'They then proceeded to assault that individual and to handcuff him and throw him in the back of the police car. A young black lady was passing by and she was subjected to physical violence. She was punched in the face and thrown to the floor by one of those police officers.'*[2] I doubted this, as most of the other accounts confirmed the story of the young constable, and an assiduous search by various means never did discover the identity of the mystery black lady.

From around 6.00 pm a series of hoax calls to non-existent incidents came in, but the situation when checked was all calm. The manufacture of petrol bombs had begun in an illegal gambling den overlooking the Villa Cross Bingo Hall. At around 7.00 pm two masked black men opened three crates of petrol bombs and distributed them. Towards 8.00 pm a disused bingo hall at the Villa Cross pub was set on fire by a group of youths. The fire crew attempting to put out the blaze were attacked with bricks, bottles and petrol bombs. A mob of some two hundred gathered in Villa Road, and the thirty three officers there were unable to break up the riot. More reinforcements were called in. One shop in the Lozells Road was looted and set ablaze, then more, until a whole row of shops was looted and burning. Within thirty minutes, more rioters arrived and started to organise. Fuel spilling from a petrol tank was used to make more petrol bombs. A supermarket and post office were among the buildings destroyed by fire. Two Asians hiding in their post office, Kassamali

---

[1] National Association for the Care and Resettlement of Offenders.
[2] Birmingham Post Sept 10th 1985.

Moledina and his brother Amirali, were burned to death, and would be discovered by firemen 7.00 am next morning.

Meanwhile the news was flashed on TV and radio. More trouble makers descended on Handsworth from as far away as Wolverhampton. Police regained control, block by block, from around 11.00 pm. Chief Constable Geoffrey Dear rushed from a conference in Eastbourne to tour the area during the early hours. Some thirty five people were in custody and more arrests were expected.

Next day Home Secretary Douglas Hurd, appointed to the job only a week previously, drove in to view the damage for himself. Walking with the aid of a stick, his immaculate white hair stood prominent among the faces of the crowd. He managed to speak to a few white and Asian residents, and then tried to talk to a throng of angry West Indian locals. A heated exchange grew to a scuffle and then to near-riot as bricks and bottles were hurled towards the Home Secretary. Camera crews were knocked to the ground and one camera stolen. A hasty retreat protected by Geoffrey Dear and local politicians steered the shocked minister to a police riot van, and the convoy sped back towards the city centre. That evening a repeat riot erupted in Soho Road, and firemen attending a blazing shop in Villa Road were forced to turn back under a hail of missiles and petrol bombs. Cars were overturned and shops looted in surrounding streets.

More than fifty shops had been badly damaged or burnt out. Seventy four policemen, two firemen and thirty one civilians were injured. Two hundred and ninety one people had been arrested, including thirty eight Asians and forty six whites, all in all more than twenty five percent non-West Indian. In spite of this, to the media, it was a *black riot*. More than five hundred police reinforcement officers from across the West Midlands had attended in vans and on foot.

***

Overnight, anger has stalked these streets and alleys, curling its wings over the rooftops, raking its claw into the heart of the people. Corner shops that other times dispense cheer to friends and family are locked in slabs of chipboard, doors and windows sealed, all light and air, the world itself, excluded. Still, the auto-pilot of society murmurs on and milkmen go their ways. Hand drawn floats whine like obedient dogs along streets pocked with droppings of the beast of yesterday, rubble and broken glass, and congealed blood.

The policemen in this quiet street are better clad. They came on duty an hour ago, with newly allocated helmets and visors and some with perspex shields. Others, still, carry dustbin lids, by now battered and misshapen. A large white van, rear doors open wide, a crouching patrol group sitting deep within, reverses slowly. Around it, padding like infantry beside an advancing tank, are more constables, dustbin lids at the ready, eyes searching every window and doorway. Smoke from a *still smouldering car loops around the corner and spirals between the line of constables. Suddenly the line hardens and closes. A young dreadlocked man is sprinting towards the now solid phalanx, behind him more policemen in inevitable chase.*

He weaves a crazy zig zag from pavement to pavement, despairing as the line closes around him, then falls and spins and rolls to his knees, gripped by many strong arms. Young children, West Indian, white, Asian, stand upon the edge of the opposite pavement, silent in Sunday best, shoes buckled and shining, white socks neatly drawn, as the flailing bodies stumble past. There, in the centre, a young black man trapped as a fish in a net, slowly subsiding, pinned by a triangle of riot shields against a garden wall. Around them, touching the black helmets with yellow pollen, hang sprays of late summer roses, petals now fading to brown.

Nearby, on Lozells Road, windows and doors are smashed, black, gaping eyes of a life now destroyed. A builder's yard, a timber merchants, a warehouse, a garage, a shop, a post office, black, burned, empty front collapsed, a tangle of melted stock and shelving, water streaming from upstairs pipes melted by the flames. On every wall and doorpost where whiteness still remains, clings the red, blue and black graffiti of an anger that passed through in the night..

In a temple along the Soho Road gather leaders of the Sikhs, red, white and yellow turbans, long beards black and grey. Two of their companions are dead, roasted alive as they cowered in the back room of their post office, built over twenty hard years. In the confusion, no-one knew they were there, their screams drowned by the cat-calls of the mob and the wail of sirens. Fire fighters, damping down the ashes next morning would find them, charred and blackened, curled like babes in the wood.

The guru speaks a strange language, his companion translates a message of peace and harmony. They stand and sing together. The sound of mourning rises above the harmonium and the deep beat of the tabla, reminding of the lament of the wanderer through the ages. Their companions are dead, the heart of the people has faltered, and in the eyes of many in Britain they remain just wogs and pakis.[1]

***

The Sun led[2] with probably the angriest media reaction, rushing out a *Blitz Issue* of seven full pages. Alongside a front page photo of a young West Indian menacingly carrying an already lit petrol bomb, it roared: *'HATE OF A BLACK BOMBER - By Ian Hepburn, who was attacked by the mob - A BLACK thug stalks a Birmingham street with hate in his eyes and a petrol bomb in his hand. The prowling West Indian was one of the hoodlums who brought new race terror to the city's riot-torn Handsworth district yesterday. And as darkness fell over the smoke-blackened*

---

[1] Based on media coverage of the 1985 Handsworth riots.
[2] 11th September 1985.

ruins of a stunned community, fresh violence flared last night as hundreds of police in riot gear faced gangs hurling petrol bombs and stones.'

Local black community leader Gus Williams laid the blame on Geoffrey Dear. *'The impression as far as the black community is concerned is that he is determined to make his reputation on the heads of the black people. There has been insensitive policing which has destroyed the good relationships they built up over the last ten years.'*[1]

Within hours the causes[2] were assiduously hunted down and, predictably, cause was confused with symptom. Jeff Rooker MP blamed sheer criminality, then later, deprivation. Clare Short MP found racism and poverty. The events outside the Acapulco Cafe were seen as the cause, a conspiracy by drug pushers was seen as the cause, or thuggishness of young blacks, or hooliganism, or greed, or unemployment, or bad housing, or softly softly policing, or reactive hard policing, or slow police reaction to the initial skirmish, or police over-reaction, or West Indian resentment of the success of the Asian shopkeepers and businessmen. Mrs Whitehouse blamed TV editors and coverage of rioting in South African townships. The City Council's housing policies, Government restrictions on funding of inner city areas were the cause. Enoch Powell's chilling logic identified immigration policies as the cause. Even I, and my concept of community policing, were said by at least one senior policeman to be the cause.

***

Perhaps *he came as young man from the Empire Windrush as it touched Liverpool Dock on that first momentous day in 1948. Now a pensioner, grey haired, collar and tie neatly pressed, his eyes are troubled.*

'I could see four policemen in the back of my house, and they pulled...' He draws breath. '... one lad... and they had him on the ground.. and they were smashing him... hitting him with their batons and so on... and he was bleeding all over his face... till he's past it... till he passed out.

So I called to them, I said, 'What do you think you're doing? What you beating him for? You have him. You've handcuffed him. Why don't you take him? And he said, 'Why don't you keep quiet.' And I said, 'This is my house, and you break my gate down to come in here. Why should I keep quiet. Do you want to kill him? You talk about peace. That's how you're going to treat the lad, how do you expect peace when you do things like this?'

Up to that night of the incident, the police was here. We gave them coffee. My wife made coffee for them out there. About twelve policemen were there, we all gave

---

[1] Wolverhampton Express & Star, Sept 10th 1985.

[2] This list is from a trawl of all those newspapers and TV programmes who covered the two days of events and the aftermath. Many of those commenting would perhaps now accept that they were restating the problem rather that finding a cause or a solution.

them coffee. But ever since then, I'd changed my mind, because I wouldn't expect...'
He swallows and hesitates. '...officers, police officers, to be doing that. I'd heard
about it, that things like that happen, but I'd never seen it, nothing like that before.'[1]

***

I was heartbroken. Around me I had watched things go downhill for years.
The people I knew, working shopkeepers, the club owners, my friends on the various
associations and neighbourhood groups, they were not fools. They could see it too.
Successful policing in Handsworth had always needed a careful touch, yet there we
were, back in Starsky and Hutch mode, just like in 1975. I fired a broadside and let
the bullets fly where they may:

'Anyone who says he is amazed by what has happened in Handsworth needs
his head examining. The area has always been a powder keg... The warning signs
have been there long enough. We have young people all over the area disaffected
because of high unemployment and the difficulty in communicating their grievances
to the authorities.'[2]

Copy cat mini-riots and skirmishes broke out across the Midlands. On
September 10th, nearby Perry Barr suffered the attention of a fifty strong mob, some
wearing masks. Terrified shop keepers cowered in back rooms as looters smashed
their way along a row of shops in the local shopping precinct. In Coventry ten people
were arrested after smashing high street windows. Stechford, the constituency of Roy
Hattersley, experienced overnight devastation of a garage owned by an Asian family.
Even the National Exhibition Centre was affected. American TV companies almost
pulled out of coverage of a World Featherweight title fight featuring local hero Pat
Cowdell. Promoter Frank Warren's dash to the USA for last minute negotiations
saved the day. Fear, tangible fear, was in the air. Mr Jashwant Sohal, representing the
traders in Lozells Road, spoke for his members. If the Police could not guarantee
protection, they would form their own vigilante groups. A magistrate involved in the
Birmingham court hearings for some of the accused rioters refused to give her name
to the press for fear of reprisals on her home or her family.

A *TV Eye* special was laid on in St Andrew's Hall, attended by people from all
over Handsworth, white, Asian, West Indian and others. On the stage was Gus
Williams, Deputy Chief Constable Les Sharpe, Alderman Neville Bosworth and
Jaswant Sohal of the Birmingham Community Relations Council. I despaired. There
we all were, shouting at each other, seeking all kinds of causes, alleging all kinds of
incidents, and talking about *community policing*. Sadly, none of those who spoke

---

[1] *Handsworth Songs,* On-camera interview of a Handsworth resident on the day after the first 1985
riot. Black Audio Film Collective, 1986.
[2] *Ex-Police chief warns of economic ghost town,* Birmingham Post 11th September 1985.

seemed to understand what they meant by the term, nor what the other speakers meant by it. I did my best to pull them together for the sake of the community, but it was a difficult meeting, and no-one was in listening mode. The producer kindly gave my section of the programme the last word in the edited version, and we ended on a positive note. Still, to the white folks across the Midlands we remained the Neighbours From Hell.

The Sunday Times of 15th November revealed that, apart from what was by then seen as a root cause, deprivation and long term unemployment, other factors had been at play. They claimed that Superintendent David Love, appointed in April 1985 to Handsworth sub-division, had little experience of community policing, coming as he did from a desk job at headquarters in the complaints and management services department. Love last served in Handsworth many years previously as a sergeant. On arrival in his new role at Thornhill Road, he promptly switched the emphasis away from community policing, to what he called more *'traditional and vigorous methods'*. Another factor was rumoured to be a drop in morale at Thornhill Road. A number of PBOs were stopped from going into pubs and clubs to talk to the locals, and had their community roles reduced. Confidence was dropping, and, at the end of August 1985, they had demanded and obtained a crisis meeting with superiors, in order to discuss their grievances.[1]

All this time a convenient labelling system was developing in the media. *Drug Barons* were rapidly promoted to *Drug Kings*. Love went public at an early stage, claiming that preliminary findings had revealed that drug dealers had 'orchestrated' the violence. He agreed that he and his officers had in recent months opted for a more forceful approach in cracking down on dealers. Love furthermore claimed that the drugs trade were a party to what had happened and may have helped stir up the riot. *'It is now clear that this disorder was not as spontaneous as it would have appeared at first'*. Preliminary investigations showed that petrol bombs were indeed ready and waiting for police and fire services arriving at the scene. *'If drug dealers thought the riot would earn them a respite from police activity they would be very wrong.'*[2]

I was fortunate, living and working among the Handsworth folk for many years, gaining a better understanding than the average police commander of what made the youth of Handsworth tick. One commentary, which today I still respect, was by Robert Kilroy Silk, in *Police Review*.[3] If there was a single nail in all this, he hit it fair and square on the head. Speaking of Douglas Hurd he said: *'Despite his view of the criminal elements behind the riot, the Home Secretary did acknowledge the serious problems of unemployment and social and economic deprivation of the area. That's why £24 million has been poured into its soulless streets in the last four years.*

---

[1] The Sunday Times, 15th September 1985 - *'Riot - Tension was rising for months'.*
[2] Birmingham Post 17th September 1985.
[3] I have one quibble - his use of the word *traditional* as meaning hard, reactive policing.

And so he should. For whatever was the immediate cause - whether it was a reaction to increased police activity, the police raid on the Villa Cross pub and its drug dealers, or the apprehending of a motoring offender - the fact remains that the young people of the area, and especially the blacks, are deprived and alienated; they have no future and are without hope. They have nothing to lose by taking to the streets and a great deal of energy and resentment and frustration to get rid of...

More important is that there appears to have been a shift away from community policing and the implementation of a more traditional and formal approach. This, it seems, not only led to a reduction in the number of officers engaged in community policing, but also a reduction of contact with local community groups and a loss of morale among local police officers.'

Alongside that opinion, was a well argued case by Wayne Francis, Home Affairs Correspondent of the Birmingham Post. *'Out of 1,434 school leavers in Handsworth this year only 99 found jobs. Asians were more successful than Afro-Caribbeans with 42 Asians finding jobs compared with eight Afro-Caribbeans and 49 other races... In the 19 to 24 age group 50.5 percent are unemployed. Against this background many social observers and some senior police officers have repeatedly said the area was a powder keg with high urban tension.'* It was uncanny. It was as if I was again reading John Brown's assessment of youth unemployment prior to the 1981 riot.

In November 1985, a local resident of Handsworth, authoress and travel writer Devia Murphy, would publish her account[1] of life inside Handsworth. Her expertise was undeniable, living as she did almost at the spot where the 1985 riot had begun. In a telling sentence, she advised that we would all do well to study the inner city situation more closely: *'It is often said that Britain would benefit from anthropologists observing our tribal rituals as we used to do in the Third World.'* She went on to describe the events leading up to the 1985 riot. Her contacts with local Rastafarians had made her aware of rising tension in the area and her account was both detailed and disturbing: *'It was noticeable how the policing changed when I was there. In about July (1985), foot patrols were replaced by police in cars - which seemed much less friendly, more threatening.'*

The reality of Chief Constable Dear's position would later emerge, not through any admission that things might have been better handled, but in what he did. On 22nd September 1985, enquiries by Sunday Times researchers Dorothy Wade and Mazher Mahmood discovered that senior police officers in Birmingham were planning to move away from the hard line policing endorsed but a few days earlier by David Love.[2] Unnamed officers senior to Love were said to be admitting that they had been unaware of rising tension. They had not understood the implications of the

---

[1] *Tales from Two Cities,* Devia Murphy, published by John Murray, 1985.
[2] *Asians oppose softer policing.* Sunday Times 22nd September 1985.

several confrontations between policemen and youths before the main riot on 9th September. They planned to intervene and modify the Handsworth policy once the enquiries into the deaths of the two Asian shopkeepers were completed. Under their new strategy, full-scale drug raids would be kept to a minimum, officers would be advised to choose the timing and location of arrests carefully to avoid street disorder, and the role of officers on the beat would be re-appraised. Still, the revised policy did not go down well with the Asian representatives, who saw it as a capitulation and a move to lax, ineffective security on the streets.

In 1987 the West Midlands Police Authority would propose the appointment of a researcher, to be paid twenty four thousand pounds a year, to examine tensions in the community. This, it was said, would save money. The chairman, Mick Ablett said: *'If tension indicators are right, we are going to save ratepayers millions of pounds because that's what it cost to police the Handsworth riots.'* A naive proposal indeed. What on earth was wrong with people in positions of power in Handsworth actually going and seeing the situation for themselves? The area was only two miles by three. You could stroll the patch in an afternoon. There were more than twenty beat constables out in the streets day after day. Did no-one see what was happening, sense the feelings and the potential? It beggared belief.

Meanwhile, back in 1985, Home Secretary Douglas Hurd, while saying some things with which many in favour of community policing could agree, nevertheless came down on the side of seeking the causes of the troubles in the way the Police had done their job across the country. The Cabinet were reported to have devoted seventy five minutes of their discussions to the Handsworth issue. They seemed reluctant to appoint yet another Scarman to discover what perhaps they knew in their hearts; that the last four years had been wasted years. Hurd ordered Chief Constable Geoffrey Dear to prepare a report focussing solely on the policing methods used before and during the riots. Dear's investigation would be overseen by John Woodcock, one of Her Majesty's Inspectors of Constabulary, allegedly to ensure that national issues were taken into account.

Liberal Leader David Steel came to see me around 15th October 1985, and we looked at Handsworth together. I had to be careful to keep a low profile. It was possible that Geoffrey Dear would regard my tour, accompanied by a prominent politician, as some kind of interference. David Steel and I reviewed action taken since 1981 on the development of some kind of employment policy in Handsworth. The City Council had tried to assist local businesses in untried and naive ways. For example, they would give someone a grant of ten thousand pounds to enable the creation of a window cleaning business. Six months later both the window cleaner and the ten thousand pounds had disappeared. The cause was simple and predictable. Many unemployed folks in Handsworth simply did not have enough money to pay a man to clean their windows. I estimated that between sixty and one hundred businesses were created in this way, and every one disappeared. You could give four thousand pounds to a local West Indian to buy sewing machines and start a small company making clothes, hats and jeans. He would make his jeans for around five pounds a pair. Down the street, an Asian, with his superior business know-how, would make an identical pair for one pound fifty. The West Indian would go out of business, and the money with him. It appeared to be waste on a grand scale, yet the reasons were more complex. It was not a question of lack of skill or lack of desire to succeed. There was no backup help and assistance, no management support, no training, no accountancy advice. Looking back, admittedly with the advantage of hindsight, it was an inevitable failure.

Many millions of pounds, somewhere between thirty and forty million, was said to have been spent upgrading Handsworth's streets. When Home Secretary Hurd made a statement on Inner City Disorders on 21st October 1985, David Steel had the opportunity to raise matters direct: *'Does the Minister accept that there is much criticism that in the past the action that has been taken through self-help scheme and the urban aid programme has been directed to outside contractors, who use outside employees and take away the profits that could be earned by local people? Does he agree that we should be looking for schemes that are designed to continue employment and business in the inner city areas?'*[1]

Members of the Birmingham Community Relations Council resolved not to co-operate with Dear's enquiry. Peter Newsam, Chairman of the national Commission for Racial Equality, rushed from London to meet with the Birmingham CRC as angry exchanges flowed across the floor of the Council Chamber. Asian shopkeeper representatives complained that policemen had stood back and allowed Asian shops to be burnt. James Hunte blamed inflammatory Police actions as the spark of all the violence. Birmingham City Council also ignored Dear's investigation and demanded, but were refused, an independent inquiry similar to the 1981 Scarman Report. So they decided to set up their own, conducted by Julius Silverman, a highly respected barrister and Labour MP in the city from 1945 to 1983. That in turn would be mainly boycotted by the people of Handsworth, who feared it would become just another Scarman report, good in itself at identifying the real causes behind the mayhem, but unacceptable to the politicians at local and national level. They understood well the twenty suggestions on social policy which, in Scarman's opinion, were the crux of the Brixton issue, and recalled that they had been studiously ignored. To add yet more confusion, West Indian representative groups resolved to set up their own study, *The Alternative Reality*, to be published in 1986. That one hundred page document would identify racism as the root of the troubles.

Police Review perceptively highlighted an issue in an article by C. H. Rolph. He focussed on something missed by every other commentator, namely the reality of police numbers and the sheer impossibility of controlling the streets on a continuous

---

[1] Hansard, Inner City Disorders 21st October 1985, col 34.

basis. His boiler house metaphor remains intriguing and apt. Under the enigmatic header *'HANDSWORTH DESTROYS A MYTH'* he wrote: *'Contrary to our cherished and confident self image, we're a nation with a history of internal violence. If ever there was a myth about Police capacity to quell riots at any moment, it ought to have been weakened when* **accessible** *policemen virtually disappeared from the streets; but even now that they are coming back, it's only the political phrase makers who call them 'the thin blue line'. They might be a dotted line, perhaps, if you could see them from a satellite, but there's an enormous space between the dots. Yet if we put ten times the number of bobbies on the streets, we should merely be tying down the safety valve rather than looking inside the boiler, and the outbursts would go on.'* (His emphasis).[1]

Predictably, when faced with a seemingly imponderable and elusive problem, the Police would generally fall back to some technological solution. So it was, with headlines national and local:- *'Hurd gets tough on rioters.'* *'Hurd gives all-clear for CS Gas and Bullets.'* *'Plastic Bullets and CS Gas end Soft Line.'* *'Police will get tough.'* I no longer could stay silent. My promise to Sir Phillip had been overtaken by events. I called Maureen Messent of the Birmingham Post and Mail. I had to declare my hand and try to stop the madness: *'The public will find it extremely difficult to have a useful rapport with policemen they have seen shooting plastic bullets. The more men are used in this way, the harder it will be for certain sections of the public to trust them... The public now baying for law and order will hate the new look Police. The country will be faced with increased violence as rioters meet force with force... Once the CS gas and the bullets are flying, it will be too late.'[2]*

Sir Kenneth Newnham, Chief of the London Metropolitan Force gave me and others of like mind an answer, warning that he was ready to use plastic bullets if further major rioting occurred. Geoffrey Dear would soon follow him. When learning of Geoffrey Dear's statement, Edwin Shore, Chairman of the West Midlands Police Committee, threatened to resign[3] and demanded an audience with Douglas Hurd. It was a matter of principle. Robin Corbett MP told the Chief Constable, *'Plastic bullets have no place on the streets of Birmingham. You cannot shoot good behaviour into people.'* Dear, on the other hand, stated that if the facility had been available to him at the start of the Handsworth riot he might have saved the lives of the two shopkeepers burned to death. He seemed determined to push it through and, after a West Midlands County Council vote directing him not to acquire plastic bullets, took his case to the people, talking of a referendum to test public opinion:

'I would be very interested indeed in the results of a properly conducted and reliable poll. If ninety percent said they were against them in any circumstances and

---

[1] *Handsworth destroys a myth,* Police Review 27th September 1985.

[2] Birmingham Evening Mail Wednesday October 9th 1985.

[3] *I'll quit if Police get riot bullet,* Birmingham Post 20th November 1985.

194

we were faced with the Handsworth riots again and I was to procure plastic bullets and fire them - it would be an impossible position to be in.' An accompanying Express and Star reader poll revealed a large majority in favour.[1]

A Birmingham Evening Mail *Insight* feature asked *'Why aid is not working for blacks.'* Rick Groves of the Birmingham University Centre for Urban and Regional Studies commented: *'Despite the Scarman Report, inner-city policies have taken a back seat. Inner city money was used to top up spending on other services in urban areas.'* An estimated twenty four million pounds had been lavished on Handsworth, but Ivan Henry, co-ordinator of the Handsworth Employment Scheme, believed that: *'The cash simply has not reached the jobless. More than half the money has gone into water-supply projects and envelope schemes to do up Handsworth's Victorian houses and shops, and much of the rest into community initiatives such as schools, day centres and nurseries. They are welcome schemes, but provide few jobs for locals. Out of work blacks see their community providing jobs alright, but for other people.'.*

The thirty thousand pound Silverman enquiry was struggling. On the first day, Thursday 1st November 1985, only four people turned up. On the top table on a raised dais adorned by three lovely baskets of flowers, sat a forlorn Julius Silverman, a secretary and an assistant. The West Indians as a group had threatened to boycott proceedings, and the Asians, too, had little confidence. Silverman and his secretary came round to see me at my Booth Street factory office. Was there anything I could do? So I spoke to the community leaders, including James Hunte, Gus Williams, Basil Clarke, and as many others as I could. I told them, *'Look, I know you think the thing's a waste of time. But Silverman is a fair man and will listen. And if you don't say anything, what is the City to do when you go asking for things? Will they believe you or not? Think about it.'*

In the event, several representatives turned up, explaining events and causes as they and the people had seen them. Chief Constable Geoffrey Dear and David Love also gave evidence. Dear claimed that *a minority of black criminals* (note, not just *criminals*) were flourishing behind a smokescreen of excuses such as unemployment and prejudice. He then went on to warn that *'... as a society we are in danger of lumping all black faces together.'*

Love declared that Handsworth had become a drugs centre for the Midlands. *'Raiding premises is still one of the options open to me and raid premises is what I shall continue to do if it rids Handsworth of drugs.'*[2]

Five days later, Deputy Chief Constable Leslie Sharpe was to tell the Dudley branch of the NSPCC that it would not be long before the rising tide of lawlessness would force policemen to arm themselves with plastic bullets. Handsworth could not be blamed on unemployment, deprivation and poverty. An orderly society could not

[1] *YES! VERDICT ON BULLET,* Walsall Express and Star, 17th December 1985.

[2] *Handsworth is a drugs Mecca - Police.* Birmingham Evening Mail 21st November 1985.

be achieved merely by more policemen, more resources and stiffer penalties in the courts. There was a need to involve children in family life. He talked of the youngsters who looted and set fire to Handsworth shops while policemen sheltered from petrol bombs. *'It was those same youngsters who complained that not enough interest had been shown in them. Yet when plans were drawn up to help them, they did not want to know.'* It would have been helpful if he had told us which youngsters, or how old they were or which schools they went to. Perhaps he had identified them during the riots, visited their homes, talked with their teachers and parents, offered them options and some hope in life. Or perhaps he hadn't. Eight weeks before, he'd praised community policing on the TV Eye programme in St Andrews Hall. To the NSPCC, however, he now maintained: *'There is some merit in ostracising this element by the rest of society. If we are not careful, this unclubbable element will get cannabis legalised, shop-lifting decriminalised. The law-abiding citizen has to stand up and be counted.'*[1] I was beginning, at last, to understand what he meant by *Community policing.*

Elsewhere, in London, police constables were being trained[2] in martial arts and the use of new weapons to deal with rioters. Detailed instructions were given on how to use their riot helmet and the cutting edge of a riot shield as weapons. Scotland Yard were said to be introducing two new truncheons, one of which was a 'flail truncheon', a ten inch ridged baton which could be whirled on the end of a chain to strike at the legs and arms, thrust into the groin, or used sideways on the philtrum (the point where the nose and the upper lip meet). In the shield chop, continued the instruction, *'If an opponent grasps the officer's right hand, instantly raise the shield and bring the edge swiftly down onto the wrist bone.'*

A Handsworth constable once secretly told John Brown, when speaking of my policies: *'Community policing? That's for wankers.'* I wondered how he would behave with such methods at his disposal.

Geoffrey Dear was to appear to soften his position. Early in 1986, in a lengthy interview[3] with John Slim of the Birmingham Evening Mail, he commented: *'Our fear is that the only thing people are going to see as an issue is hardware. Prevention is better than cure, and there are other things we should be addressing first.'* These he identified as the bringing together of the public agencies whose skills focussed on youth. *'There is a whole class which is not criminal, which is aspirant and which needs to be given a helping hand to improve its lot. They have to be stopped from under achieving. But how do you overthrow a whole culture, a matriarchal society of under-achieving. One has to start looking at issues like unemployment, bad housing, and job and educational inequality.'* The sad point is that it had taken him four years and four months to begin to contemplate this idea, and even sadder, he appeared to be

---

[1] *Rioters who 'don't want to know',* Express and Star 26th November 1985.
[2] *New Martial Arts truncheons in use.* The Observer, 6th October 1985.
[3] *Put the Blacks on the ladder of real opportunity,* Birmingham Evening Mail 13th January 1986.

speaking as a representative of society external to Handsworth telling the people of Handsworth what was good for them. Perhaps it would have been better to go and talk to the people of Handsworth prior to the development of a situation that produced the riots, and ask them directly.

In any case, his interview soon slipped back to the old agenda. Plastic bullets, when and when not to use them, plus the matter of the deployment of guns and water cannon, and how a water cannon, if your mouth is open, '... *will rip it right round to the back of your neck.'* [1] In spite of the devastating potential of such weapons, still he indicated that if faced with riots similar or worse than those of September 1985, he might use both to clear the streets. In order to minimise the chances of it all happening again, he concluded, *'My hopes are that society will come together and that agencies will subordinate their own pride and get down to addressing the fundamental problems as a matter of urgency.'* Whether he regarded the Police as one of those *agencies* I never discovered.

The Chairman of the Police Federation, Leslie Curtis, would add to the recurring confusion on policy, speaking on Thursday 5th June 1986 to rank and file officers of the West Midlands branch of the Federation.[2] He blamed the fluctuations between what he called a *'largely permissive and blind eye approach to policing'* and the firmer approach of more enlightened senior officers, in Handsworth, Brixton and Tottenham.[3] In turn the hard approach had produced resentment on the part of drug dealers, and they had organised and led the riots in those three areas. The Police should concentrate on the protection of life and property and the prevention and detection of crime, and stop *'dreaming up a whole new field of sociological, abstract, jargon-ridden theorising.'*

I will leave the last words[4] in this chapter to some of the young men of Handsworth. They may have been good honest men, or they may have had a criminal record, it matters not. I believe they spoke the truth, the reality of inner city life. Their perceptions would guide their actions and those of their friends out on the streets. I and my constables had grappled with it all before in those difficult years of the late 1970's, in our young black consultation groups, in the Holte School and other school projects, in our Citizen 80 groups, on the street outside Thornhill Road station, from all those youngsters speaking freely in 1977 to reporter Tony Francis in *Shades of Grey.* Here is the up to date version.

'They can give us a job, a decent home, but people will still look on us as black bastards. It's a question of respect. When a black boxer wins a world title, he's

---

[1] Birmingham Evening Mail 13th January 1986.
[2] *Riots blamed on blind-eye Police policy,* Birmingham Post 6th June 1986.
[3] My time at Thornhill Road was linked in the article with this blind eye approach, but to be fair to Curtis, he never said or implied this.
[4] *We don't live - we survive.* Birmingham Post 19th September 1985. Interviews by Marion Brennan.

British. When he riots, he's West Indian. They pick us up and drop us as they need us. We have no feeling.'

'After the '81 riots they gave us new roofs and pretty garden walls, but it was all show. The people inside were still hungry. Some of our parents feel we have no right to fight for something better, that we should keep silent, not rock the boat. But all we want is what you have.'

'The dole pays your rent, for some food and a couple of drinks. It doesn't pay the bills. If you want to buy clothes, you have to hustle. We don't live, we survive.'

'We are too honest. We smoke ganja and we don't deny it. It's harmless. Some Asians around here deal in heroin. That's how they make their money, not through their shops.'

'The policeman walked around my flat and asked whether my property was stolen. I couldn't believe it. To them we are just thieves, dirt. They tell us 'You lot are all the same'. Community policing doesn't exist. We have nowhere to go at night so we meet on the street and we are arrested on suspicion.'

'Now we are seeing pictures in the press of policemen posing with little black children. It's not real. Those children would be terrified of that uniform because they've seen policemen beat up their fathers.'

TWENTY SEVEN: TEA WITH THE PROFESSOR

Throughout the rest of 1985 and into the first few months of '86 I gave evidence, direct or by letter, to the Silverman enquiry. All that I spoke of was consistent with my career and experience at Thornhill Road and first hand observations in day to day contacts since retirement. I told Silverman that the Police should introduce real community policing, not just bobbies on the beat talking nicely to people. They needed the assent and co-operation of every group of citizens. No-one should be excluded. Policing policies should be founded on a deep understanding of the problems of the people living in Handsworth, how family and economic problems interacted to create a breakdown in society. Senior and junior policemen should start with the young children in the schools and work with other agencies help them to develop as citizens; help the juvenile first time minor criminal to get straight again; work alongside Government initiatives to help create jobs. If this did not happen things would not improve. Since the first tranche of immigration in the early fifties, two generations had already passed through the suburb as available jobs slowly drained away. We were now into a third wasted generation, most of whom had no job to go to. They in turn would bear children who themselves would never work.

I heard from my local contacts that parts of my evidence were not well received by the Chief Constable. He interpreted them as a criticism of himself and his Force. Such a contrast from 1978 when I had been invited to lecture at Bramshill! Then, I was saying the same things, explaining the same facts, talking about the same problems, describing the same people. For five years my systems of community policing had been a philosophy to which commanders should aspire. Now, a mere five years later, they were seen by the Government and most Chief Constables as irrelevant.

***

It was a warm July evening. Birmingham's City Council Chamber was its usual splendour. Julius Silverman had been invited to the Annual General Meeting[1] of the Birmingham Community Relations Council, to speak about his inquiry and conclusions. Forty four members were present, plus invited speakers and the media, around seventy people in total. I was there as Chairman of the Handsworth Area Community Relations Panel. Also invited were Professor John Rex, Research Professor of Ethnic Relations at the University of Warwick, and two distinguished guests, the Assistant High Commissioners of Bangladesh and India.

---

[1] This account is based on the official minutes of the meeting.

Rex had done social and policing research in Handsworth, but never during the years that I was there, and he never met with me at Thornhill Road, nor had he ever walked the streets with me. He and his colleague Sally Tomlinson had published their conclusions in 1979. They did not support John Brown's conclusions, seeing John's work, including *Shades of Grey* and *Handsworth Revisited*, as superficial. I might fairly add that Rex did not entirely share Scarman's views on Brixton or Handsworth. Silverman spoke first. I must, of necessity, do him and Rex a disservice by compressing their speeches to show the essence of their conclusions.

Silverman saw the riots of 1985 much as Scarman had seen those of 1981. Drug dealers might have been involved at the start of the 1985 affair, but the violence that ensued was a small but general uprising of frustrated people. *'It was'*, Silverman maintained, *'an orgy of destruction without any rational basis. I have no doubt that the root cause of the disturbances was mass unemployment. If society can create such a situation then society can do something to rectify it. The Government's target for the future must be that of the problem of unemployment. The regeneration of Handsworth will come when the people of Handsworth have faith in their future.'*

Rex's diagnosis was entirely different. The root cause of the 1981 and 1985 troubles was the unwitting creation of ghettos by the City's housing allocation policies. Until these were broken down by new policies, the friction would continue. The introduction of the de-segregated bussing system of the USA would create other problems. Schooling systems must change to open up opportunities for black and Asian youngsters.

I deliberately placed myself at the rear of the Chamber and kept my head down. I just wanted to see how he would play things if he thought I was not there. He did not disappoint. John Brown, he claimed, had been far from objective in his analysis of young Rastas and their activities in his book *Shades of Grey*. What Rex failed to understand was that the attitudes of the young black rastas of Handsworth in 1977 could not be easily classified. I was dealing with human beings in all their complexity, in a situation of severe deprivation. I could not wait on theories from academics who were incapable of agreement on anything. I had to act then and there, find solutions, protect Handsworth as best I could and make inevitable mistakes along the way.

He rambled on, plucking truisms out of the stifling air of the Council Chamber. *'Quite clearly, going to school in Handsworth does not give children an equal chance with children from the suburban schools ... Quite clearly, what happens to the young men and women of Handsworth is that when they have finished their segregated schooling their chances of obtaining any employment at all are minimal ... etc.'*

Then he turned to the subject of former Superintendent Webb: *'Under Sir Phillip Knights, Superintendent Webb had in fact been given considerable independence to develop his own policies and had encouraged youth work of all kinds as well as developing liaison both with the Social Service and the community. More importantly, he evolved a policy for dealing with the ganja question which involved avoiding unnecessary arrests and recognising that ganja was a part of the West Indian culture.*

Whether Webb's policies added up to community policing is another matter... For all its apparent benevolence, and perhaps because of it, Handsworth had tended to become a local police state in which the all important question was not how Handsworth was represented and fought for its interests in the City Council, but rather who was in charge of the Police.'

That was it. Thus he dismissed me, my career, my constables, the interested visitors from around the world, all our hard won projects to help the young, policemen in the schools talking to teachers and school children, community leaders who had tried for years to obtain better conditions for Handsworth, in short, everything we had achieved.

There was a polite round of applause. James Hunte as Chairman thanked the two speakers and asked if there were any questions from the floor. I put up my hand.

'Yes?...' said the Chairman.

I stood up. *'Good evening Professor Rex.'* I sat down.

He smiled: *'Oh, how lovely to see you Mr Webb. I'm glad that you're here. I hope you did not feel I was criticising you, you did a marvellous job.'*

After the proceedings were over, we took tea together.

TWENTY EIGHT: AMERICAN BEAUTY

'Twinny-three million dollars...'

It is November 1989. The speaker is Caroll Huntress, Texan American, associate of Texan oil billionaire Bunker Hunt. Standing at his side in Aston Villa's wonderful stadium is Aston Villa Chairman Doug Ellis. Huntress slowly repeats the words, rolling them gently across a green manicured centre circle towards a rank of TV cameras.

'Twinny-three million dollars... '

The Texan is here to create - with the assistance of twinny-three million dollars - a European American Football League, the *International League of American Football.* This new league, ILAF, will play between April and July in seven European cities; Rome, Milan, Barcelona, Amsterdam, Munich, Helsinki and Birmingham. The first game for an as yet un-named and unknown Birmingham team is, according to Huntress, scheduled against Rome on Easter Monday, 1990. The new league will, I fear, destroy my efforts over the previous two years on my latest project to help the young men of Birmingham's inner city.

The Birmingham Bulls were formed as far back as 1983, when American Football first featured on British TV. Young athletic men seeking an impact sport, tired of the snobbery of English rugby, flocked to new teams all over Britain. By 1988 there were almost four hundred teams, a growing market, a seemingly impressive future, and the Bulls were the cream of the nation. From their first years, they had been owned and coached by a local enthusiast American, Gerry Hartman. Gerry spent years in building the team, recruiting in the weight lifting clubs and on street corners the best athletes he could. Most of the young West Indian men lived in the deprived suburbs of Handsworth and Lozells. Gerry's team of 1986 contained many who were such good natural athletes that they would have been automatic selections for a USA college football scholarship. Some, indeed, might have made it to the NFL of America. Sadly, they were born not just on the wrong side of the track, but on the wrong side of the ocean. Frequently expressed hopes of professional success would be realised by but one of them.

In or around 1987, Gerry Hartman sold the team to a local businessman Frank Leaden. I then bought the Bulls from Frank in 1989. My son Andrew, six feet four inches in height and weighing eighteen stones, was on the squad, and a Great Britain international. They were due to play in the European Finals in Amsterdam, but could not afford to pay for the team bus and a place to stay in Holland. They needed some three thousand pounds to pay for the travel and accommodation. Andrew pleaded with me, as sons sometimes do, and I caved in, as dads always do.

I went to see the Chairman of Leisure Services on the City Council. *'Look, these young men are a multi-racial team, many from the inner city areas, a lot from*

Handsworth. They have a proud record representing Birmingham in Europe. They're damn good athletes, a credit to British sport, and they need help. So what can you do?'

The City said OK and financed the trip. Buying the Bulls proved to be an impetuous and somewhat expensive decision, but I stuck with it and still own the team today, although I lack the physical energy to get involved in the day to day running. The director for several years was a hard working Leigh Ensor, who now lives in the USA. Leigh in turn was succeeded by the ever dedicated Dave Cottrell.

Why did I do it? It occurred to me that many on the team had been around as children during the 1981 Handsworth riots. Some might have been active in the 1985 riots. Here was a chance to continue some of the supportive work that I so enjoyed in my time at Thornhill Road. Before me was an athletically talented, multi-racial team, mainly of inner city youths. It is impossible to list them here, but all were outstanding young men. Trevor Carthy[1] and Lloyd O'Neil were explosive running backs; Clive Loftman was a free safety with eyes to send a shiver down the spine of every opponent; Paul Roberts, a high jumping defensive back; silk smooth runner Mark Williams;, fearsome lineman Karl Hunter; dynamic six feet six inch tall defensive lineman Warren Billingham; and herculean giant Nigel Hoyte. So many fine young men, including team captain Colin Nash, who once stood shoulder to shoulder on the playing fields of Birmingham's Fox Hollies School with the famous Sam Mills, linebacker of the NFL New Orleans Saints. To all these, and those young men I have not listed, their memory I know still lives on among fans throughout Britain and Europe.

The team spirit and fellowship that grew among the players was uncanny. Some became family friends, and I have helped many over the years in finding jobs and sorting their lives out. Some still come to me for advice, which I am happy to offer. Frank and Gerry, pioneers in a hostile world, deserve the greatest credit.

The Bulls played many games at Birmingham's Alexander Stadium in front of up to three thousand paying fans. When the big London teams, the *Ravens* or the *Olympians* came to town we would get four thousand spectators. Inner city lads with no hope of a job would walk from the stadium tunnel to cheers and applause they would never experience on the streets of Handsworth. They found self esteem and fulfilment on a gridiron field.

Few British people understood the level of talent they possessed, nor the wonderful team skills that were achieved. Frank Leaden pulled of an amazing coup in 1987, persuading a former NFL first round draft quarterback from the St Louis Cardinals, Steve Pezarkavitch, to join the team. Frank then turned to the Los Angeles

---

[1] Trevor joined the professional London Monarchs and won a World Bowl ring in a three year career. When I last checked, he was working as a youth outreach worker in the West Midlands.

Raiders and USFL former quarterback Russ Jensen, who in turn brought with him giant lineman James Thornton, formerly of Pennsylvania University. A clutch of talented receivers included Greg Harris, former Indiana University star Tony Buford, and Yale graduate Bob Shoop.[1] After Jensen's era, in which the Bulls twice won the British title, in 1990 we recruited University of Indiana quarterback Dave Kramme and giant Chicago Bears trialist lineman Don Schrader.

On Sunday 4th August 1991, at Birmingham's Alexander Stadium, the Bulls would again win the British title under Coach Sam Timer, former Boston College coach of Doug Flutie,[2] the famous NFL quarterback. Eight thousand fans cheered themselves hoarse in a game described by the Birmingham Post as *'A pulsating Coca-Cola Bowl Final'*. Coaches who succeeded Sam Timer included Wayne Howard formerly of Long Beach State University California, and Utah University, and Wallace G English, former Offensive Co-ordinator at the Miami Dolphins.

At the end of the 1989 season, after a narrow loss to Manchester Spartans at London's Crystal Palace Stadium, for an end of season all-star event, we invited a guest coach, George Baldwin, former Head Coach of the University of Kutztown, Pennsylvania.

Which brings me back to the green turf of Aston Villa. George had been recruited by Huntress' International League as an assistant coach. Just that year, George had sold his big farmhouse in Kutztown and moved to the heat of Florida, to a condominium overlooking the blue Atlantic shores of Ormond Beach. When the League front office phoned to ask which team he preferred, George, in his usual laid-back manner, looked out from his eleventh floor window. Studying the blue, rolling waves, he murmured: *'I don't care where you guys put me. I just want to coach football.'* George would regret that statement, finding himself in the freezing land of the midnight sun in Helsinki Finland. Fortunately, or unfortunately, the League, based as it was on an excess of public relations hype, would collapse with the coaches unpaid, but not until there erupted the mother of all battles between myself and Doug Ellis. I feared that the League would arrive in Birmingham, take over everything to do with American Football, and destroy our fan base and all that I had built for those inner city young men. The Texan had the money to recruit former NFL players and top USA college players who had just missed out on the NFL. All these talented players would come to Birmingham and my own lads would not be offered an opportunity, other than as four or five token local heroes, or side line staff and water boys.

I fired a broadside at Doug Ellis. His first reply revealed his shock, then he dug his heels in. Our letters flew back and forth like exocet missiles for a couple of

---

[1] In January 2003 Bob was appointed Head Coach at Columbia University, New York.
[2] Played for New England Patriots, Buffalo Bills and in 2001 San Diego Chargers. As we complete the final edit of this book, Flutie is still leading the Chargers to victory in the 2003 season.

months, until the ILAF bubble finally burst, the Bulls went on to more British success, and a chastened Caroll Huntress flew back to Texas.

TWENTY NINE: INDIAN HOLIDAY

In April 2000, on a visit to Amritsar, a special invitation came to me via the hotel messenger service, sent by the Police, the City of Jalandar and the Ravidass Leaders. The Ravidass community worldwide has many millions of followers, including hundreds of thousands across the UK and Europe. A schism had developed between the members, dividing them fairly equally into opposing camps. One of the *Sants* in India had created a charitable Trust and the dispute centred on the way that the Trust was to be managed in the best interests of the community overall. Across the world, particularly in the Asian sub-continent, even families were becoming divided.

We, that is myself and three Sants representing the entire Ravidass peoples, sat down around the table and looked at the entire project, and then the available solutions to the problem. Over two days of meetings, and with some advice from a *former Policeman from Handsworth*, they agreed that they would instruct their people to sit down with the opposing groups and solve the difficulties to everyone's advantage. Shortly afterwards, one of the Sants came to Britain to promote to his followers the solutions we agreed in Jalandar.

By coincidence, four high ranking Ravidass leaders were on the Handsworth Festival Committee, and were in India at the same time. I did not know they were going to be there. I met one by chance in Delhi, and the others in the Punjab. They must have passed the information around their followers, as, on the way home, I had a surprise coming. I was one of the last people to arrive at Amritsar airport before take off. I went into the departure lounge, through the security screens, and as I came out of the screen there was my good friend Gurmet Suman, former general secretary of the Ravidass Association in Handsworth. He was a close family friend, always a welcome visitor at our home, and a superb supporter of the Police. I sat down with him and his lovely wife and had a chat about old times.

He got up and I thought he had gone to the toilet, and I carried on chatting to his wife. When lo and behold the doors of the lounge swung wide open and in came the Chief of Police, a Sikh, followed by eight or nine of his officers of various seniority, chief inspector, inspector and so on down the ranks. They marched up to me, shuffled in line, stood at attention, and saluted, saying how delighted they were to welcome me to India as a former chief from Birmingham and *a much respected figure, and would I please accompany them to their office for a cup of tea, a samoso and a glass of Coca-Cola.* An invitation not to be refused.

After our snack and more chat, before I left the office, the Police Chief explained that since Amritsar airport was right on the border with Pakistan, there was a massive security problem, with constant bomb and gun threats. Every move that anyone made was monitored, all were searched and cases and belongings opened and inspected. He asked me a favour: *Would I please write to the newspapers and to the Indian Government, tell them what a marvellous job is being done, how, since my last visit to Amritsar things have improved, with a thirty percent increase in efficiency, and how they are succeeding in improving relationships with the travelling public.* I said I would gladly do it. I knew for sure, everything he asked me to say was true, including the statement that the airport, by then, had installed two toilets instead of one.

They marched me to the plane like some head of state, and when we landed half way at Askabad in Turkmanistan, (one of the Russian republics), we took time in the airport lounge to recover from the long flight, waiting for the plane to be refuelled. Suddenly two young Sikhs approached, young men in their twenties with turbans and beards, wishing to be introduced. They had witnessed my reception and departure at Amritsar, and guessed who I was. Amazingly, they were two young officers from Thames Valley Police, responsible for community work and liaison. One explained that he was the area secretary for the Black Police Association.

We exchanged pleasantries, but then felt I needed to give them both a bit of a shock. The Black Police Association was not one of my favourite bodies. I reminded them that I had served as Secretary of the Police Federation for fifteen years before I became Chief Inspector. I did not like to see organisations set up within the Police that seemed to have a different agenda from the main Police representative bodies. It was their job as ethnic minority officers to integrate themselves into the main work of the Federation, not to work to another agenda. I told them *I'll be watching you carefully to make sure that you work with the Federation etc.* They assured me that that was their intention and would do as I said.

They were somewhat startled. Ever since my deafness came on after the 1981 brick throwing incident in Handsworth I've tended to talk loudly. I talked loudly before that, but even more so afterwards, so they must have been somewhat intimidated. They adjusted quickly to what I said. They had no alternative. With my loud voice, everyone on our same flight could hear everything that I said. All around the airport lounge travellers, Asian, Russian, German, leaned forward, highly interested.

On one trip to Delhi, I received a call from the leader of the Dalit Writers Association. The Writers are an organisation set up specially to promote equality and rights for India's Dalits, the *untouchables*. In Asia, when the shadow of an untouchable happens to cross that of a higher caste, a cleansing ritual has to be followed. The Writers' leader told me of a very important meeting going on at Government level in Delhi, and asked if I could please attend. It did not occur to me that the thing might be as important as he said. Yet when I walked into the room the heads turned around to look at me and I realised it was a big mistake. Governors of every Indian state were present, plus five Government ministers, and leaders of the main Trade Unions. They were present to discuss the setting up of the first Dalit

Charitable Trust, with millions of pounds donated by the Indian Government and other charitable organisations. Their intention was to assist *untouchables* all over the world, to lift them away from low status, their burden from time immemorial.

As I got my breath back, I was asked, with no preparation or research, to give a world view as a former Police Chief who had spent many years dealing with the Dalit community in Britain. I did my best, scrambling through my memory cells as fast as I could. I thought it came out quite well, and got a standing invitation to go back regularly to Delhi to assist in their deliberations. To add to all this, the world-wide Dalit Writer's Association honoured me in December 2000 with the Dr Ambedkar International Exellency Award, also received, among others, by Mother Teresa of Calcutta and President Nelson Mandela. Thanks to Dr Sumanatra, the President of the Dalit Writers, I have the opportunity to return each year on 6th December to reinforce my support and commitment for their worthy cause. I am a privileged man indeed, all thanks to the people of Handsworth.

THIRTY: THE POLICE AND FREEMASONRY

The controversy regarding the role of Freemasonry in our society is long standing. It repeatedly rears its head whenever someone is looking for a sensational headline, or an unfortunate scapegoat, and for a variety of reasons, the truth about the Masons has not always prevailed.

Does Freemasonry have any influence within the Police, the Armed Forces, with the Government local and National, and the Judiciary? Can it therefore be interpreted that Freemasonry encourages corruption in public life, and that it should be outlawed or at least viewed with extreme suspicion? More than eight thousand decent, honest, and law-abiding British citizens who are Masons, are concerned and outraged by the allegations made against them. The fight to regain public acceptance and trust is well under way. It will help if, as a Mason, I recall what is required of any man seeking to become a Mason.

WHAT A CANDIDATE SHOULD KNOW
1. Masonry consists of a body of men banded together to preserve the secrets, customs and ceremonials handed down to them and for the purpose of mutual, intellectual, social and moral improvement. Its members endeavour to cultivate and exhibit brotherly love, relief and truth, not only to one another, but to the world at large.
2. A basic condition of admission into, and membership of the Order, is a belief in the Supreme Being. This is essential and admits of no compromise.
3. It recognises no distinctions of religion, and while inculcating in each of its members the duties of loyalty and citizenship, it does not permit any of its members, either in Lodge or in their capacity as Freemasons, to discuss theological or political questions.
4. It offers no pecuniary advantages binding one Mason to deal with another, or to support him in any way in the ordinary business relations of life.
5. It has certain Charities, but is not in any sense whatever a benefit society, nor is it based upon any calculations which would render this possible. The Charities are solely for those who, having been in good circumstances, have been overtaken by misfortune or adversity. Neither a Mason, his wife, nor his children have any claim upon them.
6. Masonry teaches that a man's first duty is to himself, his wife, his family and his connections. No-one should join the Order who cannot well afford to pay the initiation fees and subscription to his Lodge as well as to the Masonic Charities, and this without detriment to the comfort and well-being of those who have any claim on his support.

7. *Therefore everyone, before offering himself as a candidate, should be well assured in his own mind:*

8. *That he sincerely desires the intellectual and moral improvement of himself and his fellow creatures.*

9. *That he is willing to devote part of his time, his means and his effort in the promotion of brotherly love, relief and truth.*

10. *That he seeks no commercial, social or pecuniary advantages.*

11. *That he is able to afford the necessary expenditure without injury to himself or his connections.*

One of the most recent additions to the Masonic debate have come about as a result of an enquiry into Masonic activity by the Parliamentary All Party Home Affairs Committee, chaired by Chris Mullin M.P. The Committee wanted to establish whether or not Police Officers, Judiciary, court officials and even press reporters involved in the celebrated Birmingham Six bombings, the Stalker-Sampson enquiry and other matters involving the West Midlands Serious Crimes Squad were Masons, and if so, had their membership in any way affected the outcome of the enquiry.

The Church, the Military and local government have also queried Masonic membership within their ranks, and whether or not such membership is compatible with their respective functions. I will return to these specific cases later in this chapter.

I make no apology or excuse. I am a dedicated Free Mason, and have been active in the Craft since my initiation into the Cloisters Lodge number 7100 in the Province of Hertfordshire in February 1967. At that time I was a young Constable serving in Letchworth. I was in the C.I.D. and, as described in previous chapters, served alongside Detective Sergeant Bert Corby and Detective Constables Tom O'Connor and Eric Clayton. We were good friends and had a rewarding working and social life together. Tom O'Connor was an Irish Catholic and we played soccer together for the Force team and our local amateur team. It was well known to me that Bert and Eric were Masons in the local Letchworth lodges. Their membership meant nothing to me whatsoever, and I had no Masonic experience in my family. Many of my local acquaintances were Masons, but at no time had the matter been discussed, nor did it have any bearings on the job or the way that we in the Force operated.

During my time on the CID I was getting older and more mature in the job, by then a family man with young children. As I was about to leave Letchworth and move to Stevenage on promotion to Sergeant, I was encouraged by Bert and Eric to maintain my contacts with them and Letchworth by joining the Letchworth Lodge. No ulterior motives were present. I liked the idea and knew that it would give me an incentive to maintain my roots in the town, enabling me to return whenever there were meetings, no matter where I was living.

The Masons that I knew were pillars of society, honest and God-fearing men to be admired and respected. If they were Masons then I would have no hesitation in joining them, if they were willing to accept me. My application was processed but before I could join I was promoted to Inspector and transferred to Walsall in the West Midlands. I did, however, promise my proposer and seconder that I wanted my application to join the Letchworth Lodge to proceed, and that even though I would be based more than one hundred miles away, I would travel to Lodge meetings and fully support their activities. I thus became a Mason and steadily progressed through the ranks to my present position of Past Provincial Grand Warden in the Province of Staffordshire, and Past Provincial Grand Standard Bearer in the Province of Hertfordshire. For the first fourteen years of membership, I made the round trip to Letchworth and served in all ranks culminating in 1981 with Mastership of the lodge. I am still a member of that lodge and have formed many lasting friendships.

When at Walsall I joined the Mercia Lodge and have been their Master on two occasions. Together with Jagit Sayoo and others I founded the Lodge of Universal Brotherhood in West Bromwich, comprising men of all races, religions and nationalities, thus helping to confound the view of many that Masonry is racist and sectarian.

My experience in Masonry is therefore of long standing. I have never gained any pecuniary advantage or precedence over anyone because of my membership. I equate it with my membership of the Round Table, the Rotary and the '41' Club, all of which have given me tremendous pleasure and inspiration throughout all these years. Nor have I ever been approached at any time to influence any decision in a way that might be illegal or that would give unfair advantage to a Mason over a non-Mason. I am, however, aware that some Masons have abused their positions. I have always believed that such individuals should be identified, punished and removed from the Organisation.

Applications to become Masons are now scrupulously monitored, and any wrongdoing by members rigorously punished. We now acknowledge that we will always be under scrutiny and that we should make ourselves more open in our activities to dispel any doubts concerning our intentions. What Masons do in their meetings is widely known, and has been the subject of countless documentaries and newspaper articles. Masonry cannot by now be described as secret.

Certain issues have however lately arisen that deserve detailed examination. In 1983, journalist Stephen Knights published a sensationalised account of Freemasonry entitled 'The Brotherhood' [1]. It has since gone through nine reprints, and was intended to be an explosive revelation of the secret world of the Freemasons, and an indictment of many alleged acts against the public committed by Freemasons and their friends. The book was well written, probably well intentioned, and given huge publicity. Before publication, Knight phoned me at my home. He identified himself and thanked me for all the information and assistance I had given to him in relation to his revelations of alleged malpractice in the old Birmingham City Police. I was more

---

[1] *The Brotherhood,* Granada Publishing 1983. Stephen Knights died in 1985.

than amazed. I had never before heard of him and had certainly never spoken to him or anyone about Masonry or its relevance to the Police service. I had never served in the Birmingham City Police and had no personal knowledge of its chief officers or functions.

Knight was equally amazed. He had based much, if not all, of his commentary on the misdeeds of the Masonic members of Birmingham City Police, on information supplied by someone purporting to be me. The information may well have been true but clearly open to question, due to its source. I have no idea who it could have been. In spite of this, Knights asked me to confirm that I was a Mason and sought my opinions on my combining Masonic membership with life as a police officer. I was happy to do so, and pages one hundred and eleven and one hundred and twelve of his book re-iterated that I had never personally experienced any wrong doing; and if I came across any, would have dealt with it in the strongest possible way. When the book was published, the allegations regarding the Birmingham City Police were not removed, nor was any mention ever made about the duplicity of Stephen Knights' informant.

A follow-up to Knights' book was *Inside the Brotherhood*, by Martin Short. It was alleged by various sources that this was the only book on Masonry that Chris Mullin had studied, prior to his campaign against Masonry. Masonic commentators saw this as hardly an objective background on which to base one's thoughts and judgements. I am familiar with much of Short's work and have much admiration for him. I still do not know why both he and Chris Mullin harboured such doubts about our organisation. Mullin is a dedicated MP and his talents are recognised by his peers in Government.

Regardless of the bad publicity generated by both these books and the fact that I was publicly identified as a Mason, I was happy to continue my Masonic career and encourage decent Masonic friends to stand firm and defend the Craft. The best defence has always been to set a good example to the world and live your life as a decent, honest God-fearing citizen.

It later came as no surprise when the Parliamentary All Party Home Affairs Committee, chaired by Mullin, turned its attention to Freemasonry. The Committee suspected that wrongdoing had occurred during the investigation of the Birmingham Six pub bombings, the Stalker-Sampson enquiry into an alleged *Shoot to Kill* policy against the IRA in Northern Ireland, and matters undertaken by the West Midlands Police Serious Crimes Squad, later to be disbanded by Chief Constable Geoffrey Dear. The Committee had a list of names of officers, judges, legal representatives and press reporters involved in these matters and wanted to know who among them were Masons.

Unfortunately, at the initial stage, the Grand Lodge of England did not wish to accede to this request, considering it to be a breach of trust and an intrusion into the private lives of individuals. A serious confrontation, therefore, seemed imminent and

Masons were seen in some quarters as preparing to defy the authority of Parliament. I was sure that this was not the wish of ordinary Masons and was against our constitution. As the most senior Masonic member and police officer in the West Midlands Police at that time, the Home Affairs Committee asked for my comments and assistance. I felt it imperative that Grand Lodge should furnish the Committee with the names of officers on the list who were Masons. I was sure that no wrongdoing had taken place, but in the event of such then those concerned should be punished accordingly. This was a personal view. I was aware that many Masons for their own reasons did not agree with me. Here is my letter:

19th February 1998

Dear R.W. Provincial Grand Master ,

I have been attempting to contact you over the past three days and I am aware that you have been away from your home on a well deserved holiday.

It was brought to my attention that our Grand Lodge Secretary was about to appear before the Parliamentary Home Affairs Committee on Thursday the 19th February 1998 to answer questions in respect of certain matters of particular interest to those August Parliamentarians.

The questions related particularly to Police Officer involvement in the Stalker enquiry, the West Midlands Serious Crimes Squad and the Birmingham Pub Bombings, and whether or not any of those Officers were Freemasons. The implication being that there might be a suspicion that those Officers had misused their authority both as Policemen and Masons and that a miscarriage of Justice had occurred.

Prior to the hearing I was approached by the Chairman of the Committee, Mr. Chris Mullin M.P. who I have known for a number of years. I informed him that I was not aware of the list of names he intended to submit to the Grand Secretary and that I would wait until after I knew what his questions to the Grand Secretary would be and his response to them.

Mr. Mullin knows of my former Police rank and that I was the Police Commander in Handsworth from 1975 to 1981 responsible for pioneering Community Policing, victim Support Schemes and assisting with the Scarman Report on Policing inner cities. I was also Chairman of the Community Relations Council in Birmingham.

Mr. Mullin also knows of my Masonic activities and involvement and that these matters have been public knowledge since the publication of Stephen Knight's book on Freemasonry and subsequent television and newspaper articles in all of which I was featured, albeit without my prior knowledge or authority.

I have publicly stated my position on Masonry and the Police, and my belief that we should never allow the public to think there exists some secret agenda which excludes them or pursues activities which are subversive, unlawful and to their detriment.

Personally I have never encountered any such activity during my thirty two years as an active Mason, and my twenty seven years as a Police Officer. It cannot be denied however that malpractice has occurred within our ranks in the not too distant past, and that we have thankfully taken steps to prevent a re-occurrence.

It is my wish that my personal views are made known to Grand Lodge having regard to my former Senior Police rank in the Force and my rank in the Province. This vested interest prompts me to hope that Grand Lodge consider my views. I believe we have nothing to hide, and that we should be proud to have our association with Masonry made public.

I have been identified as a Mason nationally for more that fifteen years and it has not hurt me in any way. Quite the contrary effect, however, and the formation of our Lodge of Universal Brotherhood in Handsworth was helped by the public perception that Masonry was not secretive, racist or dishonest and encouraged those from all groups to actively participate. A view quite contrary to that indicated in The Daily Mail article about Freemasonry on the 18th February 1998.

The present situation involving Grand Lodge and Parliament has unfortunately done little to raise the image of Freemasonry in the eyes of the general public. I do not wish to apportion any blame for this perception, but we must recognise that it exists and we must take urgent and immediate steps to remedy the situation.

We must not act contrary to the wishes of Parliament, and should set about repairing and alleviating the fears expressed by the Media, Parliament and the public at large. Conversations with my Masonic friends and those in Rotary, and other organisations I represent on a daily basis in the West Midlands, have convinced me that any members of the Police Force, serving or retired, if they are Masons, should have no qualms whatsoever in going public. Those who were involved in any of the investigations named in the Parliamentary questions should immediately agree to their identity and involvement in Masonry being disclosed, and should be encouraged to do so by Grand Lodge.

It necessarily follows that if any of them are guilty of malpractice then they should be dealt with both by criminal courts and exclusion from Masonry. We must take urgent steps to resolve this matter to the satisfaction of everyone concerned otherwise all the good work over the past months to project a positive image of the Craft will have gone to waste. We must never be seen to challenge the directions of those elected to represent us in Parliament and thereby bringing Masonry into conflict with the rest of society.

I have no doubt Mr. Mullin and the Press will continue to pursue me and Freemasonry if this matter is not resolved, and they will gain more support as it drags on. I was not a member of any of the investigating squads concerned and do not believe we or any of them have anything to fear from giving the Parliamentary Committee what they require. Being ordered to do so will be demeaning and an insult to those Masons who wish Grand Lodge to accede to Parliament's request without any more delay or prevarication, however well intentioned.

In the televised part of the Hearing seen by millions of viewers all over the countr,y our Grand Secretary told Robin Corbett MP that we had no records of the occupations of our members. My belief was that we have such records, certainly at ordinary Lodge level, and they are circulated to our members each time a prospective candidate is proposed for membership.

It is my sincere wish that this request is passed to Grand Lodge as a matter of urgency. I have every reason to believe that they will consider it with due regard to the feelings of those of us at the sharp end of this situation, and they can be assured of my continued support. I have made it clear to Mr. Mullin and the media that my views are my ow,n and that they do not in any way represent what might be those of either Grand Lodge or Provincial Grand Lodge. I have told Mr. Mullin that I will pass my views to Grand Lodge and my Provincial Grand Master, and that they might also receive communications expressing thoughts different from my own.

Yours sincerely and fraternally,

David Webb P.Pr.J.G.W.

Fortunately, Grand Lodge decided to comply and a serious confrontation was sensibly avoided. I transpired that of one hundred and seventeen persons on the list, only sixteen were Masons.[1] As far as I am aware, none of the sixteen had allegations made against them. All in all it was a veritable storm in a teacup, but it has alerted Freemasonry to the fact that we must make every effort to communicate with the public at large, prove what we stand for and demonstrate the great contribution that we have made and continue to make to community life. I believe that our decision is welcomed by everyone among the general public and in politics.

Lodges are now actively encouraged to publicise their activities. Stricter vetting of applicants and monitoring of their personal and public lives can only serve to reassure the public that Masonry is a perfectly legitimate activity binding men of similar interests working together in peace and harmony for the benefit of mankind regardless of colour, creed, religion or personal status. It is likely that this subject will never go away, but hopefully a more balanced and informed view will prevail.

---

[1]The list is securely held by David Webb and is not for publication.

THIRTY ONE: CONFUSION IN THE RANKS

The story of my life serving the wonderful people of Handsworth is nearing its end. As my eighth decade approaches, soon will come a warm autumn day when I will retire to a deckchair in my tiny garden and drift away for ever. There may be one or two acquaintances from my past who cannot wait for the moment. Sadly for them, that moment must wait its turn. There are several themes relating to the youth of Handsworth and the nation's Police that still deserve attention.

For more than twenty years government, public, Police and media have dragged us in opposing directions. At intervals a different, supposedly new, concept is advocated. I firmly believe that the confusion stems from the background and training of the many men and women who make up the Force, and is to some extent to be anticipated.

One example was an interview[1] that Chief Constable Geoffrey Dear gave to the Birmingham Mail in 1989, shortly before he moved up to become an H.M Inspector of Constabulary, a powerful and influential role in our society. He boasted: *'We are probably better at public order than anywhere in the country.'* After an account of how he now had the armour, the shields, the helicopters, the *'... highly trained fire-arms teams and others trained to be able to contain a situation without being expected to go in and penetrate a stronghold...'* he added: *'Handsworth today is alright. Handsworth is nowhere near the problem it was other than in terms of petty drug dealers. Handsworth today is not a bad place to live in at all. In many ways it is quite a desirable place to live in.'*

From there he moved to the other side of the coin: *'... we are concentrating on community relations and increasing the numbers of beat officers and the strength and influence of consultative committees: all the network of Dixon-type policing, to try to head off a riot in the first place.'* It saddened me to see this summary of what the Police had become, a reactive army deriving strength from superior technology, with just a passing reference to Sergeant Dixon and local consultation. Where, I wondered, were the children in all this?

A contrasting impression was conveyed that same year in a visit by journalist Steve Platt, born in Handsworth in the late fifties. On a visit commissioned by *The Independent* he found a depressing picture. Four years after the 1985 riots, *'Some of the shops are still burnt out and empty, the former proprietors having been refused compensation from either their insurance companies or the government. It is impossible to travel along Lozells and Villa Roads without being aware of the countless scars of the fury that raged around here in September 1985.'* True, he found alongside the dereliction many signs of regeneration, but still his overall

---

[1] *The Dear Years,* Birmingham Evening Mail, 13th December 1989.

impression was one of sad resignation and despair among the poorest. *'Outside, the policemen sit in their squad car watching from across the road. They know there is drug-dealing going on in the Acapulco, and the people who are doing it know that the policemen know. What is more, in case anyone is unaware of the fact, one disaffected local resident has painted the Acapulco frontage in three-feet-high graffiti saying:* 'DRUG DEN OWNED BY BIRMINGHAM CITY COUNCIL'. *The people in the cafe haven't bothered to clean it off, so there it stays, like a great billboard advertisement for the place.'*

In 1990 the lessons of the Broadwater Farm riots were examined[1] by Leonard Jason-Lloyd of the University of Leicester. He recalled that the deployed policemen had been bombarded with missiles for several hours, and felt they had been used as *'Aunt Sallys'*. The advantages and disadvantages of the use of CS gas and rubber bullets and other techniques were considered in what to me was a spine-chilling analysis. After indicating that none of the usually advocated technology would have worked in the close confines of occupied multi-storey blocks of flats at the estate, nevertheless he delved into the subject as a scientist dissects a dead animal. *'Finally, the use of rubber bullets in conjunction with the plastic variety may help to overcome the problems associated with (water cannon). Because they cause less injury, rubber bullets are to be preferred unless it is necessary to hit specific targets, with plastic ones regarded as a last resort. Such a progression occurred in Northern Ireland. It may be appropriate to duplicate this process on the mainland, thus giving greater credibility to the concept of reasonable force in dealing with serious public disorder.'* (My brackets).

My successor at Thornhill Road, Superintendent Martin Burton, joined the debate in the same year. Writing on the subject of the Poll Tax riots in London and a prison riot at Strangeways in Manchester, he asked: *'Surely the time is right for the Home Secretary seriously to consider the introduction of a third tier of policing. What we need is an elite team of police officers specifically selected to form a riot or public disturbance squad. The extremists have demonstrated their ability to amass thousands of supporters and it is not beyond comprehension that prisoners are also easy recruits for them, as are the inhabitants of our deprived inner city areas... The crisis demands severe action.'*[2]

In February 1991 the Walsall Force claimed a return to 'old style' policing[3], with an emphasis on strengthening community links. Many components that had been key to our Handsworth approach were, however, missing. It seemed to me to be just a cosmetic move towards a concept of the beat policeman. It lacked the key

---

[1] *The Broadwater Lessons,* Police Review, 5th October 1990. The cover of that edition featured a photograph of an armoured, helmeted, visored Policeman holding a rubber bullet gun at the ready, over the caption: *'BOUNCING BACK - A role for the rubber bullet'.*
[2] *Next time, we must be ready,* Express and Star, 2nd April 1990.
[3] *More bobbies to go on the beat as crime rate soars.* Express and Star, February 27th 1991.

commitment to a school and juvenile programme. That same month, George Esson, Chief Constable of Dumfries and Galloway hoped to develop his own concept [1]of community policing: *'When I see a police officer on foot, I find it reassuring. And if I as a senior Police officer feel that, then I can only conclude that it must be much more so for John Citizen.'* That was it, community policing Scottish style.

In contrast, the cynicism that had greeted Lord Scarman's views on the causes of the Brixton riots of 1981 was replaced, in April 1991, by a thoughtful article in *Police Review*. Under the title *Keeping Brixton's Peace,*[2] Ken Hyder examined the history of the riots with a more dispassionate view. The hint regarding seeing the young man as a criminal simply because he is black is interesting. I, too, had found this in the late 70s among some of my colleagues. Of the *Swamp 81* operation, he commented: *'When they launched Swamp 81... police commanders knew that the majority of those responsible for these crimes were black. This was hardly surprising. Many of the criminals were young, and 40 percent of pupils in Lambeth were black; in Brixton itself, the proportion was even higher.*

But as officers stopped black youngsters on Brixton streets they were making a serious error of judgement, since corrected by a more scientific approach to the problem. While black youths made up a sizeable proportion of criminals, this did not mean that all young people - or all young black people - were criminals.

The incident which sparked (the riots) was relatively trivial and the policemen involved were completely blameless... But such was the gulf between them and the black community at the time, that bystanders who were present were prepared to believe the worst... The prevailing problems should have been obvious before the riots happened. The community was struggling against high unemployment, poor overcrowded housing, a dearth of facilities and a sense of hopelessness. Racial discrimination hit black school leavers entering a precarious job market. Many turned to crime.' (My brackets). Such views in a Police magazine in 1981 would have incurred acute displeasure both at local and Government level. This was Brixton, Toxteth, Bristol, St Paul's and Handsworth, every inner city riot throughout the UK, in a nutshell.

In April 1991, my local paper, the Sunday Mercury[3] talked of the latest ideas: *'Robocop gears up for action.'* Alongside a shot from the latest hit movie *Robocop* was a photo of a self-conscious young constable, armoured and padded, helmet and mask, with a shield reminiscent of the protective devices used by some Roman soldiers. I attempted to correct matters with a contribution to a special feature in the Independent on the anniversary of the publication of the Scarman Report, plus an

---

[1] *Back to Basics,* Police Review February 1st 1991.
[2] *Keeping Brixton's Peace,* Police Review, 12th April 1991.

[3] *Robocop gears up for action,* Sunday Mercury 14th April 1991

.

interview in the same edition of the Sunday Mercury: *'The appearance of the policeman in riot gear and in possession of the equipment thought necessary to subdue unruly British subjects is a reality not just in inner cities but at industrial disputes, soccer matches and other public gatherings... The patrolling officer on the beat will be an historical oddity... isolated and marooned... no longer able to wander freely on the streets and of necessity must either patrol with other officers on a team policing system or be held in reserve... ready to respond in a reactive manner to situations as they develop...*

The policeman no longer lives in the area where he works and has already lost the local involvement long treasured by his county and rural counterparts. No longer does he socialise in the inner city areas, and he no longer advertises the fact that he is a police officer when off duty or perhaps on holiday... The inevitable conclusion is that the Service will only be able to recruit people who accept this kind of isolation and who see themselves as a race apart.'

I am not blaming policemen. They are afraid. When they are in the pub, or on holiday, few wish to tell anyone that they are police officers. They do not want anyone to know they are in the Force, in case someone might pick an argument with them or do something unpleasant to their car or their home or their family. In short, hey dare not admit to their own profession. It must have a devastating effect on the morale and effectiveness.

I regret those wasted twenty years, when the Force could have been so different if it had chosen to be so. There is always the temptation of the retired - *'Why don't they do it like we did all those years ago etc...?'* We all, as our lives move on, show signs of *Victor Meldrew*. Memories too can be selective and nostalgic. Still, I hope I have been true to my library of evidence.

***

The background to all this is, of course, that the poor are always with us. A depressing picture emerged from the North in an Observer[1] investigation into the crime and racial problems in Tyneside. Barry Hugill and David Rose found a generation of lawless young rioters and a police Force in danger of being swamped by a wave of violent crime. No surprise, unemployment among sixteen to twenty-five-year-olds was high, fluctuating between seventy and ninety percent. *'The children are so frustrated, no jobs, no money, no hope. They ask, 'What's the use of living?''*

As the years passed, things were no better for the youngsters of Handsworth. The Observer's Vikram Dodd returned in September 1995 to discover male unemployment at forty three percent overall.[2] Among Afro-Caribbeans and some Asian communities it was estimated to be as high as seventy percent. No longer was

---

[1] *No hope in No-go Land,* The Observer, 15th September 1991.
[2] *Life's far from a carnival 10 years after riots,* Observer, 10th September 1995.

it just the dole. Ever stricter rules in the job centres made it harder to be out of a job. Yet still the despair remained. Eric McKenzie of the Afro-Caribbean Resource Centre found that in addition to society's breakdown, it was now the individual's turn. Disproportionate numbers of West Indian and Asian people were seeking the sanctuary of psychiatric care. *'Why? It's the pressure. People have little chance of any decent life. You either end up banging your head against a wall in an institution, challenging the system politically or violently, or dossing and becoming completely apathetic.'*

Visiting Leicester MP Keith Vaz noted: *'After visiting the area we were left with the impression that, while no-one wants to be a prophet of doom, the lessons of the riots haven't been learned in the last ten years.'* Muhammed Idrish, an Asian community leader, watched the tension day by day. *'The potential for an uprising remains. No-one can predict when it will happen again, what the spark will be.'*

Many of the older immigrant families have now moved out of inner city areas, doctors, surgeons, pharmacists, lawyers, company directors, to the suburbs. Now a different mix is forming, containing a higher proportion of the unemployable, the old, the handicapped, the mentally ill, of all races. Unless we change our policies, the problems may reveal themselves in new and unexpected ways.

Over the last twenty years, governments of various persuasions have poured millions of pounds into Handsworth to improve the exteriors of whole streets of houses, but still the core problem remains, of an underclass who have no work or hope. You could put a family in a brand new house, and they still have neither work nor hope. If you have real poverty and not even enough for your next meal, and sometimes not even that, then stealing or some other anti-social occupation is a risk you will take. And now we have guns, imitation and real, in the hands of teenagers. If politicians cannot understand this highly potent cocktail, they will forever reap a harvest of social unrest and crime. For many of those young people remaining in Handsworth and our other inner city areas, even a young offenders' prison seems not such a bad exchange.

THIRTY TWO: RACE MEMORIES

This chapter carries a health warning. It is easy, when surveying a decade of examples of dissatisfaction with the Police to conclude that many policemen are stupid, cruel, bigoted and racially prejudiced. I believe that such men and women are in a tiny minority. Yet as the old adage goes, and as many retired Government ministers have discovered to their cost: *Spend ten years building a reputation and ten minutes losing it.* The answer lies in the hands of every chief constable and officer in command, and the nation needs their good intent as much as in any previous century since the Force was first created.

***

'You know why there are not more black coppers? They're too -----ing lazy, that's why. I think they're scared of their people and I don't think they've got the brain power for it either. I'm sorry, but that's how I feel. You can get a whole community, you wouldn't get an 'O' level between them.'* (Detective sergeant in the Home Counties)

'Policemen are insulting about everyone. It's not especially against the coons. You hear remarks about poofs, Pakis, lesbos, women, students, the rich, the media, politicians, all foreigners, the Scots, the Irish. You name it, we hate everybody.' (A constable).

'I could do things that are evil, which I couldn't dream of doing before. I can see how Hitler got there... I can see how it happens, how violence is applied, how people are fitted up, where all the nasty, sordid signs of fascism start from. I can see them now.' (Woman sergeant, Metropolitan Police).

The above comments were recorded in 1989, along with those of five hundred other policemen as part of a confidential survey[1] of Police attitudes. Not all five hundred were of like mind, but enough was revealed to suggest just how some might act when faced with a black or brown citizen at bay.

We had seen indications years before of similar pockets of racialism and abuse of power among officers. During the Brixton riots, the Daily Star[2] captured a photo of a member of the Brixton Robbery Squad, a detective donstable, wearing a leather jacket and jeans carrying a pick-axe handle. We were not told whether this rather stupid example of policing resulted in any form of discipline by superior officers. In the same edition, the Star interviewed a practising inspector from a

---

[1] *Talking Blues,* A research study by Roger Graeff, published by Collins Harvill, 1989. Based on face to face interview with 500 officers in Britain and Northern Ireland.
[2] Published 6th May 6th 1981

221

'traditional' area: *'I've known a PC in the Special Patrol Group who was almost mentally racially prejudiced. You just could not talk to him about it. Even in uniform, passing by in the coach on duty he would make monkey noises at black people through the window. His attitude was an embarrassment to everybody who worked with him. I know this must sound strange, but I can honestly say that I never saw him give vent to his prejudice while actually performing his duties.'* Not of course if someone was watching.

Reporters Shedkar Bhatia and Tony Wedderburn were allocated by the Star to Brixton to investigate the events. They were both black. As a police van slowly passed them on Railton Road, the young constable driving the van gave them the 'V' sign and mouthed the words *'Black bastards...'.* They described how they had lived in London all their lives, and had as journalists come into contact with policemen every day. Never before had they experienced racial prejudice. *'We felt angry and ashamed, not for us, but for them. That grown men should have to call out playground abuse from the safety of a van, to people walking peacefully in the street... Every black youth we spoke to in Brixton told horrifying stories of arrests, beatings-up and racist abuse. They cannot all be telling lies.'*

In May 1990 I was invited to speak on Carlton TV's *Central Weekend* alongside David Mellor. That of itself was not especially newsworthy. I did, though, receive a letter from a polite, well educated lady. It seemed to contain a little of the spirit of the age, at least for some middle class whites. *'I am writing to thank you very much indeed for taking part in 'Central Weekend' on May 25th. I was so glad to hear you speaking out as you did - also for Mr Mellor and the 'people' who all believed in the Police.*

As soon as I saw the 'black' people in the audience I thought 'Here we go again - More trouble for the Police. What is the matter with these people? They're forever going on about being black! Are they ashamed of it or something? They certainly have a 'chip' on their shoulders regarding being black. Why blame us - or our Police? After all, its not our fault they are black, anymore than we can help being white.'

A friend of mine, white, middle class, lives in an attractive suburb on the edge of Worcestershire. He has an adopted son of West Indian birth. The young man played for my team the Birmingham Bulls between 1989 and 1992. He trained hard, running the hills, sometimes at night. Each season he was stopped several times by local panda patrols, and repeatedly asked, sometimes aggressively interrogated, as to where he was going and what he was doing. After they had had their few minutes of hassling him the constables would allow him on his way. If challenged their justification would be no doubt that he was running, and a running black man in a prosperous white suburb must be up to no good. My friend knew of no white runners who were stopped. It was a small local force. The same patrolmen must have gone over the area many times and got to know his son. Did the boy make the mistake of running in a white area, or even running at all? What impression, I wondered, did he carry in his mind from then on as to the nature of policemen generally?

I have spoken elsewhere of the Stephen Lawrence Enquiry and Report. Few are aware that one of the authors of the report, the Bishop of Stepney, was stopped and searched by a policeman. He was flagged down late one night[1] near St Paul's Cathedral and ordered to open the boot of his car. The Bishop told the journalist, *'I asked him why he was searching me but he became gruff, and it was clear that he did not want me to ask any more questions.'* It was only when the bishop removed his scarf to reveal his clerical dog collar and said who he was that the officer went white and said *'Oops!'*. The Bishop added: *'Everybody in this country is entitled to be treated equally and the fact that he stopped as soon as he learned I was the Bishop of Stepney is the offensive part.'*

Another prominent person recounted that he had been stopped while running near his West London home. A car pulled up and two policemen started shouting, demanding to know where he was going. The runner was Tory peer Lord John Taylor, and he, like the Bishop, is black. As respected members of the establishment, each had ready access to the media and understanding journalist friends.

In 2002 undercover BBC journalist Mark Daly successfully applied to join the Greater Manchester Constabulary and trained as part of a group intake of seventeen recruits at the Bruche national training centre in Warrington, Cheshire. The group included a single Asian recruit who would in time be excluded, then criticised, and then effectively expelled by the group simply because he was an Asian.

Daly's intention was to investigate repeated allegations of racism among the Manchester Force. A meticulously planned operation by the BBC saw him undergo eye laser surgery to ensure that he would pass the physical tests, and hidden cameras, including one fitted within his personal body armour suit, were designed to record his experiences of trainee life.

The findings were shocking and chilling. Overt hatred of Asians, all labelled as *Pakis*, was revealed by five recruits in the immediate circle within which Daly moved. All professed an acceptance of *blacks, that is real blacks*, but a deep hatred of Asians. All five had passed through the recruitment phases without any hint of their inner feelings. Yet statements recorded on video included, *'That ****** (name of Asian recruit) - I f**** hate him. I'd pull my (Ku Klux Klan) hood on my head and f**** chase him down the road.'*

Of Stephen Lawrence, the same recruit said: *'He f**** deserved it and his mum and dad are a f**** pair of spongers - they've f**** seen a good opportunity and sponged it for everything they can get their hands on. Those who killed him*

---

[1] *Whoops!*, Daily Mail, 24th January 2000. The Daily Mail was one of the most vociferous in commenting on the black crime issue at various times during the late 90's.

223

should be given diplomatic immunity - they've done for England what others should do.'

Four other recruits voiced similar feelings of racism, but the most chilling feature was the attitude of the entire group of seventeen to the single Asian recruit who was among them. From rumblings of discontent that the man had been especially encouraged by senior officers to join the Force, the group moved to a willing acceptance of innuendoes against the man's abilities, savage criticisms and mimed violence in the privacy of trainees' rooms. The secret camera recorded a final murmur of approval mixed with sarcastic laughter when the course co-ordinator, with no apparent sign of regret, broke the news that the Asian recruit had been 'back-coursed' by five weeks and moved to another trainee group. The worst example among the group, PC Rob Pulling, spent time in London with friends, shortly after the passing out parade. He was filmed during a journey to Scotland boasting that the Metropolitan Force had been just as he had hoped.

Q. Are the Met racist?

*A. F**** hell! The Met?*

Would Constable Pulling even kill as Asian because he was an Asian? *'It's a hatred thing... I would go as far as I could get away with burying the f**** under a train track, he's f**** going under the train track.'*

Even the most restrained discussions revealed abuse of Police discretion. One newly trained constable boasted that he had used his warrant card discretion to fine an Asian man several hundred pounds with added penalty points for not being insured, because *'He was a Paki'*. He then recounted how a similar offence by a white driver had resulted in a caution. The effect on crime figures as measured by ethnic origin might therefore suggest, if such attitudes prevailed generally, that the figures are not always what they seem.

What were the reactions of senior officers at the revelation of a BBC investigation? BBC journalist Daly was arrested on 15th August 2003 on suspicion of obtaining a pecuniary advantage by deception, and released on police bail. He was also accused of damaging police property by installing a hidden camera with a pin-hole aperture in his body-armour suit. Shortly after the arrest, Chief Constable Michael Todd noted: *'If true, we deplore this tactic, which would appear to be an outrageous waste of public funds to train, equip and pay this individual. It has also deprived a genuine recruit of the opportunity to join the Service.'*

A Police spokeswoman added the comments: *'[The behaviour of this journalist] if true, is reprehensible and only serves to undermine the work of the Police Service. The journalist is also in breach of an oath of attestation that he made in becoming a police constable as he has failed to act with integrity. In condoning this act of unethical journalism, the media organisation may well have breached people's human rights.'*

The programme[1] was shown on the evening of Tuesday 21st October 2003. Senior officer reactions then indicated a more reflective attitude. Greater Manchester Deputy Chief Constable Alan Green was '... *shocked, ashamed, and very saddened by what I saw.. While [we] have made great strides to improve the situation, the programme showed that we have not done enough, and we need to do more... These types of people should be prevented from getting into the service, and that is what we are committed to doing.'*

Home office minister Hazel Blears commented: '*I was shocked at the stupidity and immaturity of the people who had got through that training programme.'*

All five constables identified in the programme were not dismissed, but allowed to resign from the force. In spite of the assurances from ministers and senior officers that recruitment methods would be tightened up, the damage was done. As far as we can estimate, the journalist Daly was allocated to the training group purely by chance. Could it be that the distribution of racist trainees, that is, five out of seventeen, including the journalist Daly, might be repeated throughout the entire intake? If so, how might they in future be exposed at the early recruitment phase? At the time of writing, the Police and Home Office are urgently seeking methods of such exposure and expulsion from the process. One force has come up with the idea of planting informers in the intake groups. That of itself may breed suspicion and distrust among trainee colleagues; we shall see. It may be possible to use psychometric testing to reveal inner feelings of racism. Whatever the solution, it is simply not good enough to use the excuse that since the Police recruit from the population at large, therefore we should expect a similar proportion of racist officers. As members of society we willingly give the Police power over each of us, often in time of stress or vulnerability. Society, therefore, has a right to demand that the Police observe significantly higher standards than the general population, and that they protect us from unjust and undeserved bias of any kind.

Those were just a few examples of how the Force can lose the confidence of the people, tiny steps down the ladder of trust and support for an organisation that must, like biblical salt, for society's sake remain above suspicion. I recalled those woolly hatted youngsters in that 1975 Handsworth squat and Jacky, that cheeky young black girl harassed to her own front door and arrested and taken to Thornhill Road Station by a misguided officer. Who in the national press would have believed or spoken for them at the time?

As a background theme throughout the nineties and lately, we have seen indications that significant numbers of our politicians are at heart against immigration, especially of non-whites. During the Thatcher years, Ministers at a series of Party conferences would draw easy laughter and applause from the party

---

[1] *The Secret Policeman.* BBC TV 21st October 2003

faithful with jokes about incoming immigrants, middle European, usually speaking French or German, asking for directions to the nearest Social Security Office[1].

One notorious example popped up in the Conservative leadership election in August 2001. Edgar Griffin, a party activist in Wales and member of Iain Duncan Smith's Welsh campaign team, foolishly became associated with the British National Party, supporting unreservedly the policy of voluntary repatriation of all immigrants and descendants of former immigrants. When questioned on the *Today Programme* on Radio Four[2], he could not explain why his policy applied solely to people of coloured skin. Under pressure he admitted that it might also apply to white immigrants, for example Australians. He added: *'Its simply common sense.'* He and his family had been active in the Welsh Conservative party at a high level throughout the 80's and 90's. His son was in a senior position in the British National Party, and his wife stood as BNP candidate in the 2001 election against Duncan Smith. Many in his area of mid-Wales must have tolerated or even agreed with his views throughout his political career, though we can only speculate as to the nature of their local debates when the subject of race and immigration was raised.

Enoch Powell, MP for Wolverhampton, in spite of expressing views on voluntary repatriation more extreme than to those of Edgar Griffin, was never expelled from the party and continued as a back-bencher for many years. Events of themselves perhaps not of major significance, but they do suggest something of the prevailing attitude at ministerial level to those who were *different.* It is a well known fact that the *Monday Club*, a core activist group officially outside the Conservative party, but nevertheless restricting its membership solely to conservatives, had, as late as 2001, a policy of voluntary repatriation. I am sure too that racism exists in many areas within the Labour Party. And now both parties and the press - tabloid and broadsheet - are focussed on a new theme, illegal immigrants.

As more erudite folks move from inner city areas to the suburbs, we face a new and more corrosive variation[3] of the race issue. Within several of our major cities we have seen the exodus of those, white and non-white, who had amassed sufficient wealth to enable them to escape from inner city poverty. The residue of population remaining are the poorest, the least equipped to survive, but survive they do. Pockets of racial groups, now mainly poor white and of Asian origin, compete for city resources. Jealousies and rumours abound to create racial and economic strife.

---

[1] The Rt. Honourable Peter Lilley was notorious for such speeches. He never referred to non-whites, but we could guess that they were in the minds of many in the conference hall.

[2] *The Today Programme*, BBC Radio Four, 24th August 2001.

[3] *No no-go areas in Oldham - Areas of Oldham hit by recent riots will not be fenced off to keep white and Asian people apart, according to Home Secretary David Blunkett,* BBC Internet News, 15th June 2001.

Bradford, Oldham and other cities[1] undergo street conflict born of poverty, where inner city poor fight each other and destroy their own community for no reason other than each is *different,* while police riot squads attempt to keep the peace, stoned and hammered from both sides.

Of course, all this evidence just restates the problem. We have to find a solution. I have believed firmly, ever since I first walked the streets of Handsworth, that we have the solution staring us in the face. However insoluble the problem may seem to the external viewer, basic principles causing such tensions are forever the same; an equation born of unemployment, poverty, bad housing, weak local political structures and cultural misunderstanding and suspicion. The Police have a critical role in firstly understanding what are the causes, and then *taking the lead* in addressing those causes, starting in the schools, alongside the leaders of other public agencies. There is no other way. Regiments of armoured policemen may suppress street disorder for a while, but the basic causes and unhappiness will remain[2], with all their long term damaging and costly effects on society.

So, whither racism in the Police at the turn of the millennium? Have things changed in a way that will assure the man in the street that he will in future be policed fairly and openly? It is hard to determine. Yet for some to claim that the Police are just a reflection of the society from which they recruit is, to me, a counsel of despair. I know from my own experience that a local commander who knows his men personally and socially can do something about it, if he wants to.

I attended a weekend conference in October 2000 in Wolverhampton with community leaders from all over the world, yet not a single policeman, junior or senior, attended. Perhaps force commanders no longer think that such gatherings are relevant, even though the word *community* is frequently used in the media when such commanders are interviewed.

Imagine a superintendent with a Station to run. His phone is by the bed. Does he want to know everything that is happening? Of course not, it's out of fashion, it's not the way that a modern commander should operate. Yet if that same superintendent goes to the station in the morning, and there has been trouble the previous night, or the station is surrounded by protesters, then he needs to know why. He should not have to walk into his office, and not know what to do, or who to talk to in the community to discover what is the cause. He is responsible for his men, and they cannot afford to hang around while things are investigated and discussed. He needs to move fast, yet reactive policing may not be the best option. He has to know, before any trouble occurs, what drives the leaders of the community and the local criminal or trouble-maker. The *why* comes from deep within society and he must

---

[1] *Labour activist hurt by riot Police,* report on Burnley inter-racial clashes, BBC Internet news 26th June 2001.

[2] *Bradford's race divisions condemned,* Report on Race Relations in Bradford, Lord Ouseley, published 11th July 2001.

understand it, must know the chemistry of his patch. To achieve this, he must be always in contact with all the leaders in the community, and the young and old. Even as I write, there are regular calls to me from serving officers in the Birmingham area, begging my assistance in putting them in touch with local community leaders. Yet this should not be for me to do. Those young policemen should be trained to do this and supported by their commanders. It should be a natural part of the job.

Time and time again the pendulum has swung away from a policy of questioning, understanding and involvement. Political party conferences sometimes bring out the worst aspects of this, when every young person with any kind of criminal record, even a minor shop lifting offence, becomes a *young thug*, a person to be locked up and taken off the streets. The logic is that while in jail they cannot commit further crimes.[1] Yet, surprisingly, in the year 2000, many cities and towns joined an initiative paralleling almost exactly one we pioneered in 1979 in our Lozells project. Across the UK, on one hundred and fifty *Splash Schemes*, thirty thousand teenagers took part in a range of activities ranging from drama and sport to music and dance.[2] A survey across all forces where schemes had been actioned, revealed that youth crime had fallen sharply. An eighteen percent reduction in theft on cars was accompanied by a thirty six percent drop in house burglaries. I was fascinated by the claim that *'Many police forces and local councils have long recognised the benefits of providing constructive activities. The schemes are being seen as more successful than curfew orders which local authorities and the Police can impose on children up to the age of fifteen to stop anti-social behaviour.'*

In case you suspect that my nostalgia leads me to exaggerate what we did between 1977 and 1981, here is a section from a report on community policing in Handsworth compiled in 1981. Among a listing of our programmes in primary and secondary schools, our courses of sixth form group discussions led by police officers, our emphasis on beat patrol officers, our Handsworth festivals, our Duke of Edinburgh Award contributions, our youth clubs, our football competitions, our cricket matches, our meetings with resident's associations and our regular discussions with leaders of ethnic minorities, churches and temples, is the following:

'The 'Citizen '80 Scheme', a joint enterprise between the educational welfare services and the Police, whereby groups of young people aged between eleven and fourteen years of age, on the recommendation of the school concerned and the educational welfare service, undertake a course during the school holidays consisting of attendance for a week at a course to learn of the role of various public services,

---

[1] The June 2001 Election campaign was dominated for several days by a Conservative claim that the Labour Government's early release scheme had actually caused more crime, including two rapes.

[2] *New findings show crime reduction.* Youth Justice Board for England and Wales, 24th August 2001. The important factor is the support and encouragement of the Home Office in the series of projects.

while the same group with as far as possible the same staff attends a five day camp in a rural setting and is encouraged to develop group responsibility.'

I sometimes wish that I could start over again as a superintendent. It seems, at long last, that the things we tried to do more than twenty years ago are finding the beginnings of recognition. Hopefully, some budding chief constable will read this book, reflect on what might have been, and do something about it.

In May 1987, Birmingham City Council published a major study on progress since the 1985 riots. The answer was, that there had been no progress. There was still mass unemployment, poor housing and a repeated failure of schemes to improve the situation generally. Unemployment had risen sharply in 1986, with firms all over Birmingham laying sometimes three quarters of their work force off overnight. Handsworth's overall unemployment stood at thirty six percent and the local Lucas Electrical Company in Hockley, where many from Handsworth worked, was scheduled to close. *'Millions have been spent in 'enveloping' the outside of homes, but the people inside still live in slum conditions... In spite of Handsworth's community policing policy, local people say that tension remains high. A recent statement by the Chief Constable described the situation as 'volatile".[1]*

Each year after the 1985 riots there were warnings that tensions were high, especially in the summer months. I will not go over these, since they seemed to me to be repeating the same old problems. There were tales in the press of a specially formed consultative and Police Monitoring Committee for Thornhill Road Station coming to blows and an exasperated new superintendent Keith Newell claiming that it was impossible to deal with the members sensibly.[2] Not that anyone questioned why such a committee was necessary. I could not understand why it was not possible for the staff of Thornhill Road to go out and meet the people as individuals, rather than wait for some committee to meet. But then, I was out of it all, my policies seen as no longer relevant.

Recently I was invited to a Ravidass gathering. I helped many years ago to start up the annual Handsworth Ravidass Convention, so as to foster better community relations between the City authorities and the ethnic minorities, especially the Asian population. It takes place on the birthday of the Guru Ravidass and is for his followers the biggest day of the year. This time, many ethnic community leaders, the Lord Mayor of Birmingham, Lord King of Handsworth, all the City dignitaries and leaders and several MP's were there. We even welcomed the head of the Fire Brigade. There was one major absence; not a single policeman was present. I kept my counsel and never asked why.

After all the other speeches had concluded, I was invited up to the stage to speak on ethnic community policing. At first I refused - I did not feel it appropriate to speak on behalf of anyone in the Force, but they insisted. I was the only person there

---

[1] *Handsworth still in grip of despair,* Birmingham Post 21st May 1987.
[2] *New forum to monitor community policing,* Birmingham Post 17th August 1988

with experience of policing, and it would have been the height of bad manners to refuse that kind invitation. But it should not have been me. It was the job of the responsible local police commander or his senior officer. When you represent your profession, the City Council see you, the press see you, the ethnic community leaders see you, the man on the street who looks at the photos in the next days papers sees you. You are seen to be mixing, talking, eating and touching, with people of a different race. You are leading by example.

Around that same period I attended a routine local housing committee meeting. A standard part of our meetings back in 1981 was for the local beat constable to give a report on crime and what was going on locally. Yet at this meeting there was no constable, no apology, no phone call, no explanation. What impression was given to those good people giving their time and energy to looking after their local area?

'Uniform Plan for detectives' was one particular headline.[1] Under a supposedly radical new scheme, Sussex Police were to move some seven hundred officers from plain clothes into uniform. The idea, agreed in September 2000 with the Home Office, was to get policemen out of their cars and into contact with the people they Police. *'We want to get away from the cultural stigma of 'being in uniform'. The ranks of PC and DC are the same and equally valued.'* Now, where had I heard that before?

Sadly the evidence suggests that such initiatives are but cosmetic. A smiling policeman visiting a school or village fete or talking on the street is just not enough. Society is a complex machine, and the Police are close to the heart of that machine in everything they do. If politicians, media and Police fail to grasp the reality of community policing, then Great Britain will be an unhappy place. The fuel protests[2] that took place in the year 2000 were a perfect example of a complex society, forever on the edge of fragmentation. We depend on each other for all our needs, including crime prevention and safety in our homes. Old policemen like me can sit in our houses, watch it go by and criticise, but we must do more. We have a responsibility to show how it can be, and hopefully educate enough of the public to accept that real community policing is worth fighting for.

---

[1] *Uniform plan for Detectives,* BBC Internet News 27th August 2001.
[2] In the autumn of 2000, over a spell of two weeks, groups of protesters picketed oil and petrol supply depots, bringing the nation to within 24 hours of a complete standstill.

THIRTY THREE: MEASURING SUCCESS

A 1990 Home Office report of a survey done in 1988 examined the public's view of the Police, and the outcome was discussed in *Police Review*. Overall, there was a drop in public esteem of seven percentage points, and the most significant area for Police unease concerned the views of racial minorities. *'It is hardly surprising that... racial minorities, together with the young and the unemployed, came away less satisfied with the results of their encounters with officers. But it is interesting to note that Afro-Caribbeans and Asians are more likely to telephone the Police and visit police stations than whites. Put another way, the service's biggest customers are its most dissatisfied ones.'*[1]

Writing in the Daily Express, Columnist Jean Rook[2] told of her own encounter with the men in blue. Opening with the comment *'Our panda-protected Police have become an estranged force which is no longer with us'*, she described being stopped, driving at twenty eight miles an hour in London, by a policeman and policewoman who vetted and questioned her, but refused to say what reason they had to pull her over. Jean Rook then contrasted this with the recent case of a superintendent who refused nine separate requests by an officer to breath into a breathalyser, yet was let off by magistrates on the grounds that he was under stress at the time, and that made it difficult for him to breathe. Jean's conclusion saddened me. Here was a well paid, white, intelligent journalist challenging a key assumption in our society; that the Police are always to be trusted. It fitted, for a slightly different reason, so much of my experience and those of the young black and Asian men I had met in my career. She concluded: *'There is one law for us and another for those who dole it out. If you can't wholly trust and confide in a policeman, what's left?'*

How then shall we measure our policing success? Do we mark the number of street riots and congratulate ourselves that things have been quiet for a while? Do we list our technology, our armour, CS gas, water cannon, helicopters, fast response armed squads, and comfort ourselves with improvement since the last riots? Do we count reported crimes and be happy that figures are down in some parts of our society? Do we survey our ever fuller prisons, and rest assured that all are for the time being safely locked up? And when we have filled the prisons, when we have suppressed street riots with masked armoured warriors and helicopters, when potential rioters fear for their lives, when we have displaced crime to new activities even more expensive to society, how then will we measure success? Will our people as a whole be happier, more fulfilled, or will our affluent suburbs and villages and farms hide behind security gates and private patrols employing retired policemen?

---

[1] *Cracks in the image,* Police Review 28th September 1990.
[2] *We must remove this thin blue line of fear,* Daily Express, 29th March 1989.

Will the poor on the fringes of our nation continue, as they are beginning to do now in parts of our major cities, to survive in ghettos of unemployment, decaying housing and dying schools? Will they bumble along committing those crimes best confined, with no trouble for the rest of us, to their own streets?

Lord Scarman highlighted the corrosive effects of unemployment on our inner city peoples. He knew it was not that simple. It runs through the generations, each age reinforced by its predecessor. Unemployed children become unemployed parents, those parents become unemployed grandparents; three generations of wasted potential, three generations of trouble for someone else, and at the centre of it all, the constable in car or on foot.

Richard Ingrams, in January 2001, dropped a number of asides into his weekly diary in the Observer.[1] He noted the recently published report by the Audit Commission which showed that confidence in the Police was at an all-time low, and recalled that almost every day there seemed to be stories of police incompetence or corruption, or an innocent man shot dead by a police marksman, or a black man persecuted by racism in the force. When things go wrong in the Police, he maintained, it seems always to be someone else's fault, either the Government's, or *We need more policemen.*

'No-one will say that the policemen who are there already are not any good. Why is this? I believe it has a lot to do with the fact that many politicians are actually rather scared of the Police. The Police have a great deal of power these days and a huge amount of information about all of us.'

I do not agree with all that he says, but he is right on one matter; the power of the force to look after its own interests. The Police are in a unique position. They are not simply the disciplinary arm of the state. They have power over the citizen, and the trust of the courts. They may stop and search and handle politely and respectfully. Or they may abuse, brutalise, lie unchallenged, their misdemeanours proved only by direct video evidence. Through his senior officers, an individual policeman can reach the ear of government, can speak with authority to politicians and teachers of the young. Through the power of membership of an association he can lead a positive debate, or he can ride the tiger of uninformed prejudice. Police superiors have the power to tell the truth, or massage the figures and the news. They may attribute all success to their own efforts, all failure to government or lack of resources. They may, when disorder or crime occurs, castigate the child, parent or criminal, or the *do-gooder*. In their gatherings and annual conferences they may show themselves once more to be a profession to be admired, or they may pressurise, barrack, even bring down, government ministers. Over the decades, the people have placed their trust and power into the hands of the Police. How will that power be used, that trust fulfilled?

---

[1] *That guttering blue lamp,* The Observer 14th January 2001.

THIRTY FOUR: INTO THE SUNSET

In my career I and several across the nation were part of a process that exposed divisions within the Police, asking questions which many were afraid, or unable, to face. Soft policing versus aggressive policing, personality clashes behind closed doors, antagonising sometimes my colleagues in the West Midlands, at other times the Association of Chief Police Officers and that trade union of rank and file, the Police Federation. Above all I repeatedly challenged the degree to which chief constables and their forces should be servants of society rather than its masters.

At intervals, there have been signs of hope. The Youth Justice Board report on *Splash Schemes* is an example. Yet we have around us so much evidence that the lessons of the seventies and eighties have not yet been learned. If when I retired everything had got better, if things had become sweet between the Police and the policed, I would have felt different. I could have resolved the tensions that have gnawed at me over the years. Sadly, things have not gone well and some things that worried me in the 70's and 80's may have got worse. The appointment in 2003 of a new Chief Constable of the West Midlands and his avowed belief in community policing may be a sign of hope for the future. I shall be watching how things go with great interest. If he does pursue policies similar to those that we pioneered, and his ideas are continued, then he deserves every support and recognition of his achievements. The wheel will indeed have turned full circle.

I walked into the hallway of Thornhill Road station a couple of times on behalf of members of our Asian Business Federation, but apart from that have never been back. The nearest I ever got was an invitation to the one hundredth anniversary of the old place, by my friend, David Baker. He was my young sergeant during my Walsall days, was promoted to Chief Superintendent, and then to Headquarters in charge of complaints. The gathering *for old times sake*, sadly, was not at Thornhill Road, but at the police social club at Tallyho in Edgbaston. All the other chief superintendents who served there in the past were there, and listened to me talk about the old times. It really hurt.

Apart from that one invitation, from the day I walked out of Thornhill Road Station all official contact stopped. There were no phone calls, no letters, nothing from all those former colleagues. Did my knowledge disappear? Was I infirm or incapable? It's hard to believe that there was no instruction down the line from as high as the Home Office that I was not to be approached. They could not take the chance. I'd been seen as a loose cannon, and I became a virtual leper. Even today, in spite of the international prominence we had for five years and the praise throughout the Force for my concepts of community policing, my name appears nowhere in police journals or training manuals anywhere in the country. My personal file, when I enquired at Headquarters, was not available.[1] I was not told why.

In 2002 I was invited to a meeting of Handsworth's No 1 Residents' Association, the very first group I became involved with in 1977. Working from an old schoolroom in Rookery Road, they get a regular grant from the City to enable them to look after their area. Donald Nelson, the secretary since 1977, worker/chairman and member of the local rotary club, asked me to come along and tell about the old days. At least, that is what he told me on the phone. That night they saw me coming. There I was, sitting quietly, trying to keep out of it, when they sprung a trap. After all these years I am back on their committee, this time as an ex-policeman and current Chairman. The group I used to work with so closely twenty four years ago, has finally got me again. We call ourselves the North Handsworth Project, more affectionately known as *Squirrels* The people are wonderful and irresistible, and I repay their trust by helping them find ways of extracting the maximum amount of money out of the City Council. It is a sweet kind of revenge.

I'm still very much involved with Rotary, but my biggest preoccupation is with the Federation of Asian Businesses, with its four hundred members. It keeps me in touch with people I used to know, and have grown to love. I sold the factory in 1992 to devote my time to the Federation, and visit India three or four times a year. Comfortable in my semi-detached, sitting in my deckchair, eyes closed with a warm sun on my face, I feel a happy, lucky man. I know that the richest man in the world is probably working harder than me to keep his fortune. The Birmingham Museum and Art Gallery, how that rolls off the tongue, put my photo in the reception area of Soho House, owned between 1766 and 1809 by Matthew Boulton, world famous engineer and metal craftsman of Birmingham. I am proud to say that it is not just a portrait; it is a real event captured by a journalist in 1977 when I was surrounded by a crowd of wonderful young West Indian men surviving on the streets.

My story is almost finished. What we achieved in Handsworth is now on record, and my unique files are to be preserved for posterity. Some say that I should have spoken out earlier. I can only hope that Home Secretary David Blunkett and his successors will look again at the solutions we pioneered. It is often said that a man's reputation is the most precious thing he can own. I can walk the streets in safety anywhere in Handsworth. Wherever I go in this world, inevitably I will meet someone who knew me or heard of me and remembers the good things I did. I have chaperoned child revolutionaries, talked with criminals, befriended and discussed my policies with a prime minister of a great nation, eaten with untouchables, faced angry mobs and smiling children, known triumph and failure, rejection and despair. Through it all, it was among the poverty-racked streets of the rainbow people of Handsworth that my true understanding of humanity began.

---

[1] Under current rules, all Policemen are entitled by law to see their personal files.

FURTHER READING

The following list is a good place to start. More studies are available through Amazon.com and major booksellers. Sadly some books written in the 1980's and conveying the feelings of the age may be out of print.

Shades of Grey and Handsworth Revisited. John Brown. A Cranfield Institute Study 1977, published as a complete volume 1982. Bedford Square Press of the National Council for Voluntary Organisations. May be difficult to find. ISBN 0 7199 1087 0.

The Downing Street Years. Margaret Thatcher. 1993. Harper Collins.

Tales from Two Cities. The life of a citizen of Handsworth, vividly described. Devia Murphy. Published by John Murray, 1985.

The Power in Our Hands. Lord Scarman et al. Jon Carpenter Publishing, 1996.

The Scarman Report: The Brixton Disorders 10-12 April 1981. Lord Justice Scarman. Cmnd 8472. Published by Penguin, 1982.

Scarman and After: Essays reflecting on Lord Scarman's Report, the Riots and Their Aftermath. J. Benyon. 1984. Pergamon Press.

Colonial Immigrants in Great Britain - a Class Analysis. John Rex. 1979. Routledge and Kegan Paul, London.

Law and Order in Multi-Racial Areas - the Problem after Scarman. An Essay: Law and Order in British Politics. John Rex. 1985. (ed.) Norton, Phillip, pp 100-115.

The Roots of Urban Unrest. Life in the Ghetto. John Rex, 1986. Benyon J. and Solomos J. Pergamon Press, pp. 103-111.

Talking Blues. A study by Roger Graeff. 1989. Published by Harper Collins.

From Scarman to Lawrence. Stuart Hall. Open University, History Workshop Journal, Volume 48, published 1999, Oxford University Press.

Race Relations in Bradford. The Ouseley Report. Lord Ouseley. 2001. Commission for Racial Equality.

The Violent Society. Eric Moonman. Published by Frank Cass, 1987.

International Perspectives on Community Policing and Crime Prevention. Dilip K Das, Steven P Lab. Published by Prentice Hall, 2003.

Community Policing and Problem Solving: Strategies and Practices. Kenneth J Peak and Ronald W. Glensor. Published by Prentice Hall, 1995.

INDEX